THE PURSUIT
OF POETRY

*A Guide to Its
Understanding and Appreciation
With an Explanation
of Its Forms and a
Dictionary of Poetic Terms*

BY

LOUIS UNTERMEYER

Simon and Schuster
NEW YORK

FIRST PRINTING

SBN 671–20409–2
Library of Congress Catalog Card Number: 78–79640
Designed by Irving Perkins
Manufactured in the United States of America
Printed by Mahony & Roese, Inc.
Bound by American Book–Stratford Press, Inc.

ACKNOWLEDGMENTS

The author thanks the following for permission to reprint the copyright material included in this volume. In the event of any unconscious errors or omissions, he will be pleased to make the necessary corrections in future editions of the book.

Ruby Fogel for "E = MC2: A Sestina Proving the Equation," reprinted with her permission.

Grove Press, Inc., for "Heat" from *Selected Poems by H.D.* Copyright © 1957 by Norman Holmes Pearson. Published by Grove Press, Inc.

Adrian Henri for "Adrian Henri's Talking After Christmas Blues," which originally appeared in the *London Times Literary Supplement* and is contained in his volume *Tonight at Noon.* First published in England, the book is published in the U.S.A. by David McKay Company, Inc. Reprinted with Mr. Henri's special permission.

Holt, Rinehart & Winston, Inc., for "The Cow in Apple Time" and "Stopping by Woods on a Snowy Evening" from *Complete Poems of Robert Frost.* Copyright 1916, 1923 by Holt, Rinehart & Winston, Inc. Copyright 1944, 1951 by Robert Frost. Reprinted by permission of Holt, Rinehart & Winston, Inc. For "Epitaph on an Army of Mercenaries" from *The Collected Poems of A. E. Housman.* Copyright 1922 by Holt, Rinehart & Winston, Inc. Copyright 1950 by Barclays Bank Ltd. Reprinted by permission of Holt, Rinehart & Winston.

Houghton Mifflin Company for four stanzas from "You, Andrew Marvell" by Archibald MacLeish, from *Collected Poems: 1917–1952,* copyright by Archibald MacLeish.

The Macmillan Company for the first ten lines of "The Wood Weasel" from *Nevertheless* by Marianne Moore. Copyright 1944 by Marianne Moore.

David McCord for a double dactyl, two symmetrics, and "History of Education," all of which are reprinted with his permission.

The Estate of Merrill Moore for the sonnet "How She Resolved to Act."

New Directions for "The Red Wheelbarrow" by William Carlos Williams from his *Collected Earlier Poems.* Copyright 1938 by William Carlos Williams. For "Do not go gentle into that good night" from *Collected Poems by Dylan Thomas.* Copyright 1952 by Dylan Thomas. Both poems reprinted by permission of New Directions Publishing Corp.

The Nodin Press for two haiku from *Seventeen Chirps* by Gerald Robert Vizenor. Reprinted by permission of the author.

Edgar Pangborn for "Sapphics for Icarus," reprinted with his permission.

Charles Scribner's Sons for "Epitaph on the Waiter" from *Bay Window Ballads.* Copyright 1935 by Charles Scribner's Sons; renewal copyright 1963 by David McCord. Reprinted with the permission of Charles Scribner's Sons.

Wesleyan University Press for "Early Supper" from *Light and Dark* by Barbara Howes. Copyright © 1959 by Barbara Howes. Reprinted by permission of Wesleyan University Press. This poem was first published in *The New Yorker.*

The poems by the author and Michael Lewis are copyright by Louis Untermeyer.

Finally I wish to record my gratitude to Henry W. Simon for many suggestions and emendations, and also to my wife, Bryna Ivens Untermeyer, to whom this book is not only dedicated but deeply indebted.

FOR BRYNA,
always

CONTENTS

PROLOGUE

OF ENGLISH VERSE

Poets may boast, as safely vain,
Their works shall with the world remain;
Both, bound together, live or die,
The verses and the prophecy.

But who can hope his lines should long
Last in a daily changing tongue?
While they are new, envy prevails;
And as that dies, our language fails.

When architects have done their part,
The matter may betray their art;
Time, if we use ill-chosen stone,
Soon brings a well-built palace down.

Poets that lasting marble seek
Must carve in Latin or in Greek;
We write in sand, our language grows,
And, like the tide, our work o'erflows.

Chaucer his sense can only boast,
The glory of his numbers lost!
Years have defaced his matchless strain,
And yet he did not sing in vain.

The beauties which adorned that age,
The shining subjects of his rage,
Hoping they should immortal prove,
Rewarded with success his love.

This was the generous poet's scope,
And all an English pen can hope,
To make the fair approve his flame,
That can so far extend their fame.

Verse, thus designed, has no ill fate
If it arrive but at the date
Of fading beauty, if it prove
But as long-lived as present love.

EDMUND WALLER (1606–1687)

A FOREWORD

The title of this book is to be taken in two ways. *The Pursuit of Poetry* represents (1) an effort to pursue and, if possible, capture the elusive essence of the art, and (2) an attempt to describe the profession or pursuit of the poet.

It is a two-part book. The first part is devoted to an examination of poetry: whether it can be defined, how it is conceived and shaped, how sound is transmitted into sense, how the music intensifies the meaning. The second part is a poetry handbook: an explanation of techniques, devices, and forms, plus a dictionary of poetic terms. I hope that the two parts will give the reader a realization of the sense of poetry.

The book is not addressed to the advanced scholar or to the trained analyst. It may (I hope) evoke responses from practitioners of verse, but it is designed chiefly for those who, whether or not they fully understand poetry, are drawn to it. I have tried to show not only the purpose and the use of poetry but also the need for it.

Following the example set by Shakespeare's editors, practically all the poetry quoted appears in modern spelling.

L. U.

I

THE ANATOMY
OF POETRY

The Definition of Poetry

Before any discussion of the poetic art, the reader may feel he has a right to a straightforward definition of poetry. It is a right that is, in almost every instance, denied him. Poets, critics, and analysts have failed to agree on the basic purpose, the experience, the use, and even the nature of poetry. Nevertheless, there have been notable illuminations.

Shakespeare in *A Midsummer Night's Dream* delineated, if he did not define, the imaginative power of poetry.

> *The poet's eye, in a fine frenzy rolling,*
> *Doth glance from heaven to earth, from earth to heaven,*
> *And, as imagination bodies forth*
> *The forms of things unknown, the poet's pen*
> *Turns them to shapes, and gives to airy nothing*
> *A local habitation and a name.*

Matthew Arnold was both more definite and more dogmatic. Arnold declared that poetry is "a criticism of life," a criticism which he said accorded with conditions fixed "by the laws of poetic truth and poetic beauty." He failed, however, to state or establish what the "laws" of either truth or beauty might be. Keats maintained the immutability of such laws when he concluded the "Ode to a Grecian Urn" with:

> *Beauty is truth, truth beauty—that is all*
> *Ye know on earth, and all ye need to know.*

It was truth which Samuel Johnson emphasized when he wrote that "poetry is the art of uniting pleasure with truth by calling imagination to the help of reason."

Keats had no patience with such distinctions. He maintained that "the poetic character lives in gusto, be it foul or fair, high or low, rich or poor, mean or elevated—it has as much delight in conceiving an Iago as an Imogen."

As for laws, Keats insisted that poetry must work out its own salvation in man; it cannot be matured by precepts, but only by sensations. "Poetry," he wrote to his publisher, John Taylor, "should surprise by a fine excess and not by singularity. It should strike the reader as a wording of his own highest thoughts and appear almost a remembrance. Its touches of beauty should never be halfway. The rise, the progress, the setting of imagery should, like the sun, come natural to him."

Wordsworth had a sterner view of the function of poetry. To him poetry was not, as Matthew Arnold assumed, a criticism of life but a sustainer and enlarger of life, an ennobler of all toward which man strives. "The poet," said Wordsworth, "is the rock of defence for human nature; an upholder and preserver, carrying everywhere with him relationship and love. In spite of difference of soil and climate, of language and manners, of laws and customs, in spite of things silently gone out of mind and things violently destroyed, the poet binds together by passion and knowledge the vast empire of human society as it is spread over the whole earth and over all time."

Coleridge echoed Wordsworth. He amplified the poet's role when he wrote: "The poet brings the whole soul of man into activity. . . . He diffuses a tone and spirit of unity that blends and (as it were) *fuses*, each into each, by that synthetic and magical power to which we have exclusively appropriated the name of Imagination."

William Hazlitt was no less sure of poetry's spiritual than of its therapeutic power. "Poetry," said Hazlitt, "is the universal language which the heart holds with nature and itself. . . . Poetry is that fine particle within us that expands, rarefies, refines, and raises our whole being . . ."

The exuberant Shelley not only reaffirmed the poet's fervor as a record "of the best and happiest moments of the best minds" —a blithe overstatement when some of the greatest poems were written out of unhappiness and immedicable woe—but also returned to the matter of its message-bringing, truth-conveying function. "A poem," he insisted, "is the very image of life expressed in its eternal truth."

Modern poets were quick to challenge so large and loose a definition. "Poetry," wrote T. S. Eliot, "is not the assertion that something is true, but the making of that truth more fully real to us." Ezra Pound went further when he announced that "Poetry is not greatly concerned with what a man thinks, but with what is so embedded in his nature that it never occurs to him to question it; not a matter of which idea he holds, but of the depth at which he holds it."

Perhaps the most radical refusal to believe that the intellect is the fount of poetry was stated by A. E. Housman in a half-expostulating, half-teasing lecture entitled "The Name and Nature of Poetry," delivered at Cambridge in 1933. "Even when poetry has a meaning, as it usually has, it may be inadvisable to draw it out," said Housman, and went on to quote Coleridge to the effect that poetry gives the most pleasure when only generally and not perfectly understood. Moreover, Housman implied that perfect understanding often extinguishes pleasure.

Having established for himself the unimportance of complete comprehension, Housman turned to the matter of limitation. To a request from America for a definition of poetry, Housman replied that he could no more define poetry than a terrier can define a rat,

> but I thought we both recognized the object by the symptoms which it provokes in us. One of those symptoms was described in connection with another object by Eliphaz the Temanite: "A spirit passed before my face: the hair of my flesh stood up." Experience has taught me, when I am shaving of a morning, to keep watch over my thoughts because, if a line of poetry strays into my

memory, my skin bristles so that the razor ceases to act. This particular symptom is accompanied by a shiver down the spine; there is another which consists in a constriction of the throat and a precipitation of water to the eyes; and there is a third which I can only describe by borrowing a phrase from one of Keats's last letters, where he says, speaking of Fanny Brawne, "everything that reminds me of her goes through me like a spear." The seat of this sensation is the pit of the stomach. . . . Poetry indeed seems to me more physical than intellectual.

Emily Dickinson was equally capricious. Had she heard Housman, she would have agreed with him. Characteristically refusing to be tied to any definition, she wrote: "If I read a book and it makes my whole body so cold no fire can ever warm me, I know it is poetry. If I feel physically as if the top of my head were taken off, I know this is poetry. Is there any other way?"

Since no single, simple definition can be final, the reader must content himself with approximations, with diverse and even differing opinions, expressions of response, mood, and temperament. Irritated by the failure to produce a pronouncement that would satisfy every kind and occasion, one might sum up by saying that poetry is the power of defining the indefinable in terms of the unforgettable.

I remember what struck me as a fitting if not final reply to the perennial question "What is poetry?" The query was asked during the question period that followed a lecture given by a professor who was also a professing poet. He began his answer confidently: "Poetry is . . ." and then he stumbled. "Well," he began again, "poetry is a thing that . . ." and again he hesitated. Then, flinging all reservations aside, he said flatly, "Poetry is that which is written by poets."

The nature of poetry is somewhat less elusive. What gives life to a poem is not too hard to determine; its viability can be felt even before it can be apprehended. Subject matter is not the answer. A good subject does not make a good poem; there is no such thing as a bad subject. It might be thought that fleas and lice can only provoke disgust, yet a flea was the subject of one of Donne's most impassioned poems and a louse inspired some of

Burns's nimblest as well as some of his most serious and peren-nially quoted lines. Nor is a sound philosophy any guarantee of a poem's virtue. The sentimentality of Edgar Guest's once popular verse is not redeemed by its cheerful optimism any more than the vigor of Robinson Jeffers' tragic confrontations is diminished by his uncompromising pessimism. Byron's immorality does not lessen the brilliance of *Don Juan* nor does Tupper's exemplary moralism lift the dullness of his *Proverbial Philosophy*. The life of a poem depends wholly upon the life the poet puts into it.

Reality is no more a test of true poetry than is subject matter. The poet can make an imagined world, with the forms of things unknown, as vivid and as vast as the real world of everyday. Edgar Allan Poe sought for and achieved a blurring of rational content. At its best his is a poetry of another sphere, of a world out of space, out of time; it moves us with the very power of its unreality. One of his most characteristic poems, "The Haunted Palace," may be read as an allegory or as the expression of Poe's nightmare life, a life and "a mind haunted by phantoms," but it is as a series of vague, wavering sensations that it both excites and lulls the readers.

THE HAUNTED PALACE

In the greenest of our valleys,
  By good angels tenanted,
Once a fair and stately palace—
  Radiant palace—reared its head.
In that monarch Thought's dominion—
  It stood there!
Never seraph spread a pinion
  Over fabric half so fair.

Banners yellow, glorious, golden,
  On its roof did float and flow;
(This—all this—was in the olden
  Time long ago.)
And every gentle air that dallied,
  In that sweet day,
Along the ramparts plumed and pallid,
  A wingèd odor went away.

Wanderers in that happy valley,
    Through two luminous windows, saw
Spirits moving musically
    To a lute's well-tunèd law,
Round about a throne, where sitting,
    (Porphyrogene!)
In state his glory well befitting,
    The ruler of the realm was seen.

And all with pearl and ruby glowing
    Was the fair palace door,
Through which came flowing, flowing, flowing,
    And sparkling evermore,
A troop of Echoes, whose sweet duty
    Was but to sing,
In voices of surpassing beauty,
    The wit and wisdom of their king.

But evil things, in robes of sorrow,
    Assailed the monarch's high estate.
(Ah, let us mourn!—for never morrow
    Shall dawn upon him, desolate!)
And round about his home the glory
    That blushed and bloomed,
Is but a dim-remembered story
    Of the old time entombed.

And travellers, now, within that valley,
    Through the red-litten windows see
Vast forms that move fantastically
    To a discordant melody,
While, like a ghastly rapid river,
    Through the pale door
A hideous throng rush out forever,
    And laugh—but smile no more.

Apart from the almost hypnotic effect of the sounds, such a poem suggests one of the functions of poetry, which is to move the reader's mind with what has moved the mind of the poet and to stir it with the power of the poet's imagination. The meaning of Poe's poem may be variously interpreted, but it vividly communicates something which is both a personal experience and a hallucination.

A sonnet ("London: September, 1802") written by William Wordsworth is a complete contrast to Poe's phantasmagoria.

> *O friend! I know not which way I must look*
> *For comfort, being, as I am, oppressed*
> *To think that now our life is only dressed*
> *For show; mean handy-work of craftsman, cook,*
> *Or groom!—We must run glittering like a brook*
> *In the open sunshine, or we are unblest;*
> *The wealthiest man among us is the best.*
> *No grandeur now in nature or in book*
> *Delights us. Rapine, avarice, expense,*
> *This is idolatry; and these we adore:*
> *Plain living and high thinking are no more:*
> *The homely beauty of the good old cause*
> *Is gone; our peace, our fearful innocence,*
> *And pure religion breathing household laws.*

Here everything is plain, simple and obvious. The reader is at ease with the situation; there is nothing to confuse him. Yet he is also aware that he is in touch with a sensitivity that transforms the obvious into more than a statement. The statement has achieved something beyond the facts; it has attained the movement, the emotional stress, which is the language and the life of poetry. If some of it seems prosy, Wordsworth asserted that "a large portion of the language of every good poem can in no respect differ from that of good prose." Wordsworth further maintained that "the language of such poetry is, as far as possible, a selection of the language really spoken by men." Replying to the question "What is meant by the word Poet?" Wordsworth continued, "He is a man speaking to men—a man, it is true, endowed with more lively sensibility, . . . who has a greater knowledge of human nature and a more comprehensive soul than are supposed to be common among mankind; a man pleased with his own passions and volitions and who rejoices more in the spirit of life that is in him, delighting to contemplate similar volitions and passions as manifested in the goings-on of the universe."

As "a man speaking to men," the poet constantly shares his experience with us; his emotion becomes ours. Lascelles Abercrombie chose three of Herrick's lightest lines to illustrate this sense of participation:

> *Whenas in silks my Julia goes*
> *Then, then (methinks) how sweetly flows*
> *The liquefaction of her clothes.*

Speaking of those seventeenth-century rhymes, Abercrombie said that "as she glides past, Herrick's Julia becomes everyone's Julia. And it is not Herrick merely *describing* what he loves to admire; our minds have become a moment of Herrick himself."

It is this sharing of emotion and experience which makes poetry the supreme communication. Even before one fully understands a poem one feels it. One feels and believes it even before the thought unfolds itself. It does not always begin with a well-defined concept, but with a vague sensation which gropes toward an idea and assumes shape as the idea reaches out toward words. A poem begins, said Robert Frost, "as a lump in the throat, a sense of wrong, a homesickness, a lovesickness. It is at its best when it is a tantalizing vagueness. It finds its thought or it makes its thought. . . . It makes us aware of things we always knew but had forgotten. It begins in delight and ends in wisdom."

The Experience of Poetry

It may be said that we inherited poetry from the universe. Creation was set in form and framed in rhythm long before man became a part of it. There was a balance of light and dark, of day and night. The sun sank, the moon climbed the heavens, with rhythmic regularity. The planets revolved in a precise pattern. The seasons were evenly quartered; the earth turned to a metrical pattern. The tides rose and fell with a never-varying, never-ending repetition.

Everything in the physical world—all energy and force—flowed in rhythm, in rise and fall, in measure and countermeasure. It flowed recurrently in waves—water waves, light waves, air waves. It never lost its rhythmical movement.

When man inherited the earth he could not help but respond to the sway of these rhythmic forces; he came to it with a built-in sense of measure. The universal balance was repeated in his body—in the beat of the heart, the rise and fall of the breath, the alternation of sleeping and waking, the moon-prompted menstrual periods. Everything within him was controlled by natural organic rhythms.

The poet speaks for his fellowmen when he verbalizes these rhythms. He becomes the interpreter of man's inarticulate responses not only by articulating his emotions but also by giving them a form. It is his inborn sense of the formal but flexible play between impulse and control, the essence of the poetic spirit, that makes man the measure of all things. "The recurrent beat of verse is not a superadded ornament," writes Frederick Clarke Prescott in *The Poetic Mind,* "but a vital and inevitable accompaniment of the poetic feeling, going back, we imagine, to the poet's heart.

The poet's feeling starts the rhythm, and the rhythm in turn will arouse feeling in the hearer, as the heart is aroused at the beat of a drum. Just as Shakespeare's words convey his sense, so his rhythm conveys to us his feeling; and it is one of the miracles of language that not merely his thought but his very emotion is thus reconstituted for us after three hundred years."

The nature of the poet is revealed not only in his idiom but also in the rhythm in which he expresses the thought of his age. This is true of every poet, of poets as radically unlike as, say, Tennyson and Whitman. Tennyson disclosed himself in conventionally precise, strictly schooled rhythmical patterns, while Whitman sounded his "barbaric yawp" in loose, seemingly wild rhythms which, like the tides, have an accumulating power. Both reflected valid and divergent reactions to the *mores* of the nineteenth century; they could not help but express themselves and their aspects of the age through disparate emotional rhythms.

"Poetry is not a turning loose of emotion," wrote T. S. Eliot in *The Sacred Wood*, "but an escape from emotion; it is not an expression of personality but an escape from personality." However, Eliot conceded that only those who have personality and emotion "know what it means to want to escape from these things." Edmund Wilson was among those who refused to confirm Eliot's disposal. In *Axel's Castle* Wilson argued that while this rejection of emotional involvement was valid and even noble in 1920, "today, after years of depersonalized and overintellectualized verse, so much of it is written in imitation of Eliot that the same sort of thing in the mouths of Eliot's disciples sounds like an excuse for *not* possessing emotion and personality."

A painter rather than a poet provided a confirmation of the creator's need for emotional sustenance. Writing to his friend Christian Zervos, Picasso held that nothing can be accomplished without a yielding to (a "turning loose" of) the emotions and whatever they suggest. "The artist," said Picasso, "is a receptacle for emotions that come from everywhere: from the sky, from the earth, from a scrap of paper, from a spider's web. That is why we must not discriminate between things. Where things are concerned there are no class distinctions."

Picasso's remark had its American counterpart in William

Carlos Williams' conviction that nothing, neither emotions nor subjects, however "unpoetic," should be rejected. His credo was: "No ideas but in things." For Williams nothing was without beauty and a significance waiting to be perceived. An emotion may be stripped to a single sensory image, but bare though the image may be, it does not lose emotional impact. Williams proved it in the verbal economy of "The Red Wheelbarrow."

> *so much depends*
> *upon*
>
> *a red wheel*
> *barrow*
>
> *glazed with rain*
> *water*
>
> *beside the white*
> *chickens.*

The precision, the final effect—the red of the wheelbarrow heightened by the glaze of rainwater and the contrasted whiteness of the chickens—suggests and even intensifies the emotions "that come from everywhere" and emanate from the very thinginess of things. Williams condensed, with the brevity of a haiku, an esthetic as well as an emotional experience in a few word-strokes.

"The Red Wheelbarrow" serves to remind us that poetry, as Shelley said, "strips the veil of familiarity from things" and reveals glories beneath the commonplace, miracles of everyday wonders that we are too unimaginative to see or too busy to appreciate.

It is too often assumed that poets are creatures so delicate that they avoid anything gross or ugly and are attuned only to what is impalpably beautiful. However, some of the poems which have lasted longest are those which have emphasized the unbeautiful, the mean and sordid. Mention has already been made of poems with such unalluring titles as Burns's "To a Louse" and Donne's "The Flea." Donne was one who saw holiness in the unholy; he disdained nothing which might be considered scarifying; there was neither high nor low in his agonizing. Burns rollicked in the disreputable. "The Jolly Beggars" displayed his delight in vulgarity, in the high spirits of low life; it is obvious that he enjoyed the orgy as much as any of the participants. Burns had a mocking tongue in his cheek when he subtitled his poem "A Cantata," for it was meant to be a rough burlesque of all the devout arias sung in churches. After a sly "recitative," a dirty soldier trolls a song about the wench on his knee, whereupon she counters with a lusty roll call of her lovers, beginning:

> *I once was a maid, tho' I cannot tell when,*
> *And still my delight is in proper young men.*
> *Some one of a troop of dragoons was my daddie;*
> *No wonder I'm fond of a sodger laddie.*

The poem ends in an uproar of annihilating humor as the poet himself furnishes the coda which combines reckless amorality and defiant contempt for law and order.

Dryden may not have been as vulgar as Burns, but his satires were no less vicious. His *MacFlecknoe* was considered too libelous for circulation; when it finally was published it appeared anonymously. Browning held that God was in his heaven and that all was right with the world, but this did not stop him from writing one of the most unbeautiful of monologues, "Soliloquy of the Spanish Cloister," in which a supposedly holy man luxuriates in a murderous hymn of hate as passionately as another man might chant a litany of love.

"Euclid alone has looked on beauty bare," declared Edna St. Vincent Millay. The poet, however, had to learn to look on beauty's opposites: on banality and brutality; to learn to encompass frightfulness as well as loveliness. In *The Sacred Wood* Eliot shrugged off the charge that he was obsessed with the tawdriness of life and with the repulsive not only in nature but also in human nature. "The contemplation of the horrid or sordid or disgusting, by the artist," wrote Eliot, "is the necessary and negative aspect of the impulse toward the pursuit of beauty." In *The Use of Poetry* he amplified that statement: "The essential advantage for a poet is not to have a beautiful world with which to deal; it is to be able to see beneath both beauty and ugliness; to see the boredom, and the horror, and the glory."

The submerged wonder that resides in all that is too often condemned as crude and commonplace is at the very heart of poetry.
It is that which both embraces and enhances life. "The poetry
of exaltation will be always the highest," wrote J. M. Synge in a
preface to his posthumously published *Poems*. "But when men
lose their feeling for ordinary life and cannot write poetry of ordinary things, their exalted poetry is likely to lose its strength of
exaltation in the way that men cease to build beautiful churches
when they have lost happiness in building shops. Even if we grant
that exalted poetry can be kept successfully by itself, the strong
things of life are needed in poetry also, to show that what is
exalted or tender is not made by feeble blood."

It should be plain, although it is not always conceded, that the
true poet mirrors the world in which he lives. And, since his
world is a cultural and political as well as an actual battleground,
the poet cannot be expected merely to charm, to rely on the spell
of incantation and wistfully try to enchant his readers. His times
always demand a sterner appraisal, one which gives his words a
greater impact. Stirring the sluggish mind, probing and provoking
it with acuteness, the poet makes us conscious of the things of
this world and aware of their unconscious influence upon us.

The purpose of poetry, if it may be said to have a purpose, is to
explore rather than to explain, not so much to interpret as to in-
tensify. Since the word "poetry" is derived from the Greek *poiesis*,
meaning a construction, a poet is literally a maker. He may not be
able to save the world, but he can help to make it worth saving.

In a fragment of verse Robert Louis Stevenson paid tribute to
the role of the poet as maker. The tone is light, but it is not
light-minded.

> *Bright is the ring of words*
>   *When the right man rings them;*
> *Fair the fall of songs*
>   *When the singer sings them.*
> *Still they are carolled and said—*
>   *On wings they are carried—*
> *After the singer is dead*
>   *And the maker buried.*

The Province of Poetry

It used to be thought that the poet was possessed, controlled—or driven beyond control—by something outside of himself. A divine madness seemed to inspire him; he breathed prophecies because his breath was that of a spirit using him as a mouthpiece. That the poet was dependent on a Muse or a Daemon or a God to transport him was accepted as a fact. It was a tradition that survived the centuries. When verse refused to flow from his usually facile pen, the post-Elizabethan Robert Herrick prayed to be possessed:

> *'Tis not every day that I*
> *Fitted am to prophesy;*
> *No, but when the spirit fills*
> *The fantastic panicles*
> *Full of fire, then I write*
> *As the Godhead doth indite.*
>
> *Thus enraged, my lines are hurled,*
> *Like the Sibyl's, through the world.*
> *Look how next the holy fire*
> *Either slakes or doth retire;*
> *So the fancy cools, till when*
> *That brave spirit comes again.*

As late as the nineteenth century, Wordsworth (in "The Recluse") invoked the Daemon, the

> . . . *prophetic spirit, that inspir'st*
> *The human soul of universal earth,*
> *Dreaming on things to come* . . .
> 　　　　　　*upon me bestow*
> *A gift of genuine insight* . . .

The tradition, though not the fact, persists. Sometimes the poet is fortunate. Sometimes he is truly possessed, and the poem springs complete, unblemished, perfectly formed and phrased, from his brain. Emotion, thought, and words unite spontaneously, and the initial conception is also the fulfilled creation. Usually, how-ever, the poem is not only born but made, written and rewritten, with as much labor as love. Many indeed have said (echoing Edison's remark about genius) that poetry was ten percent in-spiration and ninety percent perspiration. Most often a poem be-gins as a vague idea, a gleam, an image, a rhythm, a musical phrase. If the poet is lucky, the vision or image or melody grows. It assumes a form which is then shaped by application, by the conscious labor and acquired skill of the craftsman. The true poem, said Robert Frost, "is one where the emotion has found the thought and the thought has found the words."

The possessed poet and the patient craftsman have this in com-mon: both seek to charm the listener, to charm him in both senses of the word. They desire not only to allure and delight, but also to capture the reader with the spell of incantation, the original magic of poetry.

"Why should a phrase come to you out of the ground and seem to be exactly right?" asked the poet-critic Howard Nemerov. "The mystery appears to me as a poet's proper relation with things, a relation to which language, that accumulated wisdom and folly in which the living and the dead speak simultaneously, is a full part-ner and not merely a stenographer." The phrase which springs from the poet's "accumulated wisdom and folly" and prompts the poem has the distinctive characteristics of incantation, a magic that varies with the associations of the one who utters the phrase. The magic may be associated with many things—a spectacular sun-set or a sensational event, the opening of the first crocus or the

closing of a tragic life, the hoarse cries of a revolutionary crowd
or the hushed syllables of a cradle song, the feverish consumma-
tion of desire or the cool touch of a quieting hand—but its most
lasting power is evoked by the balance of sound and sense achieved
by a few magic words.

"A poem," said Archibald MacLeish as a conclusion to his *Ars
Poetica*, "should not mean/But be." Whatever meanings a poem
may have for different individuals, its meaning, its very "being,"
is implicit in its magic. In the logical sense there is little meaning
in the opening lines of one of the most stirring poems ever written:

> *Tiger, tiger, burning bright*
> *In the forests of the night*

but the leap of Blake's imagination is so compelling that we do
not stop to question the logic. We know that a tiger does not
burn and that night is not a tract of trees, but we accept the
image because it is magic, an incantation which prepares us for so
magnificent a vision as:

> *When the stars threw down their spears*
> *And watered heaven with their tears,*
> *Did he smile his work to see?*
> *Did he who made the lamb make thee?*

The response to such a poem is immediate; its sense lies in its
effect. The meaning and the magic are one. We cannot grasp the
wonder of a poet like Blake if we read him for literal understanding. It is the almost-but-not-quite-grasped mystery which is both
allusive and elusive. It is the meaningful-mystical suggestiveness
that excites us in such lines of Blake as:

> *Earth raised up her head*
> *From the darkness dread and drear.*
> *Her light fled,*
> *Stony dread!*
> *And her locks covered with grey despair.*

or:

> *To find the western path*
> *Right through the Gates of Wrath*
> *I urge my way . . .*

or:

> *The lost traveler's dream under the hill . . .*

or:

> *In every cry of every man,*
> *In every infant's cry of fear,*
> *In every voice, in every ban*
> *The mind-forged manacles I hear.*

or:

> *O rose, thou art sick!*
> *The invisible worm*
> *That flies in the night,*
> *In the howling storm,*
>
> *Has found out thy bed*
> *Of crimson joy,*
> *And his dark secret love*
> *Does thy life destroy.*

or:

> *Bring me my bow of burning gold!*
> *Bring me my arrows of desire!*
> *Bring me my spear! O clouds, unfold!*
> *Bring me my chariot of fire!*
>
> *I will not cease from mental fight,*
> *Nor shall my sword sleep in my hand*
> *Till we have built Jerusalem*
> *In England's green and pleasant land.*

or:

> *Ah, Sunflower, weary of time,*
> *Who countest the steps of the Sun,*
> *Seeking after that sweet golden clime*
> *Where the traveler's journey is done:*

Where the Youth pined away with desire,
And the pale Virgin shrouded in snow,
Arise from their graves, and aspire
Where my Sunflower wishes to go.

or:

We are led to believe a lie
When we see not through the eye,
Which was born in a night, to perish in a night,
When the soul slept in beams of light.

or:

To see a world in a grain of sand
And a Heaven in a wild flower,
Hold Infinity in the palm of your hand
And Eternity in an hour.

"For me," said Housman, "the most poetical of all poets is Blake. I find his lyrical note as beautiful as Shakespeare's and more beautiful than anyone else's. . . . Blake's meaning is often unimportant so that one can listen with all our hearing to his celestial tune."

That poetry often escapes definite rationalization is proved again and again, most notably by Coleridge's "Kubla Khan" which is without cumulative meaning or message but which is a marvelous hypnotic vision that is sheer sorcery.

In Xanadu did Kubla Khan
*   A stately pleasure-dome decree:*
Where Alph, the sacred river, ran
Through caverns measureless to man
*   Down to a sunless sea.*
So twice five miles of fertile ground
With walls and towers were girdled round:
And here were gardens bright with sinuous rills,
Where blossomed many an incense-bearing tree,
And here were forests ancient as the hills,
Enfolding sunny spots of greenery.

But oh! that deep romantic chasm which slanted
Down the green hill athwart a cedarn cover!
A savage place! as holy and enchanted
As e'er beneath a waning moon was haunted
By woman wailing for her demon-lover!
And from this chasm, with ceaseless turmoil seething,
As if this earth in fast thick pants were breathing,
A mighty fountain momently was forced,
Amid whose swift half-intermitted burst
Huge fragments vaulted like rebounding hail,
Or chaffy grain beneath the thresher's flail:
And 'mid these dancing rocks at once and ever
It flung up momently the sacred river.
Five miles meandering with a mazy motion
Through wood and dale the sacred river ran,
Then reached the caverns measureless to man,
And sank in tumult to a lifeless ocean:
And 'mid this tumult Kubla heard from far
Ancestral voices prophesying war!
    The shadow of the dome of pleasure
    Floated midway on the waves;
    Where was heard the mingled measure
    From the fountain and the caves.
It was a miracle of rare device,
A sunny pleasure-dome with caves of ice!

    A damsel with a dulcimer
    In a vision once I saw:
    It was an Abyssinian maid,
    And on her dulcimer she played,
    Singing of Mount Abora.
    Could I revive within me
    Her symphony and song,
    To such a deep delight 'twould win me,
That with music loud and long,
I would build that dome in air,
That sunny dome! those caves of ice!
And all who heard should see them there,
And all should cry, Beware! Beware!
His flashing eyes, his floating hair!

Weave a circle round him thrice,
And close your eyes with holy dread,
For he on honey-dew hath fed,
And drunk the milk of Paradise.

On a much lower level, some of the simplest evocations are, in the casual sense, enchanting. In a few lines and a few seemingly insignificant details two minor nineteenth-century poets conjured up something similar and similarly unforgettable. The first flash of memory is by the English William Allingham:

Four ducks on a pond,
A grass bank beyond,
The blue sky of spring,
White clouds on the wing.
What a little thing
To remember for years—
To remember with tears.

The second nostalgic picture is by the American Thomas Bailey Aldrich.

My mind lets go a thousand things,
Like dates of wars and deaths of kings,
And yet recalls the very hour—
'Twas noon by yonder village tower,
And on the last blue noon in May—
The wind came briskly up this way,
Crisping the brook beside the road;
Then, pausing here, set down its load
Of pine-scents, and shook listlessly
Two petals from that wild-rose tree.

There is a kind of spell in the very clairvoyance of the two pictures. There are, however, countless poems which, if not devoid of rational import, are less meaningful than musical, poems that tend to constitute a kind of poetry as "pure" and meaningless as a beautiful melody or an emotional but abstract painting.

That art is not always or even necessarily rational was one of

Walter Pater's most quoted (and most controversial) statements. "All art constantly aspires toward the condition of music." Pater held that it was actually the aim of art to obliterate the distinction between content and form. "Art is always striving to be independent of mere intelligence."

Poetry cannot be said to be independent of the intelligence, but it frequently rises beyond it. A true poem may be exhaustively analyzed, but it can never be exhausted. The province of poetry is the domain of magic.

The Words of Poetry

Poetry presented no problems either to the ancients or to those who, until the industrial revolution, lived on the land. Its comprehension was there from the beginning; the poetic impulse and its reception were taken for granted. Poems were not difficult to understand. Poorly educated, cut off from the centers of news, people listened to bards and ballad-singers, to wandering students, scholarly vagrants, itinerant troubadours—all of whom recited verses or sang them to music. People learned even as they listened while the gossip of the day, the crime of the week, and the political events of the month were turned into poetry.

Communication was immediately established because the vocabulary was shared by the reciter (or singer) and the listener. No one assumed that there were some things or thoughts or words which were, in themselves, unfit for poetry. In a sense, the listeners were unconscious poets; they, too, had within them the need to be uplifted, and the spoken words had the power to release their spirits.

It was the common words that had the greatest persuasion. Some poets still take pleasure in odd idioms and strange expressions to give a peculiar flavor to their utterance. For a long time poets adhered to the artful formulas of "poetic diction." (See page 249.) But the common words are those that last longest. They continue to move us because, said Lascelles Abercrombie, "they necessarily have the greatest suggestive power behind them . . . It is everyday speech, with its innumerable variations in usage, that keeps a word alive with poetic power."

I have said that those who listened to poetry were also poets, though unconscious ones. They, too, created as well as preserved the language of poetry. Their innate feeling for poetry is found in countless ways, in none more charming than in the field of flowers. Here the evidence is so clear and so winning that I (a persistent if not always successful gardener) allow myself something of a lengthy parenthesis to prove the point. Contrast, for example, the language used by the botanist and the wildflower gatherer. In every instance the common country name is not only more charming than the botanist's appellation but also far more poetic. The object, a flower or a fern, is even more accurately described because it has been more lovingly observed. The man of science exploring the wet woods in spring finds what he calls an *Arisaema triphyllum*, which he defines as a plant with a round and larger portion tuberous, with numerous white radicles in a circle from its upper edge, the underside covered with a dark, loose, wrinkled epidermis, spathe ovate, acuminate, convoluted, etc. The nature-lover knows better. He knows, echoing the genius who first invented the name, it is a "Jack-in-the-Pulpit." His observation, united with his imagination, accurately if whimsically describes the pulpit-like structure enriched with an arching canopy, its center occupied by a ministerially upright figure. Only a botanist blind to beauty could stigmatize the fairy-like "Lady's-slipper" as a *Cypripedium pubescens* and add that it is a cure for hysteria, or see a vernal "Wake-robin" as a *Trillium erectum*, or ruin the graceful "Purple-fringed Orchis" by naming it the ugly and unpronounceable *Blephariglottis psychodes*. Rather than *Digitalis*, with its medicinal overtones, we prefer the odd and lightly humorous "Foxglove"; instead of the deadly *Aconite* our image-inspired eye sees the miniature replica of a "Monkshood." It is the poet in us all that leads us to portray the common weeds in uncommonly picturesque terms. The "Dandelion," that bold and brilliant invader which, if it were rare, would be planted in our gardens, is so-called because some fanciful Frenchman thought the leaves resembled the tooth of the lion, or *Dent de lion*. Another wayside weed suggested the startling likeness between the great golden sun high in the heavens, the "Eye of Day," and the small earthly "Day's Eye" or "Daisy" with its ray-petals shining from a sunlike center. What delight must have moved the minds of those who first so ingeniously—and so accurately—named "Black-eyed Susan," that gay hoyden flaunting an orange scarf around her dark brown head; the blue and white stars of the "Aster"; the dead-white apparition of the "Corpse Plant" or ghostly "Indian Pipe"; the happy homeliness of "Butter-and-Eggs" (so much more satisfying than the repetitive if lilting *Linaria linaria*); the proud trumpets of the "Morning-glory"; the wandering trails of "Moneywort," familiarly called "Creeping Jenny" or "Meadow Runagate"; the aspiring *Polemonium* more deservedly known as "Jacob's Ladder"; the delicate craftsmanship of the "Jewelweed" with its golden trinkets artfully hung from fine green wires. *Nigella* conveys nothing to most of us, but "Love-in-a-Mist" vividly pictures the pale flower half-concealed in its own aura. *Physostegia* is quickly recognized as the "Obedient Plant" because its buds remain at whatever angle they are manipulated.

William Cullen Bryant was on the side of the average man. The poet refused to see a fringed gentian as a variety of *Dasystephana* but hailed it rather as a flower singular and startling because of its peculiar blueness, holding something of heaven in its intense color:

> *Blue—blue—as if the sky let fall*
> *A flower from its cerulean wall.*

To quote again from *The Theory of Poetry*, Lascelles Abercrombie considers the magic of ordinary words and inveighs against confining them to their scientific or even literary associations. He maintains that it is not so much disuse as misuse which has spoiled the elasticity of many words.

> It is the familiar employment of its meaning in one constant direction that makes a word rigid and takes the magic out of it. . . . English literature has never known such a display of verbal magic as in the Elizabethan period; the least of the Elizabethans can thrill us with the sheer vitality of his words. It is because the accent and idiom of Elizabethan poetry was always as close

as possible to the accent and idiom of speech. Poetry then found its prime material not in a language broken in by literature, but in the language of people talking, full of the rapid shades and gleams, the expressive irregularities and careless experiments, of conversation. It could not be otherwise. An Elizabethan poet had hardly any other language to draw on except the literature of speech; English as printed literature scarcely existed for him. Elizabethan poetry took place in the midst of life, and it used the language, even the slang, of life.

Abercrombie went on to examine Milton's vigorous mixture of common and "poetic" idioms, his continual shifting from pompous to colloquial phrases and back again from the colloquial to the pompous. "Milton, having triumphed through all the lordly splendors of which English is capable, ended by relying chiefly on the words and idioms of common speech."

Another kind of triumph is apparent in the first part of William Cowper's *The Task*. Cowper's subject is "The Sofa" and he writes a small mock-epic to man's rise from squatting and sprawling to sitting and his eventual graduation to stretching-out on the luxury of the sofa. The poem traces the progress of man's postures from his use of the rough, three-legged stool to the only slightly more comfortable four-legged chair:

> . . . *The back erect*
> *Distress'd the weary loins that felt no ease;*
> *The slippery seat betray'd the sliding part*
> *That press'd it, and the feet hung dangling down.*
> *Anxious in vain to find the distant floor.*

Finally the sofa is evolved.

> *The ladies first*
> *'Gan murmur as became the softer sex.*
> *Ingenious fancy, never better pleas'd*
> *Than when employ'd t'accommodate the fair,*
> *Heard the sweet moan with pity and devis'd*
> *The soft settee; . . .   So slow*
> *The growth of what is excellent; so hard*
> *T'attain perfection in this nether world.*

Here, it is obvious, the poet uses words most effectively when they are most ridiculously affected. The poetic diction is not only burlesqued by overstatement but by overelegance, by rhetorical absurdities, comic anticlimaxes, double meanings, and fundamental puns about "the slippery seat," "the softer sex," and the ultimate difficulty of attaining perfection "in this nether world."

The fun of employing words seemingly for serious purposes but actually reducing them to mockery is an artifice which is something of an art. It is an art of which even so pure a poet as Paul Valéry would have approved when he contended that the condition of the poet was a "willed inquiry," an alert and conscious curiosity about everything, a need to examine every aspect of the word and "the mobility of things . . . to prolong in some measure the happiness of the moment" and to change "what passes into what endures."

Cowper's lines are an amusing example of verse-making which is not poetry but merely one of the ways by which poetry is achieved. A perfect poem is a fusion of imperfect elements—a prevailing though not necessarily regular rhythm, a basic though not always rational idea, an imagery which is suggestive rather than exact, and a balance of sense and sound—all of which is achieved by an association of the most effective words, and, moreover, the right words in the right places.

The subtly evocative power of words is illustrated by two twentieth-century poems. They show marked differences in the authors' tastes, in tone, and in technique. Oliver St. John Gogarty's "Verse" is straightforward, direct in statement, while Humbert Wolfe's "Iliad" is more elaborate and spiced with suspended rhymes. Yet, besides the mutual reference to hexameters (see page 207), both attest to the verbal power as well as to the permanence of poetry.

VERSE

What should we know
For better or worse
Of the Long Ago
Were it not for Verse:
What ships went down;

What walls were razed;
Who won the crown;
What lads were praised?
A fallen stone,
Or a waste of sands;
And all is known
Of Art-less lands.
But you need not delve
By the sea-side hills
Where the Muse herself
All Time fulfils,
Who cuts with his scythe
All things but hers,
All but the blithe
Hexameters.

ILIAD

False dreams, all false,
mad heart, were yours.
The word, and nought else,
in time endures.
Not you long after,
perished and mute,
will last, but the defter
viol and lute.
Sweetly they'll trouble
the listeners
with the cold dropped pebble
of painless verse.
Not you will be offered,
but the poet's false pain.
You have loved and suffered,
mad heart, in vain.
What love doth Helen
or Paris have
where they lie still in
a nameless grave?
Her beauty's a wraith,
and the boy Paris

muffles in death
his mouth's cold cherries.
Yes! these are less,
that were love's summer,
than one gold phrase
of old blind Homer.
Not Helen's wonder
nor Paris stirs,
but the bright, untender
hexameters.
And thus, all passion
is nothing made,
but a star to flash in
an Iliad.
Mad heart, you were wrong!
No love of yours,
but only what's sung,
when love's over, endures.

The Sound and Sense of Poetry

Scholars delight in the never-ending argument concerning poetry's dependence on sound *contra* its dependence on sense. Before the analysts decided (and differed) about how to count syllables, place accents, distribute stresses, and define patterns of prose, Pope summed up the matter when he concluded:

> *'Tis not enough no harshness gives offense,*
> *The sound must seem an echo to the sense.*

Commenting on the mixture of auditive and psychic stimuli, Valéry wrote that "each word is an instantaneous coupling of a sound and a sense that have no connection with each other. Each sentence is an act so complex that I doubt whether anyone has yet been able to provide a tolerable definition of it . . . The poet is at grips with this verbal matter, obliged to speculate on sound and sense at once, and to satisfy not only harmony and musical timing but all the various intellectual and aesthetic conditions, not to mention the conventional rules . . . Of all the arts, poetry is that which co-ordinates the greatest number of independent factors: sound and sense, the real and the imaginary, as well as logic, syntax, and the double invention of content and form."

Sound alone has carried many of the greatest passages in poetry. Marlowe's "mighty line" was largely the result of his use of sonorous and almost savage luxuriance. *Tamburlaine the Great* is a riot of rhetoric; one can sense the pleasure with which Marlowe

rolled over on his tongue the syllables of such place-names as
Natolia, Sinus Arabicus, Samarcanda, and Babylon. No reader can
fail to share the delight Marlowe must have felt in the rich music
of such a passage as:

> Now crouch, ye kings of greatest Asia,
> And tremble when ye hear this scourge will come
> That whips down cities and controlleth crowns,
> Adding their wealth and treasure to my store.
> The Euxine sea, north to Natolia;
> The Terrene, west; the Caspian, north-north-east;
> And on the south, Sinus Arabicus;
> Shall all be loaden with the martial spoils
> We will convey with us to Persia.
> Then shall my native city, Samarcanda,
> And crystal waters of fresh Jaertis' stream,
> The pride and beauty of her princely seat,
> Be famous through the furthest continents,
> For there my palace-royal shall be placed,
> Whose shining turrets shall dismay the heavens
> And cast the fame of Ilion's tower to hell . . .
> So will I ride through Samarcanda's streets,
> Until my soul, dissevered from this flesh,
> Shall mount the milk-white way, and meet him there.
> To Babylon, my lords. To Babylon!

Milton was scarcely less enchanted with verbal resonance. In
the midst of austerities he could indulge in the sonority of exotic
proper names:

> And all who since, baptized or infidel,
> Jousted in Aspramont or Montalban,
> Damascus, or Morocco, or Trebizond,
> Or whom Bizerta sent from Afric shore,
> When Charlemagne with all his peerage fell
> By Fontarabbia.

Echoes of both Marlowe and Milton are heard in Archibald
MacLeish's evocation in "You, Andrew Marvell" with its colorful

suggestions of strange enchantment as the shadow of night sweeps over the world.

> *And strange at Ecbatan the trees*
> *Take leaf by leaf the evening strange*
> *The flooding dark about their knees*
> *The mountains over Persia change*

> *And now at Kermanshah the gate*
> *Dark empty and the withered grass*
> *And through the twilight now the late*
> *Few travelers in the westward pass*

> *And Baghdad darken and the bridge*
> *Across the silent river gone*
> *And through Arabia the edge*
> *Of evening widen and steal on*

> *And deepen on Palmyra's street*
> *The wheel rut in the ruined stone*
> *And Lebanon fade out and Crete*
> *High through the clouds and overblown*

The larger works of W. J. Turner are almost forgotten. But this twentieth-century poet, born in Australia, lives in the anthologies because of a single small lyric. His "Romance" is an incantation, a lyric of escape that justifies its title in the mere sounds and musical spell of a few faraway places.

> *When I was but thirteen or so*
> *I went into a golden land,*
> *Chimborazo, Cotopaxi*
> *Took me by the hand.*

> *My father died, my brother too,*
> *They passed like fleeting dreams,*
> *I stood where Popocatepetl*
> *In the sunlight gleams.*

> *I dimly heard the master's voice*
> *And boys far-off at play,—*
> *Chimborazo, Cotopaxi*
> *Had stolen me away.* \

I walked in a great golden dream
To and fro from school—
Shining Popocatepetl
The dusty streets did rule.

I walked home with a gold dark boy
And never a word I'd say;
Chimborazo, Cotopaxi
Had taken my speech away.

I gazed entranced upon his face
Fairer than any flower—
O shining Popocatepetl,
It was thy magic hour.

The houses, people, traffic seemed
Thin fading dreams by day;
Chimborazo, Cotopaxi,
They had stolen my soul away!

Shelley's "To a Skylark" is an almost perfect example of a poem in which sound sometimes takes the place of sense. Readers yield quickly to its rapturous effluence which begins with a salutation and rises quickly to an exaltation. Yet in that ascent the poem veers and dips into a rhetoric which is resounding and little more. Sound overrides sense in such stanzas as:

The pale purple even
Melts around thy flight;
Like a star of Heaven
In the broad daylight
Thou art unseen, but yet I hear thy shrill delight,

Keen as are the arrows
Of that silver sphere,
Whose intense lamp narrows
In the white dawn clear
Until we hardly see—we feel that it is there.

The phonetic aspect of language, the combination of euphony and cacophony is brilliantly exemplified in the passage from Pope's *Essay on Criticism* which begins:

> *True ease in writing comes from art, not chance,*
> *As those move easiest who have learned to dance.*

Pope then goes on to illustrate the continual interplay of shifting tones and tempi, of smooth and rough, fast and slow, in these lines:

> *Soft is the strain when Zephyr gently blows,*
> *And the smooth stream in smoother numbers flows;*
> *But when loud surges lash the sounding shore,*
> *The hoarse, rough verse should like the torrent roar.*
> *When Ajax strives some rock's vast weight to throw,*
> *The line too labors, and the words move slow;*
> *Not so, when swift Camilla scours the plain,*
> *Flies o'er the unbending corn, and skims along the main.*

More than other poets, Robert Browning touched the limits of sound and sense; as a consequence he was subjected to the extremes of disparagement and adulation. *The Atheneum*, which had once dismissed the poet with faint patronization, considered *The Ring and the Book* "beyond all parallel not merely the supremest poetical achievement of our time, but also the most precious and profound spiritual treasure that England has produced since the days of Shakespeare." No such laudation was accorded Browning's frequent retreat from profundities into the pleasure of playing with sounds. Even in his most somber poems Browning loved to mix melodiousness and dissonance, pitting the two against each other in contradictions of smooth and rough. "Rabbi Ben Ezra" is a perfect example of his suave and jostling effects, particularly notable in such a stanza as this with its almost unpronounceable last line:

> *Poor vaunt of life indeed*
> *Were man but formed to feed*
> *On joy, to solely seek and find and feast:*
> *Such feasting ended, then*
> *As sure an end to men;*
> *Irks care the crop-full bird? Frets doubt the maw-crammed beast?*

"Popularity" is another of Browning's well-known poems which skilfully balances euphony and cacophony. This is the tuneful first verse:

> Stand still, true poet that you are.
> I know you; let me try and draw you.
> Some night you'll fail us: when afar
>   You rise, remember one man saw you,
> Knew you, and named a star.

And this is its gratingly discordant final stanza:

> Hobbs hints blue—straight he turtle eats;
>   Nobbs prints blue—claret crowns his cup:
> Nokes outdares Stokes in azure feats—
>   Both gorge. Who fished the murex up?
> What porridge had John Keats?

Rhyme was more than a diversion for Browning. It was his delight and, all too often, his undoing. He amused himself with matching seemingly impossible pairs and coupling words which no one else would have considered joining. Sometimes he rang changes on a sound so insistently that the rhyme ran away with him. "Through the Metidja to Abd-El-Kadr" is an instance where Browning let a single vowel-sound ride rough-shod over the lines until the poem became a shambles. The mangling begins in the opening stanza:

> As I ride, as I ride
> With a full heart for my guide,
> So its tide rocks my side,
> As I ride, as I ride,
> That, as I were double-eyed,
> He, in whom our Tribes confide,
> Is descried, ways untried,
> As I ride, as I ride.

And so on for forty more monotonously jingling lines exploiting the one rhyme until both reader and rider reel with the din. The poem itself would not have been so noisy a failure had Browning known and heeded Lewis Carroll's perversion of the proverb about pence and pounds: "Take care of the sense and the sounds will take care of themselves."

The perfect union of sound and sense is rare in English poetry. It is found only sporadically, in certain anonymous Elizabethan songs, in the soliloquies of Shakespeare, in the metaphysical love poems of Donne, in the grander passages of Milton, in some of the artless lyrics of Blake and Burns, and in the odes of Keats. Never has there been a purer or more spontaneous coupling of sound and sense than in the "Ode on a Grecian Urn," "Ode to a Nightingale," "Ode to Melancholy," and "To Autumn." The faintly melancholy mood of the last blends with a muted music, music in a minor key, and suffuses the poem with a warm and "mellow fruitfulness" which poetry has never surpassed.

In *John Keats: The Making of a Poet* Aileen Ward quotes a letter which Keats wrote his good friend, John Hamilton Reynolds, describing his delight in the serenity of the autumnal landscape: "How beautiful the season is now. How fine the air. A temperate sharpness about it. Really, without joking, chaste weather—Dian skies—I never liked stubble fields so much as now—aye, better than the chilly green of spring. Somehow a stubble field looks warm— in the same way that some pictures look warm. This struck me so much in my Sunday's walk that I composed upon it." Miss Ward adds: "What he wrote that Sunday afternoon was his most perfect and untroubled poem."

TO AUTUMN

Season of mists and mellow fruitfulness,
*   Close bosom-friend of the maturing sun;*
Conspiring with him how to load and bless
*   With fruit the vines that round the thatch-eaves run;*
To bend with apples the mossed cottage-trees,
*   And fill all fruit with ripeness to the core;*
*   To swell the gourd, and plump the hazel shells*
*   With a sweet kernel; to set budding more,*
And still more, later flowers for the bees,
Until they think warm days will never cease,
*   For Summer has o'er-brimmed their clammy cells.*

Who hath not seen thee oft amid thy store?
  Sometimes whoever seeks abroad may find
Thee sitting careless on a granary floor,
  Thy hair soft-lifted by the winnowing wind;
Or on a half-reaped furrow sound asleep,
  Drowsed with the fume of poppies, while thy hook
    Spares the next swarth and all its twinèd flowers;
And sometimes like a gleaner thou dost keep
  Steady thy laden head across a brook;
  Or by a cider-press, with patient look,
    Thou watchest the last oozings, hours by hours.

Where are the songs of Spring? Ay, where are they?
  Think not of them, thou hast thy music too,—
While barred clouds bloom the soft-dying day,
  And touch the stubble-plains with rosy hue;
Then in a wailful choir, the small gnats mourn
  Among the river sallows, borne aloft
    Or sinking as the light wind lives or dies;
And full-grown lambs loud bleat from hilly bourn;
  Hedge-crickets sing; and now with treble soft
  The redbreast whistles from a garden-croft,
    And gathering swallows twitter in the skies.

The Styles of Poetry

Sound and sense are intricately bound up with the problem of style. Buffon has been interminably quoted to the effect that the style is the man, and it is generally assumed that an author cannot help but reflect himself in whatever he writes. Yet the style of a writer may undergo drastic changes, and it would be hard to prove which style represents the "real" man. If it is difficult to establish which style represents, say, Yeats, it is equally hazardous to assign a definite style to a period. The eighteenth century, for example, is usually characterized as an age of revived classicism, an age that made a fetish of scientific rationalism, an Augustan age of elegance. Yet the century that produced the precise, barbed artifice of Pope also produced the kind and quiet simplicities of Goldsmith, the mystical passion of Blake, and the earthy lyricism of Burns.

Buffon to the contrary, the style is not always the man. All too frequently style, as one of its definitions indicates, is nothing more than the fashion of the moment. The first half of the twentieth century saw the emergence of styles that were determinedly anti-traditional—surrealist, mannerist, pseudo-Marxian, psychoanalytic, imagist, projectivist—styles which were not so much created as assembled, the combined product of the library and the laboratory. For a while there was the dazzle of the achieved experiment, the technological triumph, the progress from which there was no turning back. However, as soon as the accomplishments of the avant-garde were accepted, they began to look dated. The daring styles, the innovations of the day, became the discards of tomorrow. The practitioners of the New were less interested in emotional responses, even in communication, than in methods in which the experiment was, in itself, the style. The poet of this persuasion, remarked A. Alvarez in *Beyond All This Fiddle*, "becomes so rapt with whatever is immediately at his nerve-ends that he has no time to attend to anything else or to respond at any depth. He is also so unwilling to tamper with his Muse that he ends by tolerating dross, wastage, irrelevance, obscurity, all in the paradoxical name of the aesthetic purity of his inspiration—as who should say, 'My poems are so messy because they are so pure.'"

The preoccupation with the New, the search for a fashionable style and an idiosyncratic manner, is a perennial obsession. It was exposed long before Alvarez voiced its excesses. Another essayist wrote of those who were obsessed with a need for a new style of writing. They brought in, he said, "an affected study of eloquence which then began to flourish. This grew speedily to an excess, for men began to hunt more after words than matter; more after the choiceness of the phrase, the falling of the clauses, and the varying and illustration of their words with tropes and figures than after the weight of matter, worth of subject, soundness of argument, life of invention, or depth of judgment." These sentences, so modern in their application, were written by Francis Bacon almost four hundred years ago.

It is a sense of style which determines the taste of the poet and the life of the poem. It is the manner of treatment which can lift the same theme to the height of ecstasy or drag it to the depth of banality. In the Victorian era two popular pastoral poems were to be found in most anthologies. They were "The Garden" by Andrew Marvell and "My Garden" by T. E. Brown. Here is the first:

> *How vainly men themselves amaze*
> *To win the palm, the oak, or bays;*
> *And their incessant labors see*
> *Crowned from some single herb, or tree,*
> *Whose short and narrow-vergéd shade*
> *Does prudently their toils upbraid;*
> *While all flowers and all trees do close*
> *To weave the garlands of repose!*

Fair Quiet, have I found thee here,
And Innocence, thy sister dear?
Mistaken long, I sought you then
In busy companies of men.
Your sacred plants, if here below,
Only among the plants will grow;
Society is all but rude
To this delicious solitude.

No white nor red was ever seen
So amorous as this lovely green.
Fond lovers, cruel as their flame,
Cut in these trees their mistress' name:
Little, alas! they know or heed
How far these beauties hers exceed!
Fair trees! wheresoe'er your barks I wound,
No name shall but your own be found.

When we have run our passion's heat,
Love hither makes his best retreat.
The gods, that mortal beauty chase,
Still in a tree did end their race;
Apollo hunted Daphne so,
Only that she might laurel grow;
And Pan did after Syrinx speed,
Not as a nymph, but for a reed.

What wondrous life is this I lead!
Ripe apples drop about my head;
The luscious clusters of the vine
Upon my mouth do crush their wine;
The nectarine, and curious peach,
Into my hands themselves do reach;
Stumbling on melons, as I pass,
Insnared with flowers, I fall on grass.

Meanwhile, the mind, from pleasure less,
Withdraws into its happiness;
The mind, that ocean where each kind
Does straight its own resemblance find;
Yet it creates, transcending these,
Far other worlds, and other seas;

Annihilating all that's made
To a green thought in a green shade.

Here at the fountain's sliding foot,
Or at some fruit-tree's mossy root,
Casting the body's vest aside,
My soul into the boughs does glide:
There like a bird it sits, and sings,
Then whets and combs its silver wings;
And, till prepared for longer flight,
Waves in its plumes the various light.

Such was that happy garden-state,
While man there walked without a mate.
After a place so pure and sweet,
What other help could yet be meet!
But 'twas beyond a mortal's share
To wander solitary there:
Two paradises 'twere in one,
To live in Paradise alone.

How well the skilful gardener drew
Of flowers, and herbs, this dial new;
Where, from above, the milder sun
Does through a fragrant zodiac run;
And, as it works, the industrious bee
Computes its time as well as we!
How could such sweet and wholesome hours
Be reckoned but with herbs and flowers!

And here is Brown's poem in full:

A garden is a lovesome thing, God wot!
    Rose plot,
        Fringed pool,
    Ferned grot—
        The veriest school
        Of peace, And yet the fool
Contends that God is not—
Not God! in gardens! when the eve is cool?
    Nay, but I have a sign:
    'Tis very sure God walks in mine!

Both poems are poems of praise; both celebrate the peacefulness of a garden retreat; the sentiment that prompted the poets to communicate their feeling is much the same. It is the style in which they are written that emphasizes the difference between poetry and verse-making. An exquisite taste, a fine restraint, and a delicacy of image make Marvell's lines memorable even to those who have never given a thought to gardens. Brown's stilted vocabulary, his blatant affectations and Victorian sanctimony suggest something which, in its primping archaisms, is the very opposite of "lovesome." The two poems furnish an object lesson exhibiting the difference between controlled sentiment and sentimentality, between a perfected poem and a period piece, between a dateless style and an outmoded stylishness.

The Images of Poetry

Imaging, wrote Sir Philip Sidney, anticipating the Imagists by almost four centuries, "is in itself the very height and life of poetry." Although the image may soar at "the very height and life" of poetry, it does not demand a rarefied atmosphere. On the contrary, it draws breath and flourishes in the common air. Our ordinary talk, our earthy slang with its pungent idioms, is rich in vivid images. The banal stereotypes of conversation now worn so thin they have lost all freshness were once strange and surprising. We no longer feel the excitement that some anonymous poet put into such startling images as "I jumped clear out of my skin" . . . "he is just a bag of bones" . . . "fast as greased lightning" . . . "scarce as hen's teeth" . . . "raining cats and dogs," but we continue to use the clichés because the impact of the poetic image pleases us more than the prosy statement of fact. It is hard to say someone is sly or hungry or bright or cute or crooked without completing the image by saying "sly as a fox," "hungry as a bear," "bright as a button," "cute as a kitten," "crooked as a corkscrew."

We are, as I said, pleased but not surprised. We are no longer jolted by the esthetic shock with which Eliot begins "The Love Song of J. Alfred Prufrock":

> Let us go then, you and I
> When the evening is spread out against the sky
> Like a patient etherized upon a table . . .

A less bizarre but equally fantastic image ends "Winter Remembered," a love poem by John Crowe Ransom:

> *Dear love, these fingers that have known your touch,*
> *And tied our separate forces first together,*
> *Were ten poor idiot fingers not worth much:*
> *Ten frozen parsnips hanging in the weather.*

Ransom's fingers, turned into "ten frozen parsnips," inevitably recall a similar image-effect in John Donne's "Elegy: The Comparison":

> *. . . like a bunch of ragged carrots stand*
> *The short swoll'n fingers of thy gouty hand.*

The digital image is employed more charmingly by the seventeenth-century Richard Lovelace in a tribute to "Ellinda's Glove." It is apparently a white glove, for Lovelace compares it to a "snowy farm," and the fingers become, in his image-making mind, five houses, or "tenements." It reminds him that he has come to pay the rent to his disdainful mistress who is a flirt, impartially gathering hearts and flowers.

> *Thou snowy farm with thy five tenements,*
> *Tell thy white mistress here was one*
> *That called to pay his daily rents;*
> *But she a-gathering flowers and hearts is gone,*
> *And thou left void to rude possessión.*

Matthew Arnold's "Dover Beach" is another monologue which is held together more tightly by a single unifying image. It is a disillusioned soliloquy, a dissertation on the seeming beauty but actual meaninglessness of the world, a world without joy or peace or love, a world in which the only faith is the faith of those who cling to each other. The poignance is accentuated by imagery of the sea. It is stressed and sharpened by the comparison with a sea of faith, once full but now shrunken, a sea that echoes the turbid ebb and flow of human misery in its "melancholy, long, withdraw-

ing roar," its cadences sounding "the eternal note of sadness"—
an image extended from the calmness of a tranquil bay to a dark-
ling plain where, swept with confusion, "ignorant armies clash by
night."

>The sea is calm tonight,
>The tide is full, the moon lies fair
>Upon the straits;—on the French coast the light
>Gleams and is gone; the cliffs of England stand,
>Glimmering and vast, out in the tranquil bay.
>Come to the window, sweet is the night-air!
>Only, from the long line of spray
>Where the sea meets the moon-blanched land,
>Listen! you hear the grating roar
>Of pebbles which the waves draw back, and fling,
>At their return, up the high strand,
>Begin, and cease, and then again begin,
>With tremulous cadence slow, and bring
>The eternal note of sadness in.
>
>Sophocles long ago
>Heard it on the Aegean, and it brought
>Into his mind the turbid ebb and flow
>Of human misery; we
>Find also in the sound a thought,
>Hearing it by this distant northern sea.
>
>The Sea of Faith
>Was once, too, at the full, and round earth's shore
>Lay like the folds of a bright girdle furled.
>But now I only hear
>Its melancholy, long, withdrawing roar,
>Retreating, to the breath
>Of the night-wind, down the vast edges drear
>And naked shingles of the world.
>
>Ah, love, let us be true
>To one another! For the world, which seems
>To lie before us like a land of dreams,
>So various, so beautiful, so new,
>Hath really neither joy, nor love, nor light,

> *Nor certitude, nor peace, nor help for pain;*
> *And we are here as on a darkling plain*
> *Swept with confused alarms of struggle and flight,*
> *Where ignorant armies clash by night.*

The poet's use of imagery is merely a heightening of the language employed by people in their everyday communications. The image, however, does something to their speech; it changes the pitch and raises it far above a statement. It illuminates and intensifies what would have been colorless and flat.

> *She sat like patience on a monument,*
> *Smiling at grief.*

These words spoken by Viola in *Twelfth Night* are casual words of everyday, but the image they evoke is imperishable.

The image is not essential to poetry. Some of the most profound poems do not contain a single image—Wordsworth disdained anything that was fanciful; he maintained that images were meant merely "to beguile the temporal part of our natures." But most poets have demonstrated that the image is anything but a fanciful decoration or a diverting accessory; they have shown that it is, in itself, an emanation of the poetic impulse, an overflow of the creative imagination.

As early as the 1860's Walt Whitman had declared, "We must have new words, new potentialities of speech . . . The new times, the new people need a new tongue according, and what is more, they will have such a tongue—will not be satisfied until it is evolved." Half a century later a small band of writers determined to fulfill Whitman's demand for a poetry free of affectations and shopworn poetic diction. Ezra Pound was the prime mover of a group which in 1914 published a slim volume, *Des Imagistes*. It was followed by three volumes entitled *Some Imagist Poets,* published under the aegis of Amy Lowell. Pound, though he was bitter about the "Amygists," nevertheless struck one of the keynotes of their program with his injunction "to compose in the sequence of the musical phrase, not in the sequence of the metronome." The Imagist credo was summed up in six pronunciamentos.

1. To use the language of common speech, but to employ always the *exact* word, not the merely decorative word.
2. To create new rhythms—as the expression of new moods. We do not insist upon "free-verse" as the only method of writing poetry. . . . We do believe that the individuality of a poet may often be better expressed in free verse than in conventional forms.
3. To allow absolute freedom in the choice of subject.
4. To present an image (hence the name: "Imagist"). We are not a school of painters, but we believe that poetry should render particulars exactly and not deal in vague generalities, however magnificent and sonorous.
5. To produce poetry that is hard and clear, never blurred or indefinite.
6. Finally, most of us believe that concentration is the very essence of poetry.

These principles were scarcely revolutionary. The Imagists themselves recognized that they were the essentials of all great poetry, indeed of all great literature—"these principles are not new; they have fallen into desuetude." Obvious and almost platitudinous as these statements were, they aroused a controversy; and Amy Lowell, who became their militant champion, stood embattled in a storm center. That the individuality of a poet may often be better expressed in free verse than in conventional forms was a tenet that turned into a slogan; it led unaccountably to a furore over free verse. The emphasis on the image was forgotten in attacks on "shredded prose"; exponents of verse libre were ridiculed as "vers libertines." Nevertheless, slender though their actual contribution may have been, the Imagists helped to clear poetry of its rhetorical clutter by accentuating concision, clarity, and colloquial speech. They demanded accuracy and sharply-perceived details as well as an extension of the image—principles which they frequently violated in practice.

Two examples differing in vocabulary illustrate the method. The first is from a group of "Nocturnes" by Skipwith Cannell; the second, "Heat," is by H. D. (Hilda Doolittle), the most steadfast and fastidious of the Imagists, perhaps the only true Imagist.

NOCTURNE

With the net of thy hair
Thou hast fished in the sea,
And a strange fish
Hast thou caught in thy net.
For thy hair,
Beloved,
Holdeth my heart
Within its web of gold.

HEAT

O wind, rend open the heat,
cut apart the heat,
rend it to tatters.

Fruit cannot drop
through this thick air—
fruit cannot fall into heat
that presses up and blunts
the points of pears
and rounds the grapes.

Cut through the heat—
plow through it,
turning it on either side
of your path.

Repudiating the vague poeticisms and reestablishing the need for precision and verbal economy, the Imagists performed a needed service. Yet, by overinsistence that the visual image was the core of poetry, they sacrificed not only the music but also the emotion of traditional poetry. It was an unrewarded sacrifice. "The real weakness of Imagism," wrote Stephen Spender in a lecture, *Chaos and Control*, "was a kind of deliberate cultivated externality. The aim of transforming seen objects into verbal images involved the least possible use of the imagination. For the event that is seen merely, seen in isolation and not in relation to other things within a wholeness imagined, is simply an external object translated into an external poetry."

It becomes evident that the purity of the image has to be pronounced and preserved. A mixture of images does not enlarge the effect. On the contrary, it destroys the very thing it is meant to project. The greatest of poets have been guilty of bringing together disparate elements in an effort to make an image more striking. Milton, for example, startles us with a curiously mixed metaphor when he castigates the corrupt clergy as:

> *Blind mouths! That scarce themselves know how to hold*
> *A sheep-hook . . .*

Shelley's over-rich imagery often creates incongruities that sometimes become examples of the pathetic fallacy:

> *My soul is an enchanted boat,*
> *Which, like a sleeping swan, doth float*
> *Upon the silver waves of thy sweet singing . . .*

The poet who carried mixed imagery to the limits of excess was Hart Crane. Much of Crane's poetry is connotative, often chaotic, even incoherent; imagery has seldom reached such transfigured if convulsive intensity as in that aborted epic "The Bridge." Crane's "logic of metaphor" frequently led him to invent images as fantastic as:

> *Invariably when wine redeems the sight,*
> *Narrowing the mustard scansions of the eyes . . .*
> *Into the bulging bouillon, harnessed jelly of the stars . . .*
> *We will sidestep, and to the final smirk*
> *Dally the doom of that inevitable thumb . . .*

A particular passage that puzzled many and baffled most occurred in the first verse of Crane's "At Melville's Tomb," which begins:

> *Often beneath the wave, wide from this ledge*
> *The dice of drowned men's bones he saw bequeath*
> *An embassy.*

When Harriet Monroe, editor of *Poetry: A Magazine of Verse*, objected to these obscure images, Crane composed a long letter of defense with a touch of defiance. He defended his preference for the elliptical method, his use of "poetic metaphor rather than ordinary logic," and the suggestive power of "emotional dynamics" instead of an "absolute order of rationalized definitions." Regarding the "dice of drowned men's bones" that "bequeath an embassy," Crane wrote:

> Dice bequeath an embassy, in the first place, by being ground (in this connection only) in little cubes from the bones of drowned men by the action of the sea, and are finally thrown up on the sand, having "numbers" but no identification. These being the bones of dead men who never completed their voyage, it seems legitimate to refer to them as the only surviving evidence of certain messages undelivered, mute evidence of certain things, experience that dead mariners have had to deliver.

Imagery—and ingenuity—can go no further.

The Conceits of Poetry

In its literary sense, the word *conceit* denotes an extended image, an affectation of style or expression of ideas, a witty notion, a startling or strained figure of speech. Dryden and Johnson would have agreed with Webster. Reacting against the seventeenth-century poets who used the conceit as an intellectual shock rather than a sensuous pleasure, these eighteenth-century paradigms refused to consider the conceit as a logical concept but treated it as a wayward juxtaposition of discordant comparisons. Dryden condemned the conceit as a foolish overelaboration; Johnson wondered at the perversity which created the device and scorned it as an arrangement of "heterogeneous ideas yoked together by violence."

The Elizabethans did not disdain the fantasy of finding likenesses between objects utterly unlike each other. On the contrary, it was a fashion—a fashion so favored that it parodied itself and degenerated into a veritable catalogue of clichés. The professional poet became the professional lover, and the objects of his affection were a succession of lay figures. To be more exact, they were figures of speech, and they resembled each other to the last physical detail. If the poets were true recorders, the England of three centuries ago was populated chiefly by itinerant, rhyme-turning shepherds in pursuit of modest but eventually yielding milkmaids, and affairs of state were less important than the affairs of Strephon and his Chloe. In this frolicsome world of trifling amours and elaborate protestations, of pretty languors and (apparently) no labor, the poet's lady—whether a court nymph or a country Nell

—was uniformly celebrated for her coyness or her kindness, her softness or her hardness, her redness or her whiteness. Women, so it seemed, were not regarded as women, but as metaphors. Even the better poets helped themselves to the same serviceable stock-in-trade. Sang Edmund Spenser:

> *For lo! my Love doth in herself contain*
> *All this world's riches that may far be found.*
> *If sapphires, lo! her eyes be sapphires plain;*
> *If rubies, lo! her lips be rubies sound;*
> *If pearls, her teeth be pearls, both pure and round;*
> *If ivory, her forehead ivory ween;*
> *If gold, her locks are finest gold on ground;*
> *If silver, her fair hands are silver sheen.*

Thomas Lodge's "Rosaline" differed in no detail from Spenser's inamorata:

> *Her eyes are sapphires set in snow,*
> *Resembling heaven by every wink;*
> *The Gods do fear whenas they glow,*
> *And I do tremble when I think*
> *Heigh ho, would she were mine!*

> *With orient pearl, with ruby red,*
> *With marble white, with sapphire blue*
> *Her body every way is fed,*
> *Yet soft in touch and sweet in view:*
> *Heigh ho, fair Rosaline!*

Thomas Campion threw all the stereotypes together. He declared, with horticultural abandon, in a metaphor so overburdened as to be unintentionally comic

> *There is a garden in her face,*
> *Where roses and white lilies grow;*
> *A heav'nly paradise is that place,*
> *Wherein all pleasant fruits do flow.*

The poet Barnabe Rich, who furnished Shakespeare with the plot of *Twelfth Night*, ridiculed the fulsomeness of the conceits with their foolish comparisons. Writing in 1578, Rich twitted his contemporaries:

> If he be learned and that he be able to write a verse, then his penne must plie to paint his mistresse prayse. She must then be a Pallas for her witte, a Diana for her chastitie, a Venus for her face. Then shee shall be praysed for her proportions. First her Haires are wires of golde, her Cheekes are made of Lilies and red Roses, her Browes be Arches, her eyes Sapphires, her lookes Lightnings, her mouth Corall, her teeth Pearles, her pappes Alabaster Balles, her bodye streight, her belly softe; from thence downwarde to her knees, I thinke, is made of Sugar Candie; her hands, her fingers, her legges, her feete, and all the reste of her bodie shall be so perfect, and so pure, that of my conscience, the worst parte they will leave in her, shall be her soule.

Shakespeare went further. He composed a sonnet which not only exposed the stock pattern of conceits but also burlesqued them.

> *My mistress' eyes are nothing like the sun;*
> *Coral is far more red than her lips' red;*
> *If snow be white, why then her breasts are dun;*
> *If hairs be wires, black wires grow on her head.*
> *I have seen roses damask'd, red and white,*
> *But no such roses see I in her cheeks;*
> *And in some perfumes is there more delight*
> *Than in the breath that from my mistress reeks.*

In the seventeenth century the metaphysical poets gave the conceit a new complexity. They fused the fantastic with fresh vigor and made the incongruous seem not only natural but also inevitable. Eliot characterized the startling images created by Donne and others as "the elaboration of a figure of speech to the farthest degree to which ingenuity can take it." Primarily intellectual, nevertheless the metaphysical conceit is not without sensuous and often richly sensual appeal. Thus, in "The Flea," Donne presents a situation much favored by the Elizabethans: the ardent and insistent lover held off by the impregnable virtue of his lady. But instead of clothing the subject in pretty gallantries, Donne makes the situation monstrous. Instead of the conventional flowery couch, the black body of a flea with its "living walls of jet" serves as a nuptial bed.

Mark but this flea, and mark in this,
How little that which thou deniest me is;
It sucked me first, and now sucks thee,
And in this flea our two bloods mingled be.
Thou know'st that this cannot be said
A sin, nor shame, nor loss of maidenhead;
   Yet this enjoys before it woo,
   And pampered swells with one blood made of two;
   And this, alas! is more than we would do.

Oh stay, three lives in one flea spare,
Where we almost, yea, more than married are.
This flea is you and I, and this
Our marriage bed, and marriage temple is.
Though parents grudge, and you, we're met,
And cloistered in these living walls of jet.
   Though use make you apt to kill me,
   Let not to that self-murder added be,
   And sacrilege, three sins in killing three.

Cruel and sudden, hast thou since
Purpled thy nail in blood of innocence?
Wherein could this flea guilty be,
Except in that drop which it sucked from thee?
Yet thou triumph'st, and sayest that thou
Find'st not thyself nor me the weaker now.
   'Tis true; then learn how false fears be;
   Just so much honor, when thou yield'st to me,
   Will waste, as this flea's death took life from thee.

In "A Valediction: Forbidding Mourning" Donne again relies on a curious metaphysical conceit when, by a logical yet bizarre comparison, he likens two souls to a pair of feet.

> *If they be two, they are two so*
> *As stiff twin compasses are two;*
> *Thy soul, the fixed foot, makes no show*
> *To move, but doth, if th' other do.*

The reconciliation of strange ideas and disturbing images, the conjunction of harmonies and discords, was accomplished by a continual play of intricate and often mordant wit. Eliot said it was "an alliance of levity and seriousness, by which the seriousness is intensified . . . a mechanism of sensibility which could devour any kind of experience."

The excesses of the conceit led to such theatricality in the religious metaphysical poems that they estranged many admirers. Donne himself cautioned:

> *So, when thy brain works, ere thou utter it,*
> *Cross and correct concupiscence of wit.*

Abraham Cowley did not take time to cross and correct the enthusiastic flow of his conceits. He was so excited by the discovery of the circulation of the blood that he wrote an "Ode upon Dr. Harvey" in which Nature, alarmed that all her secrets would be revealed, fled from the doctor's "violent passion":

> *What should she do? Through all the moving wood*
> *Of lives endowed with sense she took her flight.*
> *Harvey pursues, and keeps her still in sight.*
> *But as the deer, long-hunted, takes a flood,*
> *She leaped at last into the winding streams of blood;*
> *Of man's meander all the purple reaches made,*
> *Till at the heart she stayed. . . .*
> > *. . . but ere she was aware,*
> *Harvey was with her there.*

Richard Crashaw outdid them all in "The Weeper," an apostrophe to the Magdalene's eyes, in a series of conceits which, for the unimaginative, Crashaw explained as he went along.

> *Hail, sister springs!*
> *Parents of silver-footed rills!*
> *Ever-bubbling things!*
> *Thawing crystals! Snowy hills!*
> *Still spending, never spent! I mean*
> *Thy fair eyes, sweet Magdalene.*

Nineteen verses later Crashaw surpassed even himself by summoning the Saviour and concluding with one of the most grotesque images ever misconceived:

> *And now, where'er He strays*
> *Among the Galilean mountains,*
> *Or more unwelcome ways,*
> *He's followed by two faithful fountains:*
> *Two walking baths, two weeping motions,*
> *Portable and compendious oceans.*

Pope, a master of terse and telling disposals, wrote wryly about those who dared to rival him in the far reaches of the conceit:

> *Some to Conceit alone their taste confine,*
> *And glittering thoughts struck out at every line;*
> *Pleased with a work where nothing's just or fit:*
> *One glaring chaos and wild heap of wit.*

Wit, not mere cleverness, is a prerequisite for making any comparison, let alone an imaginative conceit—wit in its original sense of perception. The conceit, the odd and seemingly far-fetched metaphor, is not merely a decoration; often it is the poem itself. Cleanth Brooks (in *Modern Poetry and the Tradition*) says that the poet who, bound to decorum, plays it safe and depends on the easily recognizable similarities between things allows nothing unusual or different to disturb him. "The metaphysical conceit represents a complete reversal of this situation. The disparities are recognized and deliberately exploited by the poet and are gathered into the context of the poem."

No matter how the conceit is regarded, it is a shock image.

Sharp and swift, its success is achieved by surprise, the surprise of recognizing an unforeseen likeness between completely unlike things. It represents the image at full play, at serious if sometimes bizarre play. At its best it justifies itself by effecting a rare but logical union of opposites, a final extension and fulfillment of metaphor.

The Ambiguities of Poetry

Williiam Empson's *Seven Types of Ambiguity* is a cornerstone in the construction of poetry on intellectual foundations. In this famous and provocative work which stresses the values of compressed complexity, Empson argues that the best of literature is bound to be ambiguous. Enlarging on the principles of ambiguity, he maintains that every word "is effective in several ways at once," that two or more meanings of a word "or a grammatical structure" offer the reader a choice of meanings, and that these choices heighten as well as enrich whatever is being read. One of the most striking applications of his theory is his analysis of a line from Shakespeare's magnificent seventy-third sonnet.

> *That time of year thou may'st in me behold*
> *When yellow leaves, or none, or few, do hang*
> *Upon those boughs which shake against the cold,*
> *Bare ruined choirs, where late the sweet birds sang.*
> *In me thou seest the twilight of such day*
> *As after sunset fadeth in the west,*
> *Which by and by black night doth take away,*
> *Death's second self, that seals up all in rest:*
> *In me thou seest the glowing of such fire*
> *That on the ashes of his youth doth lie,*
> *As the death-bed whereon it must expire,*
> *Consumed with that which it was nourished by.*
> *This thou perceiv'st, which makes thy love more strong,*
> *To love that well which thou must leave ere long.*

As an example of multiple associations Empson takes the line "Bare ruined choirs, where late the sweet birds sang," considers it and holds that the comparison is valid for many reasons, "because ruined monasteries are places in which to sing, because they involve sitting in a row, because they are made of wood, are carved into knots and so forth, because they used to be surrounded by a sheltering building crystallized out of the likeness of a forest, and colored with stained glass and painting like flowers and leaves, because they are now abandoned by all but the grey walls colored like the skies of winter, because the cold and narcissistic charm suggested by choir-boys suits well with Shakespeare's feeling for the object of the sonnets, and for various sociological and historical reasons (the protestant destruction of the monasteries; fear of puritanism), which it would be hard now to trace out in their proportions; these reasons, and many more relating the simile to its place in the Sonnet, must all combine to give the line its beauty, and there is a sort of ambiguity in not knowing which of them to hold clearly in mind. Clearly," concludes Empson, leaving the reader breathless and a bit aghast, "the machinations of ambiguity are among the very roots of poetry."

Such a reading may be dismissed as a feat in ingenuity or an exhibit of willful confusion. Many who were once dazzled by Empson's erudition and his skill in associative references have tired of what they consider verbal legerdemain. Poets have been especially dubious about semantic juggling. "Along with many others," wrote Howard Nemerov, in *Poets on Poetry*, "I learned from Empson to value ambiguity. It was part of our purposeful labor in those days to fill our poems with somewhat studied puns which could be said to 'work on several different levels,' although often they did not work on even one . . . I now regard simplicity and the appearance of ease in the measure as primary values, and the detachment of a single thought from its ambiguous surroundings as a worthier object than the deliberate cultivation of ambiguity."

Other poets went further and objected flatly. In *A Primer for Poets* Karl Shapiro wrote: "A poet who talks about the four, six, or eight or ten 'levels' of meaning either has his tongue in his cheek or is trying to impress the police. Any such theory is an invitation to bedlam. Every artist by instinct should fight against the principle of multiplicity of meaning; when for some reason he finds it impossible to form his work any other way, he should admit this as failure to himself."

Nevertheless, readers must have a tolerance for the ambiguous, the more so since the most profound poetry does not yield its complete significance at a cursory reading. The modern poet, aware of the embattled world in which he lives and his insecure and insignificant part in it, cannot but reflect the complexity and disorder of his environment. Yet his poetry is often no more complicated than the poetry of John Donne, and his ambiguities are no more puzzling than the "auguries" of William Blake.

It is generally conceded that in prose words have a specific meaning and that scientific research will admit of no double meanings. Yet "in true poetry," says Frederick Clarke Prescott, anticipating Empson by several years, words "should have as many meanings as possible, and the more the better, as long as these are true to the images in the poet's mind." The skeptic might inquire how can anyone know what images were in the poet's mind and whether the secondary meaning, or any other level of ambiguity, will have the same importance as the primary meaning. At the same time he must admit that in art the shock of surprise should be as gratifying, even as necessary, as the shock of recognition. He must rid himself of prejudice against the uncertain and the unexpected; otherwise he will allow himself to be lulled by the soothing stereotypes and put to sleep by the all-too-accommodating clichés.

"One characteristic of modern poetry is that ambiguous arrangement of parts which strikes many people as being violent or obscure," writes Muriel Rukeyser in *The Life of Poetry*. "It is a method which is familiar enough on the screen; when you see the picture of a night-club, and then see the heroine's face thrown back as she sings, you make the unity without any effort, without even being conscious of the process . . . Much of modern poetry moves in terms of quick juxtapositions."

"A common source of obscurity," writes another poet,

L. A. G. Strong, in *Common Sense About Poetry*, "is the speed with which a great poet's imagination leaps from point to point. Logical connections are often left out. In a flash the kindled mind apprehends a series of conclusions and has sped across them to a new peak while the pedestrian reader is boggling at the preliminaries to the first leap."

It is, however, agreed that premeditated ambiguity is self-defeating, that difficulty per se is not a proof of distinction, that cryptic utterances are not necessarily profound. Marianne Moore, a miracle-worker in allusiveness, cautions that

> . . . *Complexity is not a crime,*
> *but carry it to the point of murkiness*
> *and nothing is plain.*

also:

> . . . *the opaque allusion—the simulated flight*
> *upward, accomplishes nothing.*

Of Empson's seven types or levels of ambiguity, one is particularly plausible. It is the one which he considers "a fortunate confusion as when the author is discovering his idea in the act of writing," or even "not holding it all in mind at once." Beyond the most carefully fashioned idea there is the perfect conception that eluded or escaped the writer. It is a truism that what gets put on paper is only an approximation of the unshaped but inspiring poem that stirred the mind of the poet. Underneath rational thought there is the irrational image or instinct, something which has little relation to reason but which stems from an unconscious impulse, a half-formed thought, a mythical association, a dream-desire. It might be said that we have exalted reason beyond its capacity to persuade and that much of poetry is an effort to restore the reader to the intimacy of the emotions. It is through the poetic imagination that floating thoughts, vague images, and ideas "discovered in the act of writing" take on coherence, and unrelated details achieve unity. Associations, private and often chaotic, originate in the welter of the unconscious and attain clarity only after they have been directed by the conscious mind. Coleridge described the process as "the streamy nature of association which thinking curbs and rudders."

> *The woods decay, the woods decay and fall,*
> *The vapors weep their burthen to the ground,*
> *Man comes and tills the field and lies beneath,*
> *And after many a summer dies the swan.*

Thus Tennyson begins his poem "Tithonus," and the reader, wooed by the lovely sounds, accepts the assemblage of unrelated details. He forgets, as Tennyson probably forgot, that the poet is portraying the king of Troy's brother who was turned into a grasshopper. He does not boggle at the ambiguities, at the doubtful statement that Man is buried in the land he cultivates, or at the irrelevant presence of the stricken swan. It is the unreasonable combination of music and imagery which, in its very vagueness, enchants him.

Again it is the buoyant power of Swinburne's surging syllables which keeps the reader mindlessly afloat in such billowing and ambiguous images as:

> *When the hounds of spring are on winter's traces,*
>   *The mother of months in meadow or plain*
> *Fills the shadows and windy places*
>   *With lisp of leaves and ripple of rain;*
> *And the brown bright nightingale amorous*
> *Is half assuaged for Itylus,*
> *For the Thracian ships and the foreign faces,*
>   *The tongueless vigil, and all the pain.*
>
> *Come with bows bent and with emptying of quivers,*
>   *Maiden most perfect, lady of light,*
> *With a noise of winds and many rivers,*
>   *With a clamor of waters, and with might;*
> *Bind on thy sandals, O thou most fleet,*
> *Over the splendor and speed of thy feet;*
> *For the faint east quickens, the wan west shivers,*
>   *Round the feet of the day and the feet of the night.*

Where shall we find her, how shall we sing to her,
  Fold our hands round her knees, and cling?
O that man's heart were as fire and could spring to her,
  Fire, or the strength of the streams that spring!
For the stars and the winds are unto her
As raiment, as songs of the harp-player;
For the risen stars and the fallen cling to her,
  And the southwest-wind and the west-wind sing.

These lines from *Atalanta in Calydon* bear little relation to the Greek legend of Atalanta and the Calydonian boar on which the drama is based. The reader, struggling uncertainly through Swinburne's turgid tragedy, is suddenly caught up in the swirl and exuberance of the rhythmic chorus, the swift alliterations—"mother of months in meadow or plain," "lisp of leaves and ripple of rain"—the rushing rhymes, and the unflagging energy of the music.

It is hard to draw a line between ecstasy and vision, but it is still harder to say where vision stops and hallucination begins. Rimbaud believed that induced hallucination was a superior form of vision. Baudelaire maintained that the very confusions of man's chaotic life drive him to visionary escapes, to the intimate and indefinable reaches of the imagination.

Poe was one who relied on visions and all that is implied in ambiguous intimations. He responded instinctively to the mysterious relations between the real and the unreal. He contended that indefiniteness was an important element of poetry, "a suggestive indefiniteness of vague and therefore of spiritual effect." In *Axel's Castle* Edmund Wilson enlarged on the effect of the mysterious

produced not merely by the confusion between the imaginary world and the real; but also by means of further confusion between the perceptions of the different senses. . . . We find Poe, in one of his poems, *hearing* the approach of the darkness, or writing a description of the sensations which follow death: "Night arrived, and with its shadows a heavy discomfort. It oppressed my limbs with the oppression of some dull weight and was palpable. There was also a moaning sound, not unlike the distant reverberation of surf, but more continuous which, beginning with the first twilight, had grown in strength with the darkness. Suddenly lights were brought into the room . . . and issuing from the flame of each lamp, there flowed unbrokenly into my ears a strain of melodious monotone."

Wilson calls attention to Poe's "notation of super-rational sensation" and "the dreamlike irrational musical poetry of 'Annabel Lee' and 'Ulalume.'" He might have cited several other of Poe's most Poe-like poems. The first twenty lines of "Dream-Land," for example, are a potent medley of ambiguous music and super-rational images.

> *By a route obscure and lonely,*
> *Haunted by ill angels only,*
> *Where an Eidolon, named Night,*
> *On a black throne reigns upright,*
> *I have reached these lands but newly*
> *From an ultimate dim Thule—*
> *From a wild weird clime that lieth, sublime,*
> *Out of Space—out of Time.*
>
> *Bottomless vales and boundless floods,*
> *And chasms, and caves, and Titan woods,*
> *With forms that no man can discover*
> *For the tears that drip all over;*
> *Mountains toppling evermore*
> *Into seas without a shore;*
> *Seas that restlessly aspire,*
> *Surging, unto skies of fire;*
> *Lakes that endlessly outspread*
> *Their lone waters—lone and dead,—*
> *Their still waters—still and chilly*
> *With the snows of the lolling lily.*

Such poetry has the impact of an instant if slightly mad communication, the emotion spontaneous, the lines unlabored. Poe accomplished this through a combination of intuition and craft.

Mallarmé distrusted easy communications. He advocated a wordless meditation, a rapt reverie, when contemplating an object or formulating an idea. What he wrote was a series of beautifully balanced ambiguities; he believed that the precise naming of a thing robbed it of its wonder. The ideal method was not to describe but to imply, to circumnavigate, to capture the essential quality of the object or idea through the magic of suggestion.

Writing in *Axel's Castle* of Poe's effectiveness and the French symbolists he affected, Wilson may well have the last word. "The medley of images; the deliberately mixed metaphors; the combination of passion and wit—of the grand and prosaic manners; the bold amalgamation of material with spiritual—all these may seem to him [the English-speaking reader of today] quite proper and familiar. He has always known them in the English poetry of the sixteenth and seventeenth centuries, Shakespeare and the other Elizabethans did all these things without theorizing about them. Is this not the natural language of poetry?"

The Interpretation of Poetry

Some of the most eloquent poems invite and, at the same time, resist interpretation. It is no literal logic but a triumph of evocativeness which gives conviction to Blake's burning tiger, to his sunflower weary of time, or to his disillusioned dialogue between a pebble and a piece of clay.

> "Love seeketh not itself to please,
>   Nor for itself hath any care,
> But for another gives its ease,
>   And builds a Heaven in Hell's despair."
>
> So sung a little clod of clay,
>   Trodden with the cattle's feet;
> But a pebble of the brook
>   Warbled out these meters meet:
>
> "Love seeketh only Self to please,
>   To bind another to its delight,
> Joys in another's loss of ease,
>   And builds a Hell in Heaven's despite."

Blake's "O rose, thou art sick" has been quoted in a preceding chapter ("The Province of Poetry") on page 31. This eight-line poem has been subjected to more differing analyses than practically any short poem in the language. One explicator decided that the ailing rose was the inevitable substitute for a young woman who had lost her virginity—the flower being traditionally feminine and the worm "that flies in the night" being phallically masculine. Another interpreter found the poem to be a portrayal of evil, an inordinate "dark secret love" and a deflowering which brings mortal sickness in its crimson wake. Still another critic, M. H. Abrams, saw Blake's worm-eaten rose as "the destruction wrought by furtiveness, deceit, and hypocrisy in what should be a frank and joyous relation of physical love." It did not occur to these analysts that the rose might be a real rose, a wilting flower, its crimson life eaten away by a real though invisible worm, a pest that actually flies in the night. In any case, the visible critics succeed in destroying the life of Blake's poem.

A more tortured example of interpretation occurs in Lawrance Thompson's biography, *Robert Frost: The Early Years.* Thompson quotes Frost's humorous "The Cow in Apple Time," which Frost laughingly said was "inspired" by a runaway cow on his farm in Derry, New Hampshire.

> *Something inspires the only cow of late*
> *To make no more of a wall than an open gate,*
> *And think no more of wall-builders than fools.*
> *Her face is flecked with pomace and she drools*
> *A cider syrup. Having tasted fruit,*
> *She scorns a pasture withering to the root.*
> *She runs from tree to tree where lie and sweeten*
> *The windfalls spiked with stubble and worm-eaten.*
> *She leaves them bitten when she has to fly.*
> *She bellows on a knoll against the sky.*
> *Her udder shrivels and the milk goes dry.*

Thompson proceeds to add this footnote: "Metaphorically considered, this characteristically puritanical farm fable may be viewed as a figurative portrait of a young married woman who runs away from home and suffers the consequences of a sinfully rebellious life." The reader—at least this reader—can only shake his head and wonder (a) by what feat of metaphor has the tale of an apple-drunk cow been turned into a "characteristically puritanical farm fable," (b) how solemnly a researcher can transform a dried-up milker into a "sinfully rebellious" married woman, and

(c) whether Thompson's serious elucidation is not funnier than the comic verses.

To critics like Thompson the poetry of Frost appears to be a mine of buried meanings, irresistibly tempting to anyone intent on digging the last nugget from seemingly inexhaustible lodes. Frost's "Stopping by Woods on a Snowy Evening" is a sad case in point. It has been interpreted to disaster if not to death. Here is the well-known lyric:

> *Whose woods these are I think I know.*
> *His house is in the village though;*
> *He will not see me stopping here*
> *To watch his woods fill up with snow.*
>
> *My little horse must think it queer*
> *To stop without a farmhouse near*
> *Between the woods and frozen lake*
> *The darkest evening of the year.*
>
> *He gives his harness bells a shake*
> *To ask if there is some mistake.*
> *The only other sound's the sweep*
> *Of easy wind and downy flake.*
>
> *The woods are lovely, dark and deep.*
> *But I have promises to keep,*
> *And miles to go before I sleep,*
> *And miles to go before I sleep.*

Four quatrains, sixteen short lines. Yet, in *Robert Frost: The Way to the Poem* (*Saturday Review*, April 12, 1958), the poet-critic John Ciardi takes more than seventy long lines, and again, in *How Does a Poem Mean?*, more than seven pages, to "explain" the levels of meaning hidden from the reader. In the Introduction to *Poetry from Statement to Meaning*, the authors, Jerome Beaty and William H. Matchett, go further in pursuit of their belief that anyone who believes the poem says what it seems to say misses the point as well as the power of the poem. "In a poetry class he [the student] might be asked what the owner of the house, the horse, and the promises contribute to the poem . . . Why is it important that the owner will not see the poet watching the woods fill up with snow? Perhaps because the owner, like the horse, would 'think it queer' for someone to sit out in the cold and watch the snow. And that brings up the horse. He is the practical one; there is no sense to stopping far from a farmhouse on a cold dark night; his 'protest'—the jangling harness bells—is the only sound interrupting the soft silence of the snow. Then there is another interruption—the recollection of the promises, the obligations, probably of everyday affairs. . . ." etcetera, etcetera.

Other similarly far-fetched interpretations have been offered. It has been said, for example, that the speaker is contemplating the quiet beauty of nature as a contrast to the horror and violence of the world, that he is about to commit suicide and waits for the snow to bury him, that the man is Man driven by necessity to travel mile after mile until the sleep of death. In *Poetry from Statement to Meaning* Beaty and Matchett cite a student who identified the owner of the woods as God, his house in the village as the church, and the speaker as an atheist whose horse, the common man, is wiser than he is and knows that God is omnipresent. The authors are apparently ridiculing such extremes of interpretation, yet, quoting another example, a short passage from *The Waste Land*, some fairly obvious seventeen lines are followed by one hundred and forty lines of prose in a search for what is apparently concealed in every other syllable.

Confounded by a complex of explanatory ambiguities, the reader, lost in a network of allusions, is too dismayed to enter, let alone find his way through, the labyrinth. Eliot himself referred to this cult of extractors, those who are determined to wring the last drop of associations from a poem, as disciples of "The Lemon-Squeezer School." He added, "Several influences converge nowadays toward the belief that to appreciate and enjoy poetry is to explain it, and that the way to explain it is to explain it away." Robert Lowell enlarged on this when (in Anthony Ostroff's *The Contemporary Poet as Artist and Critic*) he spoke of "poems processed into monthly exegeses . . . There is even a kind of modern poem, now produced in bulk, that seems written to be explained."

To revert to Frost's "Stopping by Woods on a Snowy Evening," efforts to explain the poem more fully have only succeeded in explaining it away. In *Robert Frost: An Introduction,* "a controlled research text," the poem is accompanied by nineteen pages of annotations ranging from fancy abstractions to flat absurdities. Frost's own reactions furnish a wry commentary. He said, "I've been more bothered with that one than anybody has ever been with any poem in just pressing it with more than it should be pressed for. It means enough without being pressed." Disturbed by "pressers" puzzling about the snowy woods and the miles to go, he said that all the poem means is: "It's all very nice here, but I must be getting home. There are chores to do." At another time when a critic indicated that the last three lines implied that the poet longed for an after-life in heaven, Frost smiled and shook his head. "No, it only means I want to get the hell out of there."

The poet cannot help being both amused and annoyed at the persistent ambiguity-hunting. "Too many people have been intimidated in the class room," said Frost. "They have been taught to hunt for symbols, and, as a consequence, they enjoy the search more than the poem. They regard the lines as a challenge to their ingenuity; the poem is not something to delight, but to dissect. They are determined to find that what seems to be simple is merely a symbol for something that is complex. Not that I have anything against the study and even the practice of symbols. But there are times when symbolism is as bad as an embolism. The second can kill a person, the first a poem."

Frost. would have agreed with Paul Valéry who insisted that turning a poem into prose, or making it a matter for minute examination, is an act of heresy. In his introduction to Valéry's *The Art of Poetry,* Eliot confirms this when he writes: "Especially pertinent for the reader of poetry—and for the critic of poetry— is his [Valéry's] insistence that poetry must first of all be *enjoyed* if it is to be of any use at all; that it must be enjoyed *as poetry,* and not for any other reason." Speaking for himself, Eliot concluded, "The ideal teacher will introduce pupils to modern poetry by exciting enjoyment—enjoyment first, and understanding second."

Two extreme examples of "understanding" by way of extrapolation come to mind. The first was in a classroom, the second in a textbook. In Washington I presided over a few seminars at a most progressive school for students between the ages of fifteen and eighteen. They had been studying and commenting on modern poetry. Among the mimeographed copies of poems they were to read—poems by Wallace Stevens, Ezra Pound, and Robert Lowell —I managed to slip in "The Walrus and the Carpenter." During the next session they announced strange nuances in Stevens, Pound, and Lowell with authoritarian composure. I was curious to see what they would do with Carroll. I was not disappointed.

Incredibly, none of the young offshoots of the New Criticism recognized the poem. The little explicators took "The Walrus and the Carpenter" apart with gravity and complete aplomb. One of the students maintained that the poem was an allegory of the world today, its speed, its cruelty, its apathy, its loss of security— "the fate of the oysters shows that we rush too fast, that we cannot trust anyone, and that no one cares." Another found that the meaning of the poem was in the lines about the quantity of sand:

> "If this were only cleared away,"
> They said, "it would be grand."

"That is a symbol of the poverty that surrounds us," declared the young critic, "and it is an appeal for us to clear up the mess."

A more startling interpretation was presented by a student who was specializing in political economy. He saw the figure of the Carpenter as the image of Soviet Russia, the Walrus as its weak but willing ally, and the Oysters as the gullible satellites who were bound to be gobbled up.

Only one student—a fifteen-year-old girl who had not been sufficiently exposed to the New Criticism—ventured a bald opinion.

"I may be wrong," she said timidly, "but I thought it was funny."

The textbook is Aggertt and Bowen's *Communicative Reading* (Macmillan, 1956). Following Eliot's "Journey of the Magi," E. E. Cummings' "she being Brand" is quoted in full. It begins:

she being Brand

-new; and you
know consequently a
little stiff i was
careful of her and (having

thoroughly oiled the universal
joint tested my gas felt of
her radiator made sure her springs were O.

K.) went right to it . . .

The whole poem is a lively piece of obvious double entendre, an extended, lightly pornographic metaphor in which the difficult act of intercourse with a virgin is compared to the breaking-in of a new automobile. A prefatory prose note in the textbook blandly overlooks any sexual connotations and explains to the (presumably innocent) reader that if he has ever driven a car he will appreciate the poem's subtle rhythms. "Feel the empathy of the car's movement," the student is advised, "particularly as it is so well communicated to the eye by the poet's unorthodox lines and punctuation."

Another exhibit I prize is a four-page analysis of Robinson Jeffers' twenty-line poem "Shine, Perishing Republic." Its author, Robert F. Steuding, barely mentions Jeffers' bitter disposal of democracy's "making haste on decay," the failure of Christianity, and the implication that civilization is nothing more than a corrupting disease. Instead, he praises the poem for its clever use of "the voiced apico-dental fricative," the more relaxed "voiceless apico-alveolar sibilant," "the seldom-used double appositive," and concludes that "with its perfect correlation of phonological, suprasegmental, semantic, and syntactical features" it is "a work of supreme craftsmanship."

William Carlos Williams' "The Red Wheelbarrow," that remarkably visual poem quoted on page 25, has also been subjected to interpretations that are as absurd as they are astonishing. Looking for the ineluctable meaning beyond the meaning, one searcher found that the solid utility of the wheelbarrow was a standing reproof to the short-lived foolishness of the chickens, that the poem was a picture of contemporary life with its utilitarian values ignored by the younger generation, while another explicator discovered that Williams was making a veiled statement about sexuality, the hard male impulse (red) being pitted against a flutteringly female (white) virginity.

> To examine a poem curiously, arresting it every now and then to scrutinize a line, a phrase, or a word [wrote Edwin Muir in *The Estate of Poetry*], and slowing down its movement, may bring fresh knowledge, and the knowledge may create a new emotion, but the new emotion may not be the emotion of the poem itself. Too thoroughly applied, this method may sometimes elicit from the poem a set of meanings quite different from those which strike the reader when he first comes to it. Some of those meanings may throw light on the poem. But if this does not happen, if the poem, having been submitted to analysis, does not assume a new yet natural shape, what remains is merely the analysis with its own internal interest, and the poem has been replaced by the criticism.

A poem that has been "replaced" by scientific diagnoses through the undeviating scrutiny of the analyst may not have been completely ruined, but it has been decidedly harmed. Its impact has been dulled and its essential spirit has become unimportant if not irrelevant. The story is told of a student who, fascinated and evidently satisfied by a long analysis of Yeats's "Byzantium," asked the teacher, "Now do I have to read the poem?"

I have been told of another student, a high school junior, who, on his examination paper, was asked to define poetry. "Poetry," he wrote, "is something we must learn to interrupt." His answer was not merely an error in spelling—he meant to write "interpret"— but an unfortunate though accurate estimate of what he had been taught.

It is a mistake to assume that only in the last few decades has there emerged a new kind of critic, the academic wrecker who tears into a poem and reduces it to a pile of literary rubble. There have always been those who are not after a living product but merely a process and believe that poetry is written to keep the critic occupied. In the eighteenth century Alexander Pope admonished critics in terms which are applicable to those of the twentieth century. He wrote:

> The prevailing passion of some commentators is to discover new meanings in an author, whom they will cause to be mysterious purely for the pleasure of being thought to unravel him. . . . In places where they cannot contest the truth of common interpretation they get themselves room for dissertation by imaginary *amphibologies* [which might be translated as ambiguities] which they will claim to be designed by the author . . . Men of right understanding generally see all that an author can reasonably mean, but others are apt to fancy two meanings for want of knowing one.

Speaking from the past, Pope might have been talking for any explicator-afflicted poet today. Speaking in the present, Piet Hein, the Danish inventor, essayist, and poet, put the matter neatly in one of his aphoristic quatrains:

A poet should be of the new-fashioned meaningless brand—
  Obscure, esoteric, symbolic—the critics demand it.
So if there's a poem of mine that you do understand,
  I'll gladly explain what it means till you don't understand it.

The Criticism of Poetry

Criticism is interpretation's ugly cousin. No matter how helpful or constructive criticism may claim to be, poets have always been repelled by it. They have continued to believe that the critic is the failed creator. In *English Bards and Scotch Reviewers*, Byron made himself the poets' spokesman when he wrote:

> As soon
> *Seek roses in December, ice in June,*
> *Hope constancy in wind, or corn in chaff;*
> *Believe a woman or an epitaph,*
> *Or any other thing that's false, before*
> *You trust in critics, who themselves are sore.*

In a chapter entitled "Criticism and the Poet" in *The Estate of Poetry*, Edwin Muir complained about the method of criticizing a poem by reading into it all sorts of possible meanings apart from the clear and obvious one. As an example of the method he cited a passage from Cleanth Brooks' *The Well Wrought Urn* in which Brooks interprets Tennyson's lyric "Tears, Idle Tears" to such effect that "the poem recedes into a remote academic distance, where we can hardly recognize, far less feel it." This kind of criticism, continued Muir, "so thorough and so mistaken, seems to me of very little use to any reader, and for myself it gives me a faint touch of claustrophobia, the feeling that I am being confined in a narrow place with the poem and the critic, and that I shall not get away until all three of us are exhausted."

Listening to a symphony, the listener does not refuse to enjoy it before he can read the score and learn the intricate structure of the work, nor will he fail to delight in its wonders until he can understand how they are accomplished. Children respond to verse without having every word defined for them. Similarly, the adult reader will often find that it is not necessary, or even advisable, to follow a critical standard before enjoying poetry, and that an instinctive half-understanding is better than a predetermined knowledge (often debatable) of what the poem is about.

No poetry has ever been more lucid than Wordsworth's nature transcriptions. The little poem known as "The Daffodils" is a particularly telling example of Wordsworth's clarity.

> *I wandered lonely as a cloud*
> *That floats on high o'er vales and hills,*
> *When all at once I saw a crowd,*
> *A host, of golden daffodils,*
> *Beside the lake, beneath the trees,*
> *Fluttering and dancing in the breeze.*
>
> *Continuous as the stars that shine*
> *And twinkle on the milky way,*
> *They stretched in never-ending line*
> *Along the margin of a bay:*
> *Ten thousand saw I at a glance,*
> *Tossing their heads in sprightly dance.*
>
> *The waves beside them danced; but they*
> *Out-did the sparkling waves in glee:*
> *A poet could not but be gay,*
> *In such a jocund company!*
> *I gazed—and gazed—but little thought*
> *What wealth the show to me had brought:*
>
> *For oft, when on my couch I lie*
> *In vacant or in pensive mood,*
> *They flash upon that inward eye*
> *Which is the bliss of solitude;*
> *And then my heart with pleasure fills,*
> *And dances with the daffodils.*

The simple lines have found their way into countless anthologies besides those specifically designed for children. Yet, according to more than one critic, we have read them wrong. In a full-page article in the *New York Times Book Review* (October 8, 1966) the critic Donald Hall contends that the poem is not concerned, as it seems to be, with the pleasure of observing daffodils but with the pleasure of thinking about money. Insisting that it is a poem about economics, Hall claims that Wordsworth's imagination was capitalistic, that his description of the flowers as "golden" (instead of yellow) was "an intimation of riches." By bringing together such a large quantity of blooms—"a host," "ten thousand" —and the "shine" and "twinkle" of gold, Wordsworth made "inescapable his comparison. Looking at the daffodils," wrote Hall, "was like coming into a great deal of money."

Aware that others might consider this critical appraisal ludicrous, Hall seriously concludes, "I believe that this meaning exists in the poem by a kind of unconscious intention. Far from ruining the poem, this further level increases its fascination."

I will confess that, though the poem has not been ruined for me, I can no longer read it with my former pleasure in its happy guilelessness. Thanks to the new diagnosis, I have a blurring double image of the poem. I see it through the eyes of the man who composed it in his nature-loving thirties, but I am also aware of the old Tory fingering his pension—not ten thousand but a sizable three hundred pounds—from the government.

It has been argued that the singing line is no longer in favor because its directness makes it uninteresting to the expositor, and that lyrics are rarely written today because they furnish so little material for professional criticism. It may well be true. It may well be that the poet who, in another age and another environment, expressed himself and the image of man in lyrical poetry fears to have his simplicities translated into complicated abstractions. "In a culture whose dilemma is the hypertrophy of the intellect at the expense of sensual capability," writes Susan Sontag in *Against Interpretation*, "interpretation is the revenge of intellect upon art . . . In most modern instances, interpretation amounts to the philistine refusal to leave the work of art alone. Real art has the capacity to make us nervous. By reducing the work of art to its content and then interpreting and criticising *that,* one tames the work of art."

That a work is not altogether destroyed is a proof of its viability; even a latter-day lyric sometimes has the toughness to survive. One does not have to go as far back as Hardy and Yeats and Frost and the early Eliot to realize that the lyric note has not been silenced by what Miss Sontag calls "the philistine refusal to leave the work of art alone." Criticism did not stop such contemporary poets as Conrad Aiken and Louise Bogan and Theodore Roethke and Richard Wilbur in America, Austin Clarke and Patrick Kavanagh in Ireland, Robert Graves and Philip Larkin in England, and Hugh McDiarmid in Scotland from composing in the natural and more or less precise rhythms that appeal to the inner ear. Nevertheless, criticism has too often been preoccupied with its function as a specialized form of literature, a final rationalization not only of what the writer meant to say but what he should have said. Eliot was quick to protest against such conclusiveness. "We are in danger of pursuing criticism as if it were a science, which it can never be," he wrote in *On Poetry and Poets.* "If, on the other hand, we overemphasize mere enjoyment we tend to fall into the subjective and impressionistic . . . Thirty years ago it seems to have been the latter type of criticism, the impressionistic, which caused the annoyance I felt when I wrote about the function of criticism. Today it seems we need to be more on guard against the technically explanatory."

The excesses of the scrutinizers who place the emphasis on techniques, on poetry as an exercise rather than an experience, may be traced to what was once called the New Criticism. The New Critics came into being in the 1930's—John Crowe Ransom cited William Empson, I. A. Richards, T. S. Eliot, and Yvor Winters as prime movers in his *The New Criticism* published in 1941, although some literary historians added the names of Allen Tate, Kenneth Burke, R. P. Blackmur, and Cleanth Brooks to the roster. The New Critics asserted that a work of art, and particularly the work of a poet, should be considered as an esthetic object complete in itself. The reader was supposed to disregard everything else, such as the social, political, and biographical background. The New Critics were not concerned with the emotional content of a poem but with its features as a verbal medium; they assumed the role of cool scientists determined to explore textures, timbres, overtones, and the intricate nuances of structure. After a while several of the supposed adherents to the movement, Allen Tate for example, refused to be included in the category; as noted in a previous paragraph, Eliot repudiated the aims of the technically explanatory. But for decades the impersonal logic of the New Critics had a tremendous influence, especially on the reading and, more important, on the teaching of poetry. Their doctrines became accepted dogmas; they established something like a literary dictatorship. The more progressive schools and colleges were particularly susceptible to the insistence that creative work should be divorced from its creator. As late as 1966 D. J. Enright, appraising three collections of essays in *The New York Review of Books*, wrote that literary criticism was rapidly approaching the condition of absolute autonomy. "The erstwhile mediators, in their overwhelming respect for literature, have achieved something quite remarkable. They have made themselves indispensable. They are on their way to making literature dispensable."

The cult that denied any relation between a man and his work was bound to compel a countermovement. A work of art is an act of revelation. Therefore everything we know about its maker is relevant; it reveals not only him but his work more fully. A real poem is the repercussion of a real emotion or event, a condition or a conflict in which the creator is reflected. The majesty as well as the agony of Milton burns in the heroic figures of Satan and Samson who, like Milton himself, went down to defeat in an inimically Philistine world. The two sides of Robert Herrick—the proper country preacher and the pagan who celebrated himself in a frolic of naughty lyrics—are united in his *Hesperides, or Works both Human and Divine*. No biographer has portrayed a more romantic figure than the legendary one which Byron cultivated in *Childe Harold's Pilgrimage*, glorifying and exposing himself in *Don Juan*. Anyone who reads Keats's sonnets—from the one of joyful discovery in "On First Looking into Chapman's Homer" to the one of desperation in the appeal to Fanny, "I cry your mercy—pity—love—aye, love!"—cannot fail to hear the poet's distinct and immediately recognizable voice.

Poets take this self-revelation for granted. "The truth is that a man's sense of the world dictates his subjects to him," wrote Wallace Stevens, "and this sense is derived from his personality, his temperament, over which he has little control . . . It is often said of a man that his work is autobiographical in spite of every subterfuge. It cannot be otherwise."

The Conventions of Poetry

To the traditionalist there is something not merely ancient and honorable but also sacred about convention; to the innovator a convention is an unquestioning acceptance of an outworn formula which should be scrapped. The course of poetry is a series of conflicts between those intent on holding on to convention at any cost and those who, tired of immemorial usages, remember that *tradition* is founded on *traditio*, a surrender, and regard adherence to tradition as a kind of betrayal. In *Modern Poetry and the Tradition* Cleanth Brooks remarks that "the prevailing conception of poetry is still primarily defined for us by the achievement of the Romantic poets. Every one-volume history of English literature still conceives of the Romantic period as the one far-off, divine event toward which the whole course of English poetry moves. The modern poetry of our times is the first to call that view seriously in question. . . . We are witnessing (or perhaps have witnessed) a critical revolution on the Romantic Revolt."

It is a classic platitude that every convention breeds revolt, and that the revolt of one generation becomes the convention of the next. It is a correlated truism that the world always applauds and the artist is likely to imitate what was once condemned, until it becomes so overpopular that a new revolution occurs.

Too often the reaction against convention compels a straining for novelty, the necessity of being bold or shocking or merely different. The fear of being conventional frequently leads to a bizarrerie which becomes boring. The distrust of emotion is considered a mark of sophistication, and a display of feeling is equated with sentimentality. The result is flat statement uttered, deprecatingly, in a flat tone of voice. The substitution of transition for tradition causes the poet to turn away from any responsibility to the reader, to retreat into an evasiveness of remote personal associations, private predilections, and a sensibility of alienation, an incongruous mixture of estheticism and nihilism. "If Wordsworth were alive today," said John Hall Wheelock, "he might be tempted to change his rather unsatisfactory definition of poetry to emotion remembered in anxiety and with distaste."

At the same time a rejection of customary routines and approved "poeticisms" is necessary for the continual rejuvenation of art; dead wood must be cut away to encourage new growth. Poetry has been constantly refreshed by daring experiments, by a new vocabulary, by the proliferation of new topics, new terms, new images, new media. The interplay of the still-living past and the burgeoning present, of the best of tradition and originality, is what gives poetry its flexibility as well as its vitality. Even the most privately confessional poetry, a genre that became something of a stereotype after Robert Lowell set the fashion, is preferable to the vatic apostrophes which served the poetaster, and even most of the poet laureates, for years.

It was inevitable that the attitudes and affectations, the reiterated murmurings about a prettified Nature and the innumerable salutations to a capitalized Beauty should rouse the scorn of a poet like E. E. Cummings who, in the midst of a devastating poem entitled "Poem, or Beauty Hurts Mr. Vinal," broke out with:

> *i do however protest, anent the un*
> *-spontaneous and otherwise scented merde which*
> *greets one (Everywhere Why) as divine poesy per*
> *that and this radically defunct periodical. i would*
> *suggest that certain ideas gestures*
> *rhymes, like Gillette Razor Blades*
> *having been used and reused*
> *to the mystical moment of dullness, emphatically are*
> *Not To Be Resharpened.*

Nothing changes as fast as fashion; taste is in a continual state of flux. Opinions vary not only from age to age but also from person to person living at the same period of time. Tennyson thought the songs of Burns exquisite: "in shape each of them has the perfection of the berry, in light the radiance of the dewdrop," and because of them "you forget those stupid things, his serious pieces." On the other hand, Wordsworth praised Burns for his genius in bringing poetry back to nature: "I refer," said Wordsworth, "to his serious efforts, such as 'The Cotter's Saturday Night'; the foolish little amatory songs of his one has to forget."

Who today can read Jean Ingelow, Fitz-Greene Halleck, Richard Monckton Milnes, Martin Farquhar Tupper, John Keble, Letitia Landon, Maria G. Brooks, Frances Sargent Osgood? Yet the conventions of their times united to rate them all great poets. *Poems* by Jean Ingelow went rapidly through twenty-two editions in England and more than two hundred thousand copies were sold in America. Fitz-Greene Halleck, famous for the maudlin, melodramatic "Marco Bozzaris," was the head of the Knickerbocker School and the idol of the elocutionists. Richard Monckton Milnes, a name that suggests nothing beyond a few odd syllables, was considered by Walter Savage Landor, a formidable poet and critic, the greatest poet of his time. Martin Farquhar Tupper's *Proverbial Philosophy* shared the shrine of the Bible on a hundred thousand parlor tables of the nineteenth century. A few hymns still carry the name of the Reverend John Keble, but in the mid-eighteen-hundreds one hundred and fifty editions of his *The Christian Year* were printed. A little more than a hundred years ago Letitia Landon was hailed as the Tenth Muse. The poet laureate Robert Southey christened Maria G. Brooks "Maria del Occidente," presumably because she came from Boston, and declared she was "the most impassioned and most imaginative of all poetesses." Edgar Allan Poe spoke of Frances Sargent Osgood (author of a lyric beginning "Call me pet names, dearest! Call me a bird!") with uncritical warmth and honored her with an intricate acrostic. (See page 130.) His estimate concluded that "Mrs. Osgood has assuredly no superior in America, if indeed she has any equal under the sun."

If opinions differ about individual poets, opinion-makers are even further apart when it comes to the function of poetry itself. The very size of a poem has been the subject of perpetual controversy. In "The Philosophy of Composition," an ingenious but suspect account of how "The Raven" came to be written, Poe refused to grant that there was any excuse for a long poem; he challenged the very idea of the long poem per se. "What we term a long poem is, in fact, merely a succession of brief ones—that is to say, of brief poetical effects. It is needless to demonstrate that a poem is such, only inasmuch as it intensely excites, and all intense excitements are, through a physical and psychical necessity, brief. For this reason, at least one half of *Paradise Lost* is essentially prose—a succession of poetical excitements interspersed inevitably with corresponding depressions—the whole being deprived, through the extremeness of its length, of the vastly important artistic element, totality, or unity, of effect." Valéry was among others who also believed that a poem loses its strength if it is unduly prolonged. "A hundred lines at the most," he said, "will make up a long poem." "But," said Valéry at another time, "there is no absolute truth when it comes to art. Everything is unique. Absolute judgments on works of art judge only the judges."

One cannot conceive of *Paradise Lost* being written today. We lack not only the faith to participate in such a poem but also the time to read it. The ever-increasing tempo of the times prohibits the epic. Moreover, as Poe contended, so lengthy a poem cannot sustain the pitch of poetry for any considerable duration. The degree of excitement, let alone exaltation, cannot be maintained except for short intervals. The moment of ecstasy is bound to be transient; it survives only in memory. That is why readers, while admiring the magnificence of the great epics, continue to favor the packed concentration of the sonnet and the small perfection of the lyric with its music as uncontrived and inevitable as a melody by Schubert.

Differences concerning the reading of poetry extend to the writing of it. Insisting that poetry could not be produced by determination, Shelley wrote: "A man cannot say, 'I *will* write poetry.' The greatest poet cannot say it; for the mind in creation is a fading coal which some invisible influence, like an inconstant wind, wakens to transitory brightness. . . . Could this influence be durable in its original purity and force, it is impossible to predict the greatness of the results. But when composition begins, inspiration is already on the decline, and the most glorious poetry that has ever been communicated to the world is probably a feeble shadow of the original conception of the poet." Keats differed only slightly when he asserted "innumerable compositions and decompositions take place between the intellect and its thousand materials before it [the poem] arrives at that trembling, delicate, and snail-horn perception of beauty." T. S. Eliot made the situation more explicit: "The larger part of the labor of an author is critical labor: the labor of sifting, combining, constructing, expunging, correcting, testing—this frightful toil is as much critical as creative."

It is in the act of writing—"sifting, combining, constructing, expunging, correcting, testing"—that the poet reveals whether he is depending on a convention or departing from it. He does not become "original" merely by startling us with strange ideas or inventing sensational situations; he is more likely to attain originality by giving a sense of novelty to familiar objects and bringing new perceptions to old plots. Chaucer nonchalantly took his material wherever he could find it, in medieval French romances, in classical legends, in the lewdest pages of Boccaccio. Shakespeare did not scruple to steal from his contemporaries; he also ransacked Ovid, North's translation of Plutarch, Holinshed's *Chronicles of England, Scotland, and Ireland,* Saxo Grammaticus' *Danish History,* the anonymous compilation of racy tales in the *Gesta Romanorum* and, with even greater zest than Chaucer, the narratives of Boccaccio, who also, like his adapters, appropriated whatever he wanted without bothering to acknowledge the source.

"Originality," wrote John Livingston Lowes, "is more than the saying of something never said before about something now for the first time perceived. . . . Originality is, in the main, independent of derivation. Its specific quality is the individual stamp: the pervasion of thought and expression, wherever derived, by something that gives distinction and individuality." Neither convention nor the revolt from convention can limit the power of the true originator: the poet who is able to reconcile opposing elements by uniting old and new, convention and innovation, familiarity and strangeness, in a paradox of recognition and surprise.

The Prose of Poetry

In spite of countless efforts, it is impossible to draw a sharp line between prose and poetry. It has been said that prose is consciously constructed whereas poetry is subconsciously created. It has been held that the function of prose is to state and that the purpose of poetry is to suggest, that prose is the product of the reasoning brain while poetry emanates from a wordless feeling, a vague emotion, a sense of pain or pleasure striving for expression. Valéry contended that ordinary diction starts from prose and raises itself into poetry, that poetry is to prose what dancing is to walking. He went on to say that prose, the ordinary spoken language, "is a practical tool. It is concerned with resolving immediate problems. Its task is fulfilled when the sentence has been completely abolished, annulled, and replaced by the meaning. Comprehension is its end. On the other hand, poetic usage is dominated by personal associations, by a continuous and sustained, largely musical, feeling."

It is, however, generally agreed that no one has established a demarcation to show where prose ends and poetry begins. Although it is easy enough to distinguish between prose which has a haphazard rhythm and verse which is definitely metrical, distinctions between prose and poetry are not only arbitrary but meaningless. "The farther the idiom, vocabulary, and syntax depart from those of prose," said Eliot, "the more artificial the language of poetry will become. At most, prose moves in one direction, poetry in another." "The difference between prose and poetry," wrote Stephen Spender, "lies in the kind of use to which language is put . . . We get the 'feel' of the difference between prose and poetry from the pull, the tug of language in one or the other direction." It may be said that poetry is uplifted prose, speech raised to a higher level, a greater intensity, a more memorable communication.

There is a certain uncharted borderland between prose and poetry, uncharted because the territory of prose often overlaps into the domain of poetry. And vice versa. There is a plethora of prose in Whitman's rhapsodic *Leaves of Grass*, and there is unquestionable poetry in Lincoln's *Gettysburg Address*, in the resonance of the King James version of the *Psalms*, in the ringing eloquence of John Donne's *Devotions*, in the exultations of Herman Melville. *Moby Dick* is studded with passages that are nothing less than prose poems; ecstasy has rarely reached a higher pitch than in Father Mapple's sermon with its magnificent conclusion:

> Delight is to him—a far, far upward and inward delight—who, against the proud gods and commodores of this earth, ever stands forth his own inexorable self. Delight is to him whose strong arms yet support him, when the ship of this base, treacherous world has gone down beneath him. Delight is to him, who gives no quarter in the truth, and kills, burns, and destroys all sin though he pluck it out from under the robes of Senators and Judges. Delight—top-gallant delight—is to him, who acknowledges no law or lord, but the Lord his God, and is only a patriot to heaven. Delight is to him, whom all the waves of the billows of the seas of the boisterous mob can never shake from this sure Keel of the Ages. And eternal delight and deliciousness will be his, who, coming to lay him down, can say with his final breath—O Father!—chiefly known to me by Thy rod—mortal or immortal, here I die. I have striven to be Thine, more than to be this world's, or mine own. Yet this is nothing; I leave eternity to Thee; for what is man that he should live out the lifetime of his God?

The indistinct line between prose and poetry was further thinned in the early years of the twentieth century with the invention of what was termed "polyphonic prose," an extension of free verse which combined the looseness of prose with occasional metrical moments and intermittent rhymes. Paul Fort was its prime practitioner in France; its chief exponents in America were John Gould Fletcher and Amy Lowell. It was Amy Lowell who explained that the word polyphonic was the keynote to the genre— "polyphonic means many-voiced, and the form is so called because it makes use of all the voices of poetry: metre, *vers libre*, assonance, alliteration, rhyme, and return." As an example of the form, here is the opening of Amy Lowell's "Guns as Keys: and the Great Gate Swings":

> *Due East, far West. Distant as the nests of the opposite*
> *winds. Removed as fire and water are, as the clouds*
> *and the roots of the hills, as the wills of youth and*
> *age. Let the key-guns be mounted; make a brave*
> *show of waging war, and pry off the lid of Pandora's*
> *box once more. Get in at any cost, and get out*
> *at little, so it seems. But wait—wait—there is*
> *much to follow through the Great Gate.*

> *They do not see things in quite that way, on this*
> *bright November day, with sun flashing and waves*
> *splashing up and down Chesapeake Bay. On shore, all*
> *the papers are running to press with huge headlines:*
> *"Commodore Perry Sails." Dining-tables buzz with*
> *travelers' tales . . .*

Although it was an interesting departure from the norm, most readers found that polyphonic prose was not, as its adherents maintained, a revolutionary form—Fletcher spoke of its enlarged "orchestral qualities" and related them to Bach fugues—but only an occasional device, a juxtaposition of somewhat harried prose and hit-or-miss rhythms, none of which were sustained. The result was likely to be spasmodic, jolting even when most ingenious.

The relation of prose to poetry reminds me of a practice that has irritated me whenever I have encountered it. It is a pernicious habit that still persists in too many classrooms where students are persuaded to "tell" what a poem "says" in the student's own words. The wish to extract the "meaning" of a poem by paraphrasing it seems harmless and even helpful; but, as L. A. G. Strong, a teacher as well as a poet, wrote, "it gives rise to a fundamental misapprehension which is at the root of half the popular prejudice against poetry. It encourages the wholly false belief that poetry is an artificial way of saying something which can be said equally well in prose. The truth is that poetry can never be paraphrased. . . . The effect of the poem is the effect of the poem as it stands. You cannot separate the thought from the expression. You cannot distinguish between the language and the meaning."

In short, the beauty and the power of a poem cannot be increased by rewording but can only be destroyed by paraphrase. The poem, the whole poem, and only the poem, can transmit its essential nature—its feeling, its texture and tone, its intent as well as its intensity. It is the very order of the words, or a single word, the untranslatable phrase—or the phrase which no one should attempt to translate—which, unless it is disrupted, stirs the awakened mind. To quote Valéry again, "Poetry arises from the essential arrangement of images, figures, consonances, dissonances, fusion of rhythms—avoiding anything which can be reduced to prose. To put a poem into prose is simply to misunderstand its essence." "Reordering" the arrangement of the lines of a poem to emphasize its "meaning" robs it not only of its music but of the indefinable sense of poetry. Any rearrangement or transposition or rewording will change a pure experience into a poor exercise.

I have before me an illustration of what happens when a teacher instructs a student (in this case a high school senior) to render —and the verb is apt—the meaning of a poem "in his own words." The poem chosen was Keats's sonnet "To One Who has been Long in City Pent."

> To one who has been long in city pent,
>   'Tis very sweet to look into the fair
>   And open face of heaven—to breathe a prayer
> Full in the smile of the blue firmament.
> Who is more happy, when, with heart's content,
>   Fatigued he sinks into some pleasant lair
>   Of wavy grass, and reads a debonair
> And gentle tale of love and languishment?
> Returning home at evening, with an ear
>   Catching the notes of Philomel—an eye

Watching the sailing cloudlet's bright career,
He mourns that day so soon has glided by,
E'en like the passage of an angel's tear
That falls through the clear ether silently.

Here is the student's rendering:

"Anyone who has had to live in a city is glad to visit the country and give thanks for the bright blue sky. He is happy and contented even when he is tired, for he can sink into some resting place and read a soothing story. On his way home at evening he can hear a bird or watch a cloud sailing by. He is sorry that the day has gone by so fast, like an angel's tear dropping through the air."

There is no question that the paraphrase has faithfully "translated" the prose "meaning" of Keats's sonnet. The teacher undoubtedly gained some evidence of the student's degree of attentiveness and understanding. The disturbing question is: has the poetry of the poem been lost to the student in the process of reducing it to prose?

A more amusing instance of arresting the progress of poetry and replacing communication with criticism is furnished by an anonymous teacher. Quoting the first two lines of Wordsworth's "To the Cuckoo," he mocked the tutorial method by adding two lines of his own.

"O cuckoo! Shall I call thee Bird?
Or just a wandering Voice?"
State the alternative preferred,
With reasons for your choice.

On the other hand, poets have continually turned prose into poetry. History is full of examples of prose passages lifted into magnificent verse. Agrippa's fable of the parts of the body that rebelled against the belly, in North's translation of Plutarch's *Lives of the Noble Grecians and Romans,* is transposed into Menenius' speech in Act I of *Coriolanus.* Lisabetta's planting the severed head of her lover, Lorenzo—the fifth story on the fourth day of Boccaccio's *Decameron*—is carried over and glorified in Keats's "Isabella: or, the Pot of Basil." Malory's *Le Morte d'Arthur* became the blank verse of Tennyson's "The Passing of Arthur" in *Idylls of the King*. Bernal Díaz's *True History of the Conquest of New Spain* is the basis for the terza rima in MacLeish's *Conquistador:* Turning back to Plutarch's *Lives*, here is the description of Cleopatra's barge in North's translation:

Therefore, when she was sent unto by divers letters, both from Antonius himself, and also from his friends, she made so light of it, and mocked Antonius so much, that she disdained to set forward otherwise, but to take her barge in the river of Cydnus; the poop whereof was of gold, the sails of purple, and the oars of silver, which kept stroke in rowing after the sound of the musicke of flutes, howboys, citherns, viols, and such other instruments as they played upon in the barge. And now for the person of herself: she was laid under a pavilion of cloth of gold of tissue, apparelled and attired like the goddess Venus commonly drawn in picture: and hard by her, on either hand of her, pretty fair boys apparelled as Painters do set forth god Cupid, with little fans in their hands, with the which they fanned wind upon her. Her Ladies and Gentlewomen also, the fairest of them were apparelled like the Nymphs *Nereids* (which are the mermaids of the waters) and like the *Graces*, some steering the helm, others tending the tackle and ropes of the barge, out of the which there came a wonderful passing sweet savour of perfumes, that perfumed the wharf's side, pestered with innumerable multitudes of people. Some of them followed the barge all along the river-side: others also ran out of the city to see her coming in. So that in the end there ran such multitudes of people one after another to see her, that Antonius was left post alone in the market-place in his Imperial seat to give audience: and there went a rumour in the people's mouths, that the goddess Venus was come to play with the god Bacchus, for the general good of all Asia.

This is what Shakespeare did with it in the second scene of the second act of *Antony and Cleopatra*.

The barge she sat in, like a burnished throne,
Burned on the water: the poop was beaten gold;
Purple the sails, and so perfuméd that
The winds were love-sick with them; the oars were silver,

Which to the tune of flutes kept stroke, and made
The water which they beat to follow faster,
As amorous of their strokes. For her own person,
It beggared all description: she did lie
In her pavilion—cloth-of-gold of tissue—
O'er picturing that Venus where we see
The fancy outwork nature: On each side her
Stood pretty dimpled boys, like smiling Cupids,
With divers-colored fans, whose wind did seem
To glow the delicate cheeks which they did cool,
And what they undid did. . . .
Her gentlewomen, like the Nereides,
So many mermaids, tended her i' the eyes,
And made their bends adornings. At the helm
A seeming mermaid steers; the silken tackle
Swell with the touches of those flower-soft hands
That yarely frame the office. From the barge
A strange invisible perfume hits the sense
Of the adjacent wharfs. The city cast
Her people out upon her. And Antony,
Enthroned i' the market-place, did sit alone,
Whistling to the air, which, but for vacancy,
Had gone to gaze on Cleopatra too,
And made a gap in nature.

The line between prose and poetry is the line drawn and then discarded by the poet.

The Reading of Poetry

Anyone who has anything to say has a natural desire to be heard. Even though the artist sometimes claims that he creates only for himself, he cannot help wishing to share his creation, his experience and (unconsciously, perhaps) his emotion with others. The moment a creator shows his paintings, orchestrates his symphony, or prints his poem he ceases to isolate or even protect himself. He may keep himself aloof, shun the crowd, scorn criticism, disclaim interest in any response, but he cannot pretend that his right to privacy extends to what he has exhibited.

It is a perpetually arguable question whether the poet writes for an audience or for himself. Although communication seems the logical aim of a piece of writing, most poets would deny that they have an audience in mind when writing and that, moreover, they feel any obligation to communicate. They might quote Keats in their behalf: "I feel assured I should write for the mere yearning and fondness I have for the beautiful, even if my night's labors should be burnt every morning and no eye shine upon them." Nevertheless, poetry is written to be read by someone besides the writer. The poem is conceived in the poet's inner being, but it comes to life only when it is read, and preferably read aloud.

It has been said that, with the exception of popular songs, poets no longer compose their lines for the ear but write only for the eye. Gutenberg opened up a new world for those who learned to read prose. But he did a disservice to poetry. Before the invention of movable type, poetry was recited, declaimed, sung, and chanted in every possible variety of voice. People delighted to listen to ballad singers at street corners, to jongleurs in market places, to troubadours who wandered from country fairs to regal courts. They listened and they *heard*. The poems came alive with all their multiple resonances: the open vowels and the percussive consonants, the rich rhymes and the assonances, the alternating rhythms of the breath and the ever-changing pitch of the voice.

After being put on the printed page, the poem went silent. Those who read poetry silently never heard it. The eye was a poor substitute for the ear. What was true for music was equally true for poetry. The eye can read the score of Mozart's Jupiter symphony, but the pages do not come to life until the different instruments are heard in the subtle and almost miraculous union of diverse sounds.

"The ear does it," wrote Robert Frost to his former student John Bartlett. "The ear is the only true writer and the only true reader. I have known people who could read without hearing the sentence sounds and they were the fastest readers. Eye readers we call them. They can get the meaning by glances. But they are bad readers because they miss the best part of what a good writer puts into his work."

A good writer (it cannot be said too often) is as concerned with the sound as with the sense. If he is a poet he is likely to make the sound carry the sense—even, at times, substitute for it. "Jabberwocky," that masterpiece of nonsense, is made of words that vaguely suggest sense, and there have been countless annotations tracing their meaning. In *Through the Looking Glass* Humpty Dumpty volunteers to interpret the meaning: "I can explain all the poems that ever were invented, and a good many that haven't been invented yet." He tells Alice that "slithy" is a "portmanteau" word meaning "lithe" and "slimy," that "gimble" is to make holes like a "gimlet," that the grass-plot around a sun-dial is called a "wabe" because it goes a long *way* be*fore* and a long *way* be*hind* it. But the reader is happier with the senseless sounds than with the interpretations; he resents reducing the mystery of what constitutes a "vorpal" sword to a workaday adjective. It is what wins the ear that wins our affection even before our understanding.

Yvor Winters maintained that the audible reading of poetry is as important as the understanding of it. Winters declared that "without audible reading you simply do not have poetry." He recommended the reading of poetry "not merely for the sensual ear, but for the mind's ear as well." Winters went on to quote a passage from Paul Valéry's "Discourse on the Declamation of Verse" in which the French poet-critic wrote:

In studying a piece of poetry to recite one should not take as source or point of departure ordinary conversation in order to rise from the level of prose to the desired poetic tone. On the contrary, one should take song as a base and should put oneself in the state of a singer, adjust one's voice to the plenitude of musical sounds, and from there descend to the somewhat less resonant state suitable to verse. This, it seemed to me, is the only way to preserve the musical essence of poems. . . . Above all, do not be in a hurry to arrive at the meaning. Approach it without effort and, as it were, insensibly. Remain in this pure musical state until such time as the meaning, appearing little by little, can no longer mar the musical form. You will introduce it at the end as the supreme nuance that will transfigure the passage without altering it.

Valéry failed to indicate that the reading of a poem is, necessarily, as individual a performance as the rendering of a piece of music. It varies not only with each person's sense of what the poem should convey, but also with the pitch of the reader's voice, the choice of tone, the emphasis on one phrase or another, the decision whether to give a hard or a delicate touch to the percussive consonants, the prolongation or shortening of the vowels, the accenting or slurring of the rhythm. The poem, in short, is a musical challenge; it is a score without directions of tempo or dynamics, a confrontation in which the reader is both conductor and orchestrator as well as solo performer.

The reading of poetry is, therefore, anything but a haphazard vocalization of words. The words themselves have different meanings not only for different readers but at different times. The poem we read today may not have the same power or persuasion for us that it had for those who read it in another period.

Toussaint, the most unhappy man of men!
Whether the whistling rustic tend his plough
Within thy hearing, or thy head be now
Pillowed in some deep dungeon's earless den—
O miserable Chieftain! where and when
Wilt thou find patience? Yet die not; do thou
Wear rather in thy bonds a cheerful brow,
Though fallen thyself, never to rise again,
Live, and take comfort. Thou hast left behind
Powers that will work for thee: air, earth, and skies.
There's not a breathing of the common wind
That will forget thee; thou hast great allies;
Thy friends are exultations, agonies,
And love, and man's unconquerable mind.

When Wordsworth wrote this sonnet he was still glowing with what the French Revolution promised not only to people of the eighteenth century but to the future. It brought hope to millions, particularly to the enslaved Negroes in the French Caribbeans. But the National Assembly was not ready to extend the rights of man to slaves. The blacks of Haiti then staged their own revolt. It was led by one who called himself Toussaint L'Ouverture. The struggle for freedom lasted twenty years and was finally won. But, long before independence had been achieved, Toussaint L'Ouverture was captured and taken to a French prison, where he died.

Today the sonnet lacks both the background and the indignation which inspired it. The wrath has gone out of it. We read the sonnet today more for its sound than for its sense. We dutifully accept the awkward phrases, the broken sentences and heavy rhetoric of the first eight lines for the eloquent music of the concluding sestet. We do not read the poem as the record of a noble historic event but as a gathering of noble sonorities.

There's not a breathing of the common wind
That will forget thee; thou hast great allies;
Thy friends are exultations, agonies,
And love, and man's unconquerable mind.

Every poem is not only an individual expression but also an experience, and its reading is an event, a particular moment in the mind of a particular person. Fortunately, we can sample the best of those expressions and experiences, those "events," through recordings by the poets themselves on disc and tape. That sound is one of the sources of meaning is repeatedly proved by the way poetry is read on records. Such readings not only revitalize the poem on the printed page but also reveal the characteristics and, unconsciously, the character of the poet. Poetry and the person are combined in the exuberant oratory of Dylan Thomas, in the clerically clipped but dramatic declamation of T. S. Eliot, in the sly and subtle simplicities of Robert Frost, the nervously intense vigor of Robert Lowell. One thinks of what today's recording media could do for us if some time-machine could transport the mechanism to the past. What would we not give to hear Chaucer retelling the lusty Wife of Bath's tale, or listen to Shakespeare solving the riddle of his sonnets by reading them in the right order, or hearken to Blake intoning his "Auguries of Innocence," or thrill while Burns trolled out the Hogarthian ribaldry of "The Jolly Beggars," or attend breathlessly while Keats summoned the nightingale that charmed magic casements and was not born for death!

The Translation of Poetry

Poetry, said Robert Frost, is what gets lost in translation. *Traduttore: tradditore* (blunted when rendered "translator: traitor") is the Italian disposal. A translation is not necessarily a betrayal, but it cannot hope to reproduce the poem as it was conceived and composed. A translation may even be a better poem than the original—as in the case of French and Spanish translations of Poe's "The Raven"—but it is not the same poem.

The lyrics of Heinrich Heine, for example, are so simple that, paradoxically, they defy translation. When the translator deals with description, wit, and satire, he has little difficulty carrying the meaning over from one language to another. When, however, he deals with the sound, the verbal music, the poetry *as* poetry, he fails completely. *Im wunderschönen Monat Mai* loses all its wonder when, if the translator is scrupulously literal, it becomes the banal "in the wonderfully beautiful month of May." The delicately rhymed and lightly alliterative syllables of *Leise zieht durch mein Gemüt liebliche Geläute* are lost in the maudlin English equivalent of "Lovely chiming sounds are softly drawing through my soul." To make the way of the translator (transgressor?) still harder, it is an annoying phenomenon that, whereas such constantly employed abstractions as Love, Life, Faith, Truth, Joy, Grief are firm English monosyllables, in German they happen to be standard two-syllable nouns—*Liebe, Leben, Glaube, Wahrheit, Freude, Kummer*—forcing the translator to pad or drastically disarrange his lines.

French poetry furnishes equally distracting problems. Here is the first verse of Verlaine's "Chanson d'Automne":

> *Les sanglots longs*
> *Des violons*
> * De l'automne*
> *Blessent mon coeur*
> *D'une langueur*
> * Monotone.*

What happens when it is rendered into English is this:

> *Autumn begins:*
> *Her violins*
> * Sigh and sob.*
> *They fill my breast*
> *With dull unrest,*
> * Leaden throb.*

The substance is not too badly conveyed in Brian Hill's translation, but there is not the slightest hint of the rise and fall of the sound, the hushed, half-closed vowels, the slow "dying fall." Melody can no more be translated than color can be communicated or perfume be conveyed by way of words.

There are two choices open to the translator. If he is not at home with the nuances of the foreign language he is confronting, he can settle for a "trot," a word-for-word transliteration, and give a fair idea of the meaning of the poem which approximates the sound as well as the sense. It will, perhaps, be a good poem, but it will not be the poem written by the original author. The second choice is not really a translation but a re-creation, a paraphrase, an imitation which sacrifices the word-order, the "tune" and the cadence for a response to the mood of the original. Such paraphrases, as opposed to the literal metaphrase, distinguish the translations of Ezra Pound, Dudley Fitts, Richard Lattimore, and Robert Lowell—Lowell was content to call his book of versions of Villon, Baudelaire, Rilke, Montale, and others *Imitations*.

The best that can happen to a translator, said Lascelles Abercrombie, is that "he may be poet enough to provide out of his own life and art some substitute for what has vanished. How splendidly that may happen, let the Authorized Version of *Job* remind us. Sometimes, indeed, the original has been the mere stimulus of a wholly new creation: the famous instance is Edward Fitzgerald's Omar Khayyam . . . In any translation *The Divine Comedy* must seem, moment by moment, to have suffered an intolerable loss, and yet the greatness of the whole will substantially survive. And so, too, when the translator substitutes for the original a poetic craftsmanship peculiarly his own. Chapman's Homer is quite unlike Pope's, and neither Chapman's nor Pope's Homer is like Homer himself. Yet unmistakably the greatness of both Chapman and Pope is Homer's greatness; this, in either paraphrase, is the surviving thing."

In short, a good translation is one that sounds as though it might be the original itself. But how can this be achieved? How can one translate a sound? How much of the music can be preserved without losing the meaning, and how much of the meaning can be retained without distorting the music? It is not true that if you take care of the sense the sounds will take care of themselves. The sound is the essence, if not the sense, of poetry and cannot be communicated except by itself. Even the most gifted translator can carry little more than the "plot" and, perhaps, the rhythm, but what he transports will have the same relation to the original poem that the libretto has to the fulfilled opera.

Obviously, wrote Dudley Fitts in *The Poetic Nuance*, "if translation means a carrying across, it is nonsense to suppose that we should be satisfied with carrying across anything less than the whole. A poem is a total complex. There are details of it that can be represented adequately in another language . . . But no one will mistake the details for the whole, and consequently a translation must fail to the extent that it leaves unaccounted for whatever aspects of the original it is unable to handle. Everyone knows what these aspects are: nuances of diction, of sound, of tone, that make any poem a discrete experience, an entity somehow different from any other good poem ever written."

Nevertheless, a good translation can increase our respect and (if the translator is a Pope, a Dryden, a Pound, or a Lowell) our appreciation of the source. Since his language differs radically from that of the original, he must have something beyond a gift for mimicry; he must be moved by a natural affinity of taste and temperament. He must have a more than ordinarily sensitive ear, a verbal dexterity, and the ability to sound the subtle differences inherent in a foreign language.

It is interesting to contrast four different versions of the first few lines of a poem by Horace, the thirtieth in his third book of odes. This is the Latin beginning:

> *Exegi monumentum aere perennius*
> *Regalique situ pyramidum altius,*
> *Quod non imber edax, non Aquilo impotens*
> *Possit diruere aut innumerabilis*
> *Annorum series et fuga temporum.*

The nineteenth-century poet-statesman-viceroy of India, Edward Bulwer, Lord Lytton, offered this stilted and inverted equivalent which, nevertheless, was much respected by the author's contemporaries.

> *I have built a monument than bronze more lasting,*
> *Soaring more high than regal pyramids,*
> *Which nor the stealthy gnawing of the rain-drops,*
> *Nor the vain rush of Boreas shall destroy;*
> *Nor shall it pass away with the unnumbered*
> *Series of ages and the flight of time.*

Fifty years later the classical scholar Warren H. Cudworth "Englished" the odes "into rimed verse corresponding to the original meters" with this result:

> *Outlasting bronze, a monument I rear*
> *That o'er the regal pyramids towers sheer,*
> *Which gnawing rains, nor blustering Aquilo,*
> *Nor ceaseless lapse of years, nor ages' flow*
> *Shall ever from its sure foundation start.*

Lord Dunsany, surveying the field in 1947, compromised. He
pointed out that many translators had wandered far from Horace
and that he had done his best "to steer a clear way between
Scylla and Charybdis," between beauty and exactitude. He presented this proper if flavorless version:

> A monument more durable than brass,
> Rising above the regal pyramids,
> Have I erected, which no rain nor wind,
> Nor centuries unnumbered, could destroy,
> Nor all the flight of seasons.

It remained for Ezra Pound to treat the Latin cavalierly and
give Horace's lines a characteristic colloquial ease:

> This monument will outlast metal, and I made it .
> More durable than the king's seat, higher than pyramids.
> Gnaw of the wind and rain? Impotent
> The flow of the years to break it, however many.

None of these translations is perfect; none transmits the movement of the verse nor the technique by which Horace confidently
but not vaingloriously assumes the immortality of his fame. Yet all
convey something incomparably better than Gladstone's much-
quoted version, which the four-times Prime Minister began
blithely in jogtrot rhyme:

> Now I have reared a monument more durable than brass
> And one that doth the royal scale of pyramids surpass . . .

and ended with this rhetorical flourish:

> So take thine honors earned by deeds; and graciously do thou
> Melpomene, with Delphic bays adorn thy poet's brow.

Ingenuity, even virtuosity, is not enough. It is important to
suggest the accent, feel the weight, sense the flavor of the original. It is, moreover, necessary to attempt the almost impossible:

to capture the magic concealed in the imagery, the shape of the words, the rise and fall of the syllables. In his biography of Goethe, G. H. Lewes remarks that in a poem "meaning and form are as indissoluble as body and soul, and the form cannot be reproduced. For words in poetry are not, as in prose, simple representatives of objects and ideas; they are parts of an organic whole," a whole which, Lewes implies, cannot be substituted, taken apart, or transposed.

At the same time the continual demand for communication, for a wider rapport between cultures, makes it imperative that poetry be translated, preferably by poets. Moreover, poems that have been carried over from one tongue to another should be retranslated every decade or two in an effort to achieve a new approach, another attempt to reproduce the tone, the texture, the elemental rhythm, and, most of all, the main effect: the impact of music with meaning—from Villon to Voznesensky—in terms attuned to their times.

The Playfulness of Poetry

Even when poetry is most serious, it indulges in the sidespring of fancy, the leap of the adventurous imagination and the surprising fantasia of the unconscious. It can be maintained that poetry is often as playful as it is profound, that word-play is the essence of poetry. Poetry begins with metaphor, and the metaphorical tendency—finding similarity in dissimilar things—increases with the playfulness of the poet's mind. This saying one thing and indicating another is a verbal sportiveness, a game in which the wit of the writer and the wit of the reader are matched.

The play of imagery acts to enrich reality, even to heighten it. The average man enjoys its exaggerated double-entendre so much that he employs it constantly. "My heart leaped," he says, or "my heart stood still," knowing perfectly well that it contracts and expands quietly within the pericardium. A more powerful form of poetic play is the supposedly "lowest form of wit," the so-often-despised pun. Primarily the pun is a poetic device, a verbal legerdemain, a shifting of sounds that, like rhyme, are similar yet not quite the same. It is a half-matching, half-changing of vowels and consonants, an adroit assonance, which springs from the same combination of wit and imagination that propels the poetic impulse.

Poets, from Shakespeare to Joyce, testify for the defense. Punning was important to Shakespeare not only as a comic diversion but as a multi-level significant commentary. In *The Poetic Mind* Frederick Clarke Prescott calls attention to the triple meanings invoked when Hotspur, rebelling against Henry IV, cries out:

> *We must have bloody noses and cracked crowns*
> *And pass them current too.*

"Here," says Prescott, "the 'cracked crowns' are, first, cracked coins; secondly, broken heads; and, thirdly, royal crowns upset. . . . But this triple word-play is simple compared with Hamlet's. In Act I, Hamlet, dressed in black, appears before the king and queen, who have cast off their mourning and are seated on their thrones of state.

> KING: But now, my cousin Hamlet, and my son—
> HAMLET (*aside*): A little more than kin and less than kind.
> KING: How is it that the clouds still hang on you?
> HAMLET: Not so, my lord; I am too much i' the sun.

"Besides the literal meaning borne by 'clouds' and 'sun,' which is the starting point, Hamlet declares: 1, that, in his black, he is too much in the sunshine of royal splendor; 2, that, destitute and under a cloud as he is, he is but too much in the sunshine of the king's favor; 3, that, as the common saw has it, he is 'out of God's benediction into the warm sun' (*Lear*, II, ii, 168)—that is, out of house and home; 4, that he is 'sonned' too much by the king without a son's rights. But the speech is poetry, and the meanings cannot be enumerated in prose. . . . 'Too much in the sun' means all these things together and at once. It is of imagination all compact."

Prescott cites another example of the pun's playful yet grim power. Noting that to the Elizabethan audiences, the verb "to die" suggests the climax of the sexual act, he quotes two lines from Juliet's death scene.

> JULIET: Yea, noise? Then I'll be brief. O happy dagger!
>   (*She snatches Romeo's dagger.*)
> This is thy sheath. (*Stabs herself.*) There rust and let me die.
>   (*Falls on Romeo's body and dies.*)

The phallic symbolism of Juliet's stabbing herself with Romeo's dagger becomes more apparent when we recall that Romeo had perished with the same pun on his lips: "Thus with a kiss I die."

II

THE CRAFT
OF POETRY

A Dictionary of Devices,
a Handbook of Poetic Terms,
and a Compendium of Metrical Patterns
From Ballads to Ballades,
From Lyrics to Epics,
From Sonnets to Sestinas, With Examples
of All the Forms and Variations

Word-plays served Shakespeare for a wide range of other effects, from the lightest persiflage to the coarsest jokes. *Romeo and Juliet,* the most tender of tragedies, opens roughly with a series of bawdy puns about thrusting Montague's men from the walls and thrusting his maids *to* the wall, about maids and maidenheads, about the ability to stand—" 'tis known I am a pretty piece of flesh."

In a chapter entitled "Wit and High Seriousness" in *Modern Poetry and the Tradition* Cleanth Brooks quotes Carew's fanciful song, "Ask Me No More."

> *Ask me no more where Jove bestows,*
> *When June is past, the fading rose;*
> *For in your beauty's orient deep*
> *These flowers, as in their causes, sleep.*
>
> *Ask me no more whither do stray*
> *The golden atoms of the day;*
> *For in pure love heaven did prepare*
> *Those powders to enrich your hair.*
>
> *Ask me no more whither doth haste*
> *The nightingale, when May is past;*
> *For in your sweet dividing throat*
> *She winters, and keeps warm her note.*
>
> *Ask me no more where those stars light,*
> *That downwards fall in dead of night;*
> *For in your eyes they sit, and there*
> *Fixèd become, as in their sphere.*
>
> *Ask me no more if east or west*
> *The phoenix builds her spicy nest;*
> *For unto you at last she flies,*
> *And in your fragrant bosom dies.*

Brooks points to the skill with which Carew unites playfulness and plausibility—the falling stars which find their proper place in the eyes of his beloved, the association of "orient" with the beauty and splendor of the east, that orient where the phoenix is fabled to live—and adds that the poem gives an overall effect of

seriousness "not in spite of the wit, but by means of the wit."
Carew had a reputation for profligacy—his "The Rapture" and
"The Second Rapture" are frankly lascivious—but the verses above
are not merely artful but also as plangent as they are playful.

Taking the stock situation of the importunate lover and the
reluctant lady, Andrew Marvell lifted it from casual playfulness to
genuine passion, culminating with the threat of time and the dark
finality of death. Marvell did not treat the theme with false
naïvety, like the lovesick Elizabethans, nor with terrifying ferocity,
like Donne. Marvell controlled both himself and his conceits. Before he warned the lady that "The grave's a fine and private
place/But none, I think, do there embrace," he began "To His
Coy Mistress" in half-amused raillery. The teasing tone flickers
through the lines until, with "But at my back I always hear," it
turns, by way of an implied pun, from levity to gravity.

> *Had we but world enough, and time,*
> *This coyness, lady, were no crime.*
> *We would sit down, and think which way*
> *To walk, and pass our long love's day.*
> *Thou by the Indian Ganges' side*
> *Should'st rubies find: I by the tide*
> *Of Humber would complain. I would*
> *Love you ten years before the Flood,*
> *And you should, if you please, refuse*
> *Till the conversion of the Jews.*
> *My vegetable love should grow*
> *Vaster than empires, and more slow.*
> *An hundred years should go to praise*
> *Thine eyes, and on thy forehead gaze:*
> *Two hundred to adore each breast:*
> *But thirty thousand to the rest;*
> *An age at least to every part,*
> *And the last age should show your heart.*
> *For, lady, you deserve this state,*
> *Nor would I love at lower rate.*
>   *But at my back I always hear*
> *Time's wingèd chariot hurrying near:*

And yonder all before us lie
Deserts of vast eternity.
Thy beauty shall no more be found;
Nor, in thy marble vault, shall sound
My echoing song. Then worms shall try
That long-preserved virginity,
And your quaint honor turn to dust,
And into ashes all my lust.
The grave's a fine and private place,
But none, I think, do there embrace.
  Now, therefore, while the youthful hue
Sits on thy skin like morning dew,
And while thy willing soul transpires
At every pore with instant fires,
Now let us sport us while we may;
And now, like amorous birds of prey,
Rather at once our time devour,
Than languish in his slow-chapt power.
Let us roll all our strength and all
Our sweetness up into one ball,
And tear our pleasures with rough strife
Thorough the iron gates of life.
Thus, though we cannot make our sun
Stand still, yet we will make him run.

The gap between the poets of the seventeenth and the twentieth century seems staggering, but it is bridged from Donne by way of Marvell to Eliot. There is a curious blend of Donne's cerebral sensuality and Marvell's mischievous sprightliness in Eliot's "Sweeney Erect," "Sweeney Among the Nightingales," and "Whispers of Immortality"—those early essays in metaphysical light verse—with their throwback a few hundred years in such taut, teasing stanzas as:

Donne, I suppose, was such another
Who found no substitute for sense,
To seize and clutch and penetrate:
Expert beyond experience,

> He knew the anguish of the marrow,
> The ague of the skeleton;
> No contact possible to flesh
> Allayed the fever of the bone.

> Grishkin is nice: her Russian eye
> Is underlined for emphasis;
> Uncorseted, her friendly bust
> Gives promise of pneumatic bliss.

It seems, paradoxically enough, that the poet is most serious when he is most whimsical and that the most searching poetry is the poetry of wit. Irony, a mordant form of play, can encompass mockery as well as tragedy. One of the most caustic pieces of ironic poetry ever composed is compacted in a twentieth-century epitaph by A. E. Housman. It is his "Epitaph on an Army of Mercenaries."

> These, in the day when heaven was falling,
> The hour when earth's foundations fled,
> Followed their mercenary calling
> And took their wages and are dead.

> Their shoulders held the sky suspended;
> They stood, and earth's foundations stay;
> What God abandoned, these defended,
> And saved the sum of things for pay.

In such a poem wit swings full circle from gay to grim and, far from frivolity, poetry returns to its element of serious play.

The Oddities of Poetry

The impulse to revel in poetry has led to a great variety of strange and sometimes remarkable oddities. One of the earliest practitioners of eccentric forms was the seventeenth-century churchman and churchbuilder "Holy" George Herbert. Never has there been a poetry so pious and yet so playful. Herbert was no less serious when he was making puns than when he was writing hymns. Although he delighted in metaphorical play, it was never play for its own sake but play for God's sake. He embodied his most profound reflections in rhymed anagrams and acrostics, curiously designed stanzas, and picture verses: Herbert's *The Temple* contains 169 poems, and 116 of them are in entirely different verse forms, many of which he invented. He balanced deeply religious thoughts on the point of aphorisms. He wrote solemn poems centering about a pun—"Jesu: I Ease-You," "Roma: Maro, Oram, Armo, Amor"—poems, like the one appropriately entitled "Our Life is Hid," where the key words are hidden in a kind of acrostic, and epigrams that are anagrams. Here is one of his tight, expressive couplets:

$$\text{ANA} \left\{ \begin{array}{c} \text{MARY} \\ \text{ARMY} \end{array} \right\} \text{GRAM}$$

How well her name an Army doth present,
In whom the Lord of Hosts did pitch His tent!

Another poem which is both diverting and devout is Herbert's "Paradise." It is a strictly rhymed poem, the rhymes are in three-

line stanzas, but they match each other in a curious way. The first
letter of each rhyming word is successively dropped until what began as a clever trick ends in quiet solemnity.

> *I bless Thee, Lord, because I GROW*
> *Among Thy trees, which in a ROW*
> *To Thee both fruit and order OW(E).*
>
> *What open force, or hidden CHARM*
> *Can blast my fruit, or bring me HARM,*
> *While the inclosure is Thine ARM:*
>
> *Inclose me still for fear I START;*
> *Be to me rather sharp and TART,*
> *Than let me want Thy hand and ART.*
>
> *When Thou dost greater judgments SPARE,*
> *And with Thy knife but prune and PARE,*
> *Even fruitful trees more fruitful ARE:*
>
> *Such sharpness shows the sweetest FR(I)END,*
> *Such cuttings rather heal than REND,*
> *And such beginnings touch their END.*

As early as the Elizabethan era, poets sported with echo verses.
Herbert, however, surprised his readers by adding fervor to what
had been used for mockery. In "Heaven" the purpose transcends
entertainment.

> *O, who will show me those delights on high?*
> ECHO: I.
> *Thou Echo, thou art mortal, all men know.*
> ECHO: No.
> *Wert thou not born among the trees and leaves?*
> ECHO: Leaves.
> *And are there any leaves that still abide?*
> ECHO: Bide.
> *What leaves are they? Impart the matter wholly.*
> ECHO: Holy.
> *Are holy leaves the Echo, then, of bliss?*
> ECHO: Yes.

> *Then tell me, what is that supreme delight?*
>   ECHO: Light.
> *Light to the mind. What shall the will enjoy?*
>   ECHO: Joy.
> *But are there cares and business with the pleasure?*
>   ECHO: Leisure.
> *Light, joy, and leisure; but shall they persever?*
>   ECHO: Ever.

The possibilities in echoing rhymes continued to fascinate poets. Swift mixed flippancy, cynicism, and sentiment in "A Gentle Echo on Woman."

Shepherd. *Echo, I ween, will in the woods reply,*
           And quaintly answer questions. Shall I try?
Echo.   Try.
Shepherd. *What must we do our passion to express?*
Echo.   Press.
Shepherd. *How shall I please her, who ne'er loved before?*
Echo.   Be fore.
Shepherd. *What most moves women when we them address?*
Echo.   A dress.
Shepherd. *Say, what can keep her chaste whom I adore?*
Echo.   A door.
Shepherd. *If music softens rocks, love tunes my lyre.*
Echo.   Liar.
Shepherd. *Then teach me, Echo, how shall I come by her?*
Echo.   Buy her.
Shepherd. *But what can glad me when she's laid on bier?*
Echo.   Beer.
Shepherd. *What must I do when women will be kind?*
Echo.   Be kind.
Shepherd. *What must I do when women will be cross?*
Echo.   Be cross.
Shepherd. *Lord, what is she that can so turn and wind?*
Echo.   Wind.
Shepherd. *If she be wind, what stills her when she blows?*
Echo.   Blows.
Shepherd. *But if she bang again, still should I bang her?*
Echo.   Bang her.

Shepherd. *Is there no way to moderate her anger?*
Echo.   Hang her.
Shepherd. *Thanks, gentle Echo! right thy answers tell*
            What woman is and how to guard her well.
Echo.   Guard her well.

More than a hundred years later the American humorist John Godfrey Saxe gave the old device a new turn and, influenced by the English Thomas Hood, a pert, punning vivacity.

> *I asked of Echo t'other day*
>   *(Whose words are often few and funny),*
> *What to a novice she could say*
>   *Of Courtship, Love, and Matrimony.*
>   *Quoth Echo, plainly,—"Matter-o'-money."*
>
> *Whom should I marry? Should it be*
>   *A dashing damsel, gay and pert,*
> *A pattern of inconsistency;*
>   *Or selfish, mercenary flirt?*
>   *Quoth Echo, sharply,—"Nary flirt!"*
>
> *What if, aweary of the strife*
>   *That long has lured the dear deceiver,*
> *She promised to amend her life,*
>   *And sin no more; can I believe her?*
>   *Quoth Echo, very promptly,—"Leave her!"*
>
> *But if some maiden with a heart*
>   *On me should venture to bestow it,*
> *Pray, should I act the wiser part*
>   *To take the treasure or forego it?*
>   *Quoth Echo, with decision,—"Go it!"*
>
> *But what if, seemingly afraid*
>   *To bind her fate in Hymen's fetter,*
> *She vow she means to die a maid,*
>   *In answer to my loving letter?*
>   *Quoth Echo, rather coolly,—"Let her!"*

What if, in spite of her disdain,
  I find my heart intwined about
With Cupid's dear delicious chain
  So closely that I can't get out?
  Quoth Echo, laughingly,—"Get out!"

But if some maid with beauty blest,
  As pure and fair as Heaven can make her,
Will share my labor and my rest
  Till envious Death shall overtake her?
  Quoth Echo (sotto voce),—"Take her!"

Surprisingly enough, modern poets do not despise the artifice. In the second section of "Misanthropos," a long dramatic poem which was performed on the British Broadcasting Company's Third Program in 1965, Thom Gunn employs a stinging echo-poem which begins:

At last my shout is answered! Are you near,
Man whom I cannot see but can hear?

                                                Here.
The canyon hides you well, which well defended.
Sir, tell me, is the long war ended?

                                                Ended.
I passed no human on my trip, a slow one.
Is it your luck, down there, to know one?

                                                No one.

An equally fanciful effect was favored by poets as early as the Greek Anthology. In his treatise *De Divinatione* Cicero cites the antiquity of the form and explains its method: "The verses are distinguished by that arrangement which the Greeks call 'acrostic,' where, from the first letters of each verse in order, words are formed which express some particular meaning." Sometimes the acrostic is contrived by the last letters of each line, but usually the first letter forms it. The Elizabethan John Davies wrote long philosophical poems which are interesting only to the literary historian, but his "hymns" to Queen Elizabeth were—of all forms—a set of "marble-constant" acrostics. In his ingenious exercises Davies turned a rhyming trick into a genuine tribute.

> E *arly before the day doth spring*
> L *et us awake, my Muse, and sing,*
> I *t is no time to slumber;*
> S *o many joys this time doth bring*
> A *s time will fail to number.*
> B *ut whereto shall we bend our lays?*
> E *ven up to heaven, again to raise*
> T *he maid which, thence descended,*
> H *ath brought again the golden days*
> A *nd all the world amended.*

> R *udeness itself she doth refine,*
> E *'en like an alchemist divine,*
> G *ross times of iron turning*
> I *nto the purest form of gold,*
> N *ot to corrupt till heaven wax old,*
> A *nd be refined with burning.*

A master of inspired nonsense, Lewis Carroll expressed some of his most serious sentiments by way of acrostics. Among the more than a dozen written in this form (most of which reveal the names of little girls he loved) are the verses which introduce *Sylvie and Bruno,* the prefatory poem to *The Hunting of the Snark,* and the tender epilogue to *Through the Looking Glass,* which, when the initial letters are read downward, gives the full name of the original Alice.

> *A boat, beneath a sunny sky*
> *Lingering onward dreamily*
> *In an evening of July—*
>
> *Children three that nestle near,*
> *Eager eye and willing ear,*
> *Pleased a simple tale to hear—*
>
> *Long has paled that sunny sky:*
> *Echoes fade and memories die:*
> *Autumn frosts have slain July.*

Still she haunts me, phantomwise.
Alice moving under skies
Never seen by waking eyes.

Children yet, the tale to hear,
Eager eye and willing ear,
Lovingly shall nestle near.

In a Wonderland they lie,
Dreaming as the days go by,
Dreaming as the summers die:

Ever drifting down the stream—
Lingering in the golden gleam—
Life, what is it but a dream?

The pioneer writer of mysteries solved by deductive ratiocination was also ingenious as a poet. Edgar Allan Poe's "A Valentine" is a riddling acrostic accomplished with extraordinary complexity. Reading the first letter of the first line, the second letter of the second line, the third letter of the third line, and so on, finally discloses the name of Frances Sargent Osgood, a pretty versifier whom Poe praised extravagantly.

F or her these lines are penned, whose luminous eyes,
 B r ightly expressive as the twins of Leda,
Sh a ll find her own sweet name that, nestling, lies
 Upo n this page, enwrapped from every reader.
Sear c h narrowly this rhyme, which holds a treasure
 Divin e —a talisman—an amulet
That mu s t be worn at heart. Search well the measure;
 The word s —the letters themselves. Do not forget
The trivi a lest point, or you may lose your labor.
 And yet the r e is in this no Gordian knot
Which one mi g ht not undo without a sabre,
 If one could m e rely understand the plot.
Enwritten upo n this page whereon are peering
 Such eager eyes, t here lies, I say, perdu,
A well-known name, o ft uttered in the hearing
 Of poets, by poets; a s the name is a poet's, too.

> *Its letters, althou g h naturally lying—*
> *Like the knight Pint o (Mendez Ferdinando)—*
> *Still form a synonym f o r truth. Cease trying!*
> *You will not read the ri d dle though you do the best you*
> *can do.*

No less curious is a further and more modern variation of the acrostic. In "The Wood-Weasel" (a charming euphemism for the polecat or skunk) Marianne Moore champions the little creature, lifts it from its disreputable associations and, at the same time, designs a most unorthodox arrangement. The name of the person to whom the poem is dedicated is brought out backward, that is from bottom to top instead of the usual procedure. This is the first verse:

> *emerges daintily the skunk—*
> *don't laugh—in sylvan black and white chipmunk*
> *regalia. The inky thing*
> *adaptively whited with glistening*
> *goat-fur, is wood-warden. In his*
> *ermined well-cuttlefish-inked wool, he is*
> *determination's totem. Out-*
> *lawed? His sweet face and powerful feet go about*
> *in chieftain's coat of Chilcat cloth.*
> *He is his own protection from the moth . . .*

Another poetic oddity is the poem in which the lines are composed of successive letters of the alphabet and all the words in each line begin with the letters as they follow in alphabetical order. The most famous of this genre is the anonymous tour de force, "The Siege of Belgrade." It opens with these lines:

> *An Austrian army awefully arrayed,*
> *Boldly, by battery, besieged Belgrade.*
> *Cossack commanders cannonading come,*
> *Dealing destruction's devastating doom.*
> *Every endeavor engineers essay*
> *For fame, for fortune, fighting furious fray . . .*

"Found Poetry" enjoyed a short vogue during the nineteen sixties. It was prompted by artists incorporating "found objects" in paintings and sculptures. It was so called because its practitioners "found" the substance of picturesque novelties, poetic passages, and oddments of poetry in the lush prose of advertisements, in highly colored travel brochures, even in the enticements of candymakers. The novelist Graham Greene made what looked like a poem out of an airline folder. Norman Mailer claimed he found poetry in the graffiti of Men's Rooms. Proponents of the form asserted that "poetry is where you find it" and that their rearranged or "rectified" poems were as valid as "pop" art. They pointed to what Picasso had done with forks, spoons, broken dolls, matchboxes, machine parts, and other objects lying around the house, the garden, and the garage. They neglected to say that Picasso had done something not only with but to the objects he had recovered. He had combined them with his own creativeness and given them new dimensions, a personal significance. The manufacturers of Found Poetry did nothing to their material except to break up the prose into arbitrary lines. The end result of Found Poetry was, like its beginning, prose—prose fancied and reframed but, nevertheless, prose. Here are two examples. The first alliterative *jeu d'esprit* is from a magazine display of Supp-hose Stockings; the second, obviously written with tongue, as well as chocolate, in cheek, is taken verbatim from an advertisement for Barton's "Sinful Candies."

> *Oh, the young fashion flair of being*
> *By Phoenix.*
> *Lively, light-footed luxury.*
> *All flawless fit and flattery*
> *That follows through with firmness.*
> *Pure magic in motion*
> *As you dash through the day*
> *And go dancing all night.*

*   *   *

Vienna, 1912,
Where man worshipped woman more than gold.

And his dreams were of moments
   stolen on midnight balconies.
Of secret Sundays in that little konditorei,
Lips tasting of hot chocolate,
   eyes promising eternity.
Of lonely nights of misery and bad poetry,
   of furs and jewels,
   of extravagant chocolates.
All lavished for the love of the woman
   he'd give his soul to possess, but who,
   like the Danube, belonged to the world. . . .
We've gone back to making the decadent chocolates
   of the Vienna of 1912.
Passionately continental chocolates,
   light and dark,
   teased together into one shell,
   and infused with the luscious,
   most sensuous essences . . .
Delights. Kisses. Loves.
Delicious as sin.

A more diverting departure from the poetic norm was a typographical oddity known as Concrete Poetry. The designation was questionable, for its nature was not concrete but abstract. It was something to look at rather than to read. It was also, according to its manipulators, a new kinetic form, but its movement was only for the eye, visual rather than verbal. It consisted of arranging or breaking up words in a variety of designs: fragmenting them, blowing them up, overprinting and/or superimposing them, fitting them into squares, circles, spirals, thin verticals, boxes, labyrinths, and "graphic space." *An Anthology of Concrete Poetry*, issued by the Something Else Press, Inc., in 1967, ran to 342 pages and billed itself as the newest and "most active of modern poetry movements."

The conception, as "far out" as the vanguard could go, was anything but new. It carried the idea back to the centuries-old pastime of whimsically spaced verses, to Biblical proverbs about drinking shaped like a wine glass or a bottle or decanter, to Her-

rick, whose "To Christ on the Cross" is built in the form of a
cross, and, again, to Herbert. Herbert's "Easter Wings" is so
spaced that the verses become a pair of tapered wings, while "The
Altar" is so shaped that the first four lines represent the top of
the altar, the next eight lines the upholding column, and the concluding four lines the stone base.

> A broken ALTAR, Lord, thy servant rears,
> Made of a heart and cemented with tears;
>   Whose parts are as thy hand did frame;
>   No workman's tool hath touched the same.
>   A   HEART   alone
>   Is   such   a   stone,
>   As   nothing   but
>   Thy power doth cut.
>   Wherefore each part
>   Of my hard heart
>   Meets in this frame
>   To praise thy name;
>   That if I chance to hold my peace,
>   These stones to praise thee may not cease.
> Oh, let thy blessèd SACRIFICE be mine,
> And sanctify this ALTAR to be thine.

Lewis Carroll, that ever-resourceful mathematical fantasist,
could not resist the lure of this form of entertainment. While the
Mouse is telling Alice that his is "a long and a sad tale" and
Alice is looking down and agreeing that his is indeed "a long
tail," her idea of the tale comes out concretely like this:

                    Fury said to
                  a mouse, That
                    he met in the
                      house, "Let
                        us both go
                          to law: *I*
                            will prose-
                              cute *you*.—
                              Come, I'll
                            take no de-
                          nial: We
                        must have
                      the trial;
                    For really
                  this morn-
                  ing I've
                nothing
              to do."
                Said the
                mouse to
                  the cur,
                    "Such a
                      trial, dear
                        sir. With
                          no jury
                            or judge,
                              would
                                be wast-
                                ing our
                                breath."
                            "I'll be
                              judge,
                          I'll be
                        jury,"
                    said
                  cun-
                  ning
                  old
                    Fury;
                      "I'll
                        try
                          the
                            whole
                              cause,
                                and
                              con-
                            demn
                          you to
                        death."

The Concretists were anticipated not only by poets of a much earlier epoch but also by such twentieth-century moderns as Apollinaire, whose seemingly haphazard *Calligrammes* influenced the Surrealists; by Pound, who carefully inserted Chinese ideograms into his *Cantos*; and by E. E. Cummings, who enlivened his pages with meaningful distortions. As an example of Concrete Poetry, "Language to Be Looked At," here is a poem by Ian Hamilton Finlay in which the Scottish poet does not (like another Scottish poet) compare his girl to a red, red rose but, as suggested by the shape and the slanted pun, a pear.

```
             pair g
             au pair
            girl au pa
           rl au pair g
          au pair girl a
         girl au pair girl
        pair girl au pair gir
       air girl au pair girl au
      r girl au pair girl au pa
      )air girl au pair girl au
       ı pair girl au pair girl
        ʼr girl au pair girl aʼ
         ʼ au pair girl ɘʼ
```

A concrete poem, say the Concretists, is an object "in and by itself," something in which the reader "sees the lines of force," looks at the poem rather than through it. The Brazilian Ronaldo Azeredo says he puts velocity, or "the square of speed," in a square but "we may only think of a kind of abstract iconography. The reiteration of VVV gives on the visual level the same semantic information achieved by the final line of the poem."

```
V V V V V V V V V V
V V V V V V V V V E
V V V V V V V V E L
V V V V V V V E L O
V V V V V V E L O C
V V V V V E L O C I
V V V V E L O C I D
V V V E L O C I D A
V V E L O C I D A D
V E L O C I D A D E
```

Lastly, here is a "Letter to a French Novelist," an anagrammatic poem by Edwin Morgan, first printed in the *London Times Literary Supplement* issue (August 6, 1964) devoted to "The Changing Guard."

SAPORTA:
  O satrap!
  O Sparta!
  Oars tap.
  O, a strap?
  A pastor?
  Pa Astor?
  Ps! Aorta.
  Taro sap.
  Art soap?
  A rat sop
  to paras.
  O.A.S. trap.
  So apart!
  —Pat Rosa.

The best of such contrivances are amusing word-games, playful trivialities for Saturday poets and Sunday painters. Most of them are toy constructions, verbal building blocks that fall apart as soon as they are put together. Yet, foolish and ephemeral though many of them are, they are added proofs of the range, the reach, and the resourcefulness of poetry. For poetry, as has been said before, is where you find it.

A

ABSTRACT POETRY. Edith Sitwell invented the term to describe the poems in her volume *Façade*. She indicated that they were "abstract" in the way that certain paintings are abstract, non-representational, not realistic but arrangements of pure design, "patterns in color." It was, at best, a dubious designation, for it suggested a poetry of sheer sound, whereas sense came through, if only by association. Apart from the validity of the term, Edith Sitwell often succeeded in mixing the real and the unreal on a more or less "abstract" canvas. For example:

> *Like Balaclava, the lava came down from the*
> *Roof, and the sea's blue wooden gendarmerie*
> *Took them in charge while Beelzebub roared for his rum.*
> *. . . None of them come!*

ACCENT. It has always been a question whether accent is the same as stress or whether stress is one of the constituents of accent. It has also never been established whether an accented syllable is not only stronger but pitched higher than an unaccented syllable, and whether unconsciously the voice gives it more weight. In any but the most technical interpretation, accent is the emphasis (by stress or pitch or both) given to a particular syllable when it is spoken.

ACCENTUAL VERSE is verse that maintains a fixed number of accents, not syllables, in every line. Anglo-Saxon poetry (see page 151) is composed of strictly accentual verse. Moreover, accentual verse is the norm of English poetry in which syllables may vary in number, but only the accented syllables are counted. Examples are innumerable; almost every page of English poetry yields illustrations. Here are three opening lines from three different periods:

> Lóve in my bósom like a bée . . .
>
> I sáw Etérnity the óther night . . .
>
> Lóok, stránger, at this ísland nów . . .

SYLLABIC VERSE is the opposite of ACCENTUAL VERSE. It ignores the accents and counts only the syllables. Such languages as French and Japanese, which are almost totally without accent or stress, produce poetry which is plainly syllabic. There is, properly speaking, no metrical foot in French verse. Reviewing a volume by Marianne Moore, one of the most expert practitioners of Syllabic Verse, W. H. Auden commented on the advantage of the form which "allows and encourages an unbroken run-on from line to line, stanza to stanza, and the rhyming of accented and unaccented syllables." For example:

> Subdivided by sun
> Till the nettings are legion.

A more recent employment of the form occurs in Thom Gunn's "My Sad Captains." This is the first stanza:

> One by one they appear in
> the darkness: a few friends, and
> a few with historical
> names. How late they start to shine!
> but before they fade, they stand
> perfectly embodied, all. . . .

Every line has exactly seven syllables, but the accent varies from line to line. The poet is willing to sacrifice a regular emphasis for the sake of run-on regularity, a planned conversational continuity.

Although there have been occasional successes in the use of Syllabic Verse, English poetry is founded on stress or emphasis. English poetry, as Paul Fussell, Jr., writes in *Poetic Meter and Poetic Form*, responds to "our own Anglo-Saxon lust for stress . . . In a syllabic poem like Marianne Moore's 'In Distrust of Merits' the quatrains at the end of each stanza generally remain decently syllabic, with the stresses falling apparently whimsically. For example:

> > > *. . . he holds*
> > *his ground in patience patience*
> > *patience, that is action or*
> > *beauty, the soldier's defence*
> > *and hardest armor for*
>
> *the fight . . .*

"All goes well within this syllabic system until the climactic ending of the poem, where a major assertion rather than a gentle comment is called for. It is interesting to watch the accents rising now from underground to take over the stanza and to shatter the syllabic surface as the passion and the commitment also rise:

> *I inwardly did nothing*
> *O Iscariotlike crime!*
> *Beauty is everlasting*
> *and dust is for a time."*

ACROSTIC.   To the examples of the form quoted on pages 128–131 one more may be added. This is a tribute by a twentieth-century poet laureate to a seventeenth-century English composer. It is in—of all places!—*Eros and Psyche* by Robert Bridges.

> ***P*** *athetic strains and passionate they wove,*
> ***U*** *rgent in ecstasies of heavenly sense;*
> ***R*** *esponsive rivalries that, while they strove,*
> ***C*** *ombined in full harmonious suspense,*
> ***E*** *ntrancing wild desire, then fell at last*
> ***L*** *ulled in soft closes, and with gay contrast*
> ***L*** *aunched forth their fresh unwearied excellence.*

ALBA. The alba (literally "dawn") is a sunrise song. It—and its variant, the aubade—is either a solo plaint or a dialogue-duet between lovers. It is the counterpart of the serenade, which is an evening song. (See pages 299–300.)

ALEXANDRINE. A twelve-syllable line, so called because it was popularized in the twelfth-century poem *Le Roman d'Alexandre*. It became the chief unit of French poetry and found its way to England through Spenser's *The Faerie Queene*. Spenser invented a nine-line stanza of eight iambic pentameter lines ending with a weightier line of twelve syllables, the alexandrine. In his *Essay on Criticism* Pope described it mockingly when he added an example of the form to a small catalogue of clichés.

> *Where'er you find "the cooling western breeze,"*
> *In the next line, it "whispers through the trees";*
> *If "crystal streams" with "pleasing murmurs creep,"*
> *The reader's threatened, not in vain, with "sleep";*
> *Then, at the last and only couplet fraught*
> *With some unmeaning thing they call a thought,*
> *A needless alexandrine ends the song,*
> *That, like a wounded snake, drags its slow length along.*

Swift used the alexandrine effectively in his description of a city shower that carried with it all manner of nauseous waste:

> *Sweeping from butchers' stalls, dung, guts, and blood,*
> *Drowned puppies, stinking sprats, all drenched in mud,*
> *Dead cats and turnip tops come tumbling down the flood.*

This is a grim contrast to Spenser's idyllic landscape with an appropriately musical alexandrine:

> *And at the foot thereof, a gentle flood*
> *His silver waves did softly tumble down,*
> *Unmarred with ragged moss or filthy mud,*
> *Nor might wild beasts, nor might the ruder clown*
> *Thereto approach, nor filth might therein drown:*

But nymphs and fairies by the banks did sit,
In the wood's shade, which did the waters crown,
Keeping all noisome things away from it,
And to the water's fall tuning their accents fit.

ALLEGORY. Allegory is an art of double meanings. It is a kind of extended or sustained metaphor in which the things or characters referred to have meanings apart from themselves. Many of the myths and fables are allegories which relate a narrative but imply an interpretation beyond the story. Coleridge defined allegory as "a translation of abstract notions into a picture language," a substitution of an actual or familiar object for a purely poetic conception.

Perhaps the most famous as well as the most elaborate allegory in prose is Bunyan's *Pilgrim's Progress,* in which the central figure, Christian, represents all Christians, and his tribulations mirror the trials and troubles of all mankind. Among the more notable allegories in poetry are the fabulous transformations in Ovid's *Metamorphoses,* Spenser's *Faerie Queene,* and Shelley's *Prometheus Unbound.*

ALLITERATION. Alliteration (sometimes called head-rhyme) is the repetition of the same letter or sound in words succeeding each other at close intervals. Alliterative phrases are in constant use: "bed and board," "wind and weather," "time and tide," "watch and wait," "from pillar to post," "last but not least," and "money makes the mare go." In poetry it refers to the repeated sounds at the beginning of two or more words in a single line, as in Shakespeare's "Life is as tedious as a twice-told tale," "But now I'm cabin'd, cribbed, confined," "Our dreadful marches to delightful measures," or Keats's appeal, in his "Ode to a Nightingale," for a draught of vintage with "beaded bubbles winking at the brim," or Masefield's "Cargoes," which lists:

Sandalwood, cedarwood, and sweet white wine.

Cowper, in "The Timepiece," pays his tribute to England with alliterative loyalty:

I would not yet exchange thy sullen skies
And fields without a flower for warmer France . . .

One might say that alliteration is initial-rhyme in contrast to end-rhyme, which goes under the general heading of rhyme. Old English or Anglo-Saxon poetry centered about alliteration. Anglo-Saxon poetry did not rhyme in the usual sense. Instead, each half-line contained two accented syllables, and one or both of the first two accents began with the same sound as the third accented syllable, in the second half-line. The alliteration consisted not only of consonants but also of vowels which were considered emphatic.

Alliterative verse has had a wide range and a long life. It can be traced from the Anglo-Saxon *Beowulf* which, in a modern approximation, begins:

> *Lo, we have listened to   lays of the Spear-Danes*
> *Full of the fame of   fabulous leaders*

through nursery rhymes like:

> *Sing a song of sixpence, a pocketful of rye*

to Auden's *The Age of Anxiety* with its careful casualness:

> *How well and witty when you wake up,*
> *How glad and good when you go to bed* . . .

"Apt alliteration's artful aid" (the appropriate phrase dates from eighteenth-century Charles Churchill) has been of service to poets through the years. It is found in Burns's passionate appeal:

> *Ye banks and braes of bonny Doon*
> *How can ye bloom sae fresh and fair*

and in Rossetti's light apostrophe:

> *Lazy, laughing, languid Jenny*
> *Fond of a kiss and fond of a penny*

Tennyson used alliteration lightly, particularly in "Lancelot and Elaine," where the l's—there are eight of them—are half hidden in two lines:

> *Elaine the fair, Elaine the lovable,*
> *Elaine, the lily maid of Astolat*

Shakespeare did not hesitate to let alliteration ridicule itself. In a parody of the theatrically rhetorical manner, he had Quince speak the prologue to the play-within-a-play in A *Midsummer Night's Dream* with such lines as:

> *Whereat, with blade, with bloody blameful blade,*
> *He bravely broached his boiling bloody breast,*
> *And Thisby, tarrying in mulberry shade,*
> *His dagger drew, and died.*

An almost equally amusing burlesque of alliteration—to leap from Shakespeare to Gilbert—occurs in *The Mikado* when Ko-Ko, Pooh-Bah, and Pish-Tush join in a trio contemplating their all-too-short future:

> *To sit in solemn silence in a dull, dark dock,*
> *In a pestilential prison with a life-long lock,*
> *Awaiting the sensation of a short, sharp shock,*
> *From a cheap and chippy chopper on a big, black block.*

Swinburne was so devoted to alliteration that he allowed it to dictate the movement and even run away with the meaning of his lines. He wallowed in

> *The lilies and languors of virtue*
> *And the raptures and roses of vice.*

Often parodied, Swinburne outdid all others in a burlesque of himself. His "Nephelidia" is a brilliant bit of alliterative nonsense and a pointed piece of criticism. Here alliteration is so excessive that it is hard to read the lines.

From the depth of the dreamy decline of the dawn through
  a notable nimbus of nebulous noonshine,
Pallid and pink as the palm of the flag-flower that
  flickers with fear of the flies as they float,
Are the looks of our lovers that lustrously lean from
  a marvel of mystic, miraculous moonshine.
These that we feel in the blood of our blushes that
  thicken and threaten with throbs through the throat?

No one used—and sometimes overused—the device more power-
fully than Gerard Manley Hopkins. He accentuated compound-
word effects by surcharging his lines with a breathless combination
of alliteration and internal rhymes. In one sonnet, "Felix Randal,"
there are such alliteration-packed lines as:

Fatal four disorders fleshed there, all contended? . . .

My tongue hath taught thee comfort, touch had quenched thy
                                                  tears . . .

When thou at the random grim forge, powerful amidst peers,
Didst fettle for the great grey drayhorse his bright and
                                       battering sandal!

Other characteristic Hopkins lines are even more alliterative.

. . . daylight's dauphin dapple-dawn falcon . . .

Fall, gall themselves, and gash gold-vermilion . . .

Fresh-firecoal chestnut-falls; finches' wings;
Landscape plotted and pieced—fold, fallow, and plough . . .

Cuckoo-echoing, bell-swarmèd, lark-charmèd, rook-racked,
                                       river-rounded . . .

Poets find alliteration as helpful today as in the time of Beowulf.
In *Miracles*, a collection of poems by children, an eleven-year-old
Australian boy, Peter Kelso, echoes the Anglo-Saxon bards in lines
that begin by playing with the repetition of w's and h's:

> *In poems, our earth's wonders*
> *Are windowed through*
> *Words*

> *A good poem must haunt the heart*
> *And be heeded by the head of the*
> *Hearer . . .*
> *With a wave of words . . .*

AMPHIBRACH. From a Greek word meaning "short at both ends," an amphibrach is a metrical foot which has three syllables: one accented syllable between two unaccented ones. It is expressed thus: ∪ / ∪. Words which, in themselves, are amphibrachs are words of a single strong syllable between two weak, or unaccented, ones, words like "un*want*ed," "for*got*ten," "en*dur*ing," "in*sip*id," "a*ris*ing."

Browning's "How They Brought the Good News from Ghent to Aix" is written almost entirely in amphibrachs. It begins:

> Ĭ sprăng tŏ thĕ stírrŭp, ănd Jóris, ănd hé;
> I galloped, Dirck galloped, we galloped all three.

AMPHIMACER. From the Greek meaning "long at both ends," the amphimacer, sometimes called a cretic foot, is the opposite of the amphibrach. It consists of three syllables, the first and last long, the middle one short: / ∪ /. . Almost unusable in a poem of any length, it was employed by Tennyson in "The Oak," the first verse of which follows:

> Líve thў Lífe,
>   Young and old,
> Like yon oak
> Bright in spring,
>   Living gold;

ANACREONTICS are poems, usually lyric in character, which rejoice in the pleasures of indulgence. They are so called because the Greek poet, Anacreon, devoted himself to celebrating the triple worship of Wine, Woman, and Song. It is said that an unjust fate made the wine-loving Anacreon die by choking on a grape pit. His verses have been blithely translated by Abraham Cowley, Thomas Stanley, and Thomas Moore, whom Byron called "Anacreon Moore." This is one of the seventy-five odes of Anacreon translated by Moore.

> *Observe when Mother Earth is dry,*
> *She drinks the droppings of the sky,*
> *And then the dewy cordial gives*
> *To every thirsty plant that lives.*
> *The vapors, which at evening weep,*
> *Are beverage to the swelling deep;*
> *And when the rosy sun appears*
> *He drinks the ocean's misty tears.*
> *The moon too quaffs her paly stream*
> *Of lustre from the solar beam.*
> *So, hence with all your sober thinking!*
> *Since Nature's holy law is drinking,*
> *I'll make the laws of Nature mine*
> *And toast the Universe in wine!*

ANACRUSIS. Literally "a pushing back," anacrusis is the addition of one or more unstressed syllables at the beginning of a line which would otherwise begin with an accented syllable. Two examples follow; the first is by William Blake, the second by Robert Frost:

> *Bound and weary, I thought best*
> *To sulk upon my mother's breast.*

> *And left no trace but the cellar walls,*
> *And a cellar in which the daylight falls . . .*

ANALYZED RHYME. See CONSONANCE on page 185.

ANAPEST. A metrical unit of two unaccented syllables followed by an accented one: $\cup\cup/$. An anapestic foot is the exact opposite of a dactylic foot, which consists of a strongly accented syllable followed by two short, unaccented ones: / ∪ ∪. The anapestic foot suggests hurried movement and is incorporated in such words as "disap*pear*," "inter*rupt*," "super*sede*," "Vien*nese*." James El-roy Flecker's "War Song of the Saracens" is impelled by the some-what headlong rhythm of the anapests:

> Wĕ ăre théy who cŏme fástĕr thăn fáte; wĕ ăre théy who rĭde
> eárlў ŏr láte.

ANGLO-SAXON POETRY. Anglo-Saxon poetry is divided into two types: the heroic and the religious. The heroic poetry is pagan in character and Teutonic in origin; the religious poetry is Chris-tian and meditative, Biblical in origin. Written in a language diffi-cult for all but students, it is complicated by strict rules and strange devices. Anglo-Saxon poetry does not rhyme but, to com-pensate for the lack, every line contains four strongly accented syl-lables with an irregular number of unaccented ones. Every line, moreover, is divided by a sharp caesura or pause. To give more resonance to the verse, the first three accented syllables are allitera-tive. (See ALLITERATION on page 145.) Composed between the seventh and eleventh centuries, some of the more notable Anglo-Saxon poems are *Widsith*, perhaps the oldest, *Beowulf*, *The Wanderer*, *The Seafarer*, *Wulf and Eadwacer*. This type of allitera-tive verse survived as late as the fourteenth century, in *Piers Plow-man*, which begins:

> In a summer season   when soft was the sun,
> I shaped me in shrouds   as I a shepherd were;
> In habit as an hermit   unholy of works
> Went wide in this world   wonders to hear.

Richard Wilbur is one of the modern poets who has used the de-vice with great delicacy. "The Lilacs," the first poem in his volume *Walking to Sleep*, opens:

> Those laden lilacs   at the lawn's end
> Came stark, spindly,   and in staggered file,

Like walking wounded   from the dead of winter.
We watched them waken   in the brusque weather
To rot and rootbreak,   to ripped branches . . .

APOCOPATED RHYME.   See RHYME on page 263.

APOSTROPHE. Based on the Greek for "to turn about," a
poetic apostrophe is a turning to and addressing an absent person
as though he were present, an object as though it were a person, an
inanimate thing as though it were alive. Wordsworth began his
sonnet "London: 1802" with an appeal to a dead poet: "Milton!
Thou should'st be living at this hour." Byron addressed and per-
sonified the world of waves: "Roll on, thou deep and dark blue
ocean, roll!" Bryant apostrophized the fringed gentian: "Thou
blossom, bright with autumn dew." Keats spoke passionately to a
Grecian urn: "Thou still unravish'd bride of quietness." Walt
Whitman's "O Captain! My Captain!" eulogizes Lincoln as
though Lincoln himself, not merely his dead body, were there to
receive the tribute. Robert Frost establishes the intimate personality of a tree when he speaks to it:

> *Tree at my window, window tree,*
> *My sash is lowered when night comes on;*
> *But let there never be curtain drawn*
> *Between you and me.*

ASSONANCE is a resemblance rather than a correspondence of
sounds. Rhyme is an exact matching of vowels and consonants, as
in "beam" and "dream"; assonance is a matching of the vowels but
not the consonants, as in "beam" and "teach." It is continually
found in popular poetry ("mine" and "sublime") and in old ballads ("deep" and "feet," "maid" and "rain," "bed" and "web")
and in modernized versions of the ancient "Sir Patrick Spens":

> *The anchor broke, the topmast split,*
> *'Twas such a deadly storm;*
> *The waves came o'er the broken ship*
> *Till all her sides were torn.*

Nursery rhymes are full of assonances. Here are two examples.

> *Peter, Peter, pumpkin-eater,*
> *Had a wife and couldn't keep her.*

> *Little Tommy Tucker*
> *Sang for his supper.*
> *What shall he eat?*
> *Brown bread and butter.*

Sometimes the approximation of sounds ranges widely and wildly, as in two lines from an Irish broadside:

> *I hear great lamentation the small birds were making,*
> Saying, *"We'll have no more engagements with the boys of*
> *Mullabaun."*

Once frowned upon by the purists as a mark of slipshod crafts-manship, assonance is used today not only as a welcome change from "pure" rhyme but also for the spice of surprise. It is often united with alliteration to achieve added resonance. A particularly effective blend of sound-surprises occurs in George Starbuck's "Outbreak of Spring" in *Bone Thoughts*, which changes assonance to consonance.

> . . . *Full-feasted*
> *Spring, like an ill bird, settles to the masthead*
> *of here and there an elm. The streets are misted.*
> *A Boston rain, archaic and monastic,*
> *cobbles the blacktop waters, bringing mosaic*
> *to dusty windshields; to the waking, music.*

B

BALLAD. A ballad may be said to be a short story, often a grim one, that has become a folk-song. Its origin was among the people. The ancient ballad-makers were sure of their audiences because they used the language of the folk. They paraphrased legends and gave them the feeling of myths. They recorded the common man's understanding of the natural as well as the supernatural world and translated the current news of star-crossed love, infidelity, feuds, and murders into song.

Varied though the subjects and the tunes to which they are sung may be, ballads have certain characteristics in common. Since the ballad is essentially a short story—a story that has to hold casual listeners immediately—its prime purpose is instant comprehension. There is no time for fine shades, subtle images, delicate nuances. Simple rhymes and stock phrases which everyone recognizes make the story easy to remember. Repetition of words and ideas adds emphasis and makes the ideas still easier for the listener. There is no place for preliminaries; no time can be wasted on backgrounds or explanations. The opening lines plunge into the heart of a situation; things happen at once. The action is swift, the plot is uncomplicated. Moreover, the ballad-maker is completely objective. He never moralizes. He shows no emotion when contemplating villainy. He is not horrified by murder, shocked by illicit love, outraged by betrayal. He knows that most communities consist of people who relish raw gossip and a downright bloody deed, whose sympathies are with the outlaw, and who are concerned with the event, not with a long-winded commentary about it. Thus the ballad-maker is a perfect storyteller in the sense that he is outside the story. He tells the tale for what it is worth. He does not pass upon its character or its credibility. He leaves all judgments (if any are called for) to his hearers.

Here are three typical beginnings of ballads which suggest the tenor of the tale to come and, at the same time, set the style as well as the pace of the story.

> *"Why does your sword so drip with blood,*
> *Edward, Edward?*
> *Why does your sword so drip with blood,*
> *And why so sad are ye, O?"*

> *   *   *

> *Childe Maurice hunted the Silver Wood,*
> *He whistled and he sung:*
> *"I think I see the woman yonder*
> *That I have loved so long."*

* * *

The king sits in Dumferline town
Drinking the blude-red wine.
"O where will I get a gude skipper
To sail this ship o' mine?"

Among the most notable early English ballads are the traditional "Johnnie Armstrong," "Edward, Edward," "Sir Patrick Spens," "Thomas the Rhymer," "May Colvin," "The Wife of Usher's Well," "The Douglas Tragedy," "Fair Annie," "The Queen's Maries," "Bonny Barbara Allen," "Clerk Saunders," "Fair Margaret and Sweet William," "Lord Randal," and "The Two Sisters of Binnorie." Here are the last two:

LORD RANDAL

"O where have you been, Lord Randal, my son?
O where have you been, my handsome young man?"—
  "I have been to the wild wood; mother, make my bed soon,
  For I'm weary with hunting, and fain would lie down."

"Who gave you your dinner, Lord Randal, my son?
Who gave you your dinner, my handsome young man?"—
  "I dined with my sweetheart; mother, make my bed soon,
  For I'm weary with hunting, and fain would lie down."

"What had you for dinner, Lord Randal, my son?
What had you for dinner, my handsome young man?"—
  "I had eels broiled in broth; mother, make my bed soon,
  For I'm weary with hunting, and fain would lie down."

"And where are your bloodhounds, Lord Randal, my son?
And where are your bloodhounds, my handsome young man?"—
  "O they swelled and they died; mother, make my bed soon,
  For I'm weary with hunting, and fain would lie down."

"O I fear you are poisoned, Lord Randal, my son!
O I fear you are poisoned, my handsome young man!"—
  "O yes! I am poisoned; mother, make my bed soon,
  For I'm sick at the heart, and I fain would lie down."

THE TWO SISTERS OF BINNORIE

There were two sisters sat in a bower;
  Binnorie, O Binnorie;
There came a knight to be their wooer;
  By the bonnie mill-dams of Binnorie.*

He courted the eldest with gloves and rings,
But he loved the youngest above all things.

The eldest was vexèd to despair,
And much she envied her sister fair.

The eldest said to the youngest one,
"Will ye see our father's ships come in?"

She's taken her by the lily-white hand,
And led her down to the river strand.

The youngest stood upon a stone;
The eldest came and pushed her in.

"O sister, sister, reach your hand,
And you shall be heir of half my land.

"O sister, reach me but your glove
And sweet William shall be all your love."

"Sink on, nor hope for hand or glove!
Sweet William shall surely be my love."

Sometimes she sank, sometimes she swam,
Until she came to the mouth of the dam.

Out then came the miller's son
And saw the fair maid swimming in.

"O father, father, draw your dam!
Here's either a mermaid or a swan."

The miller hasted and drew his dam,
And there he found a drowned womàn.

You could not see her middle small,
Her girdle was so rich withal.

You could not see her yellow hair
For the gold and pearls that clustered there.

* The two roman lines (the refrain) are repeated throughout the ballad.

And by there came a harper fine
Who harped to nobles when they dine.

And when he looked that lady on,
He sighed and made a heavy moan.

He's made a harp of her breast bone,
Whose sounds would melt a heart of stone.

He's taken three locks of her yellow hair
And with them strung his harp so rare.

He went into her father's hall
To play his harp before them all.

But as he laid it on a stone,
The harp began to play alone.

And soon the harp sang loud and clear,
"Farewell, my father and mother dear.

Farewell, farewell, my brother Hugh,
Farewell, my William, sweet and true."

And then as plain as plain could be,
  (Binnorie, O Binnorie)
"There sits my sister who drownèd me
  By the bonny mill-dams of Binnorie!"

Although most ballads begin grimly and end tragically, more than a few are conversationally casual; some are lightly and even coarsely comic. For plain rustic humor none surpasses "Sweet William, His Wife, and the Sheepskin." The humbling of a sullen or uncooperative wife furnished the plot for many a play besides Shakespeare's *The Taming of the Shrew*. Ballad-makers made much of the situation.

SWEET WILLIAM, HIS WIFE, AND THE SHEEPSKIN

Sweet William, he married a wife,
  Gentle Jenny called Rosemary,
To be the sweet comfort of his life,
  As the dew flies over the mulberry tree.*

* The two roman lines (the refrain) are repeated throughout the ballad.

But Jenny would not in the kitchen go,
For fear of soiling her pretty white shoe.

She would not weave, and she would not spin,
For fear of hurting her gay gold ring.

One day sweet William came in from the plow,
Saying, "Dear wife, is dinner ready now?"

"There's a little cornbread that's left on the shelf,
If you want any more you can bake it yourself."

Sweet William went out to his sheep pen,
And stripped an old wether of its sheep skin.

He laid the skin around his wife's back,
And with a stout stick went whickety-whack!

"I'll tell my father and all my kin
How you hit me hard with a hickory limb."

"You can tell your father and all your kin,
I was only tanning my own sheep skin."

Next day when William came in from the plow
He said, "Dear wife, is dinner ready now?"

She covered the table and spread the board,
And, "Yes, my dear husband," was her every word.

Now they live free from all sorrow and strife,
And they say she makes William a very good wife.

For a long time after the industrial revolution ballad-makers ceased to be popular. People who were once isolated, now eager to become part of a sophisticated civilization, were quick to exchange the rude but genuine poetry for cheap and sentimental stuff. In his *Apologie for Poetry* the sixteenth-century Sir Philip Sidney had defended the ballad-makers and their primitive appeal. He indicated the scorn with which the cultured aristocracy regarded the verse-making so attractive to the average man and registered his own irreverent delight in the ballad's persuasion. "I must confess my own barbariousness, for I never heard the old song of Percy and Douglas but that I found my heart moved more than with a trumpet."

Nevertheless, between the seventeenth and nineteenth centuries ballads were regarded as antiquated. In his preface to the second edition of *Lyrical Ballads* Wordsworth voiced his fear that they (and possibly all poetry) would disappear. "A multitude of causes, unknown to former times, are now acting with a combined force to blunt all discriminating powers of the mind, and, unfitting it for all voluntary exertion, to reduce it to a state of almost savage torpor. The most effective of these causes are the great national events which are daily taking place and the increasing accumulation of men in cities where the uniformity of their occupations produces a craving for extraordinary incidents, which the rapid communication of intelligence hourly gratifies."

Wordsworth was unduly pessimistic. Modern life did not stifle the ballad-making instinct. On the contrary, an imposing anthology might be made of ballads about ordinary as well as extraordinary events by Rudyard Kipling—compilers never tire of rifling his *Barrack-Room Ballads*—G. K. Chesterton, Alfred Noyes, John Masefield, the brothers Benét, and John Davidson, whose "A Ballad of Hell" and "A Ballad of a Nun" revive the dramatic tension of the best of ancient ballads, as well as the somewhat more dated narratives by Alfred, Lord Tennyson, Henry Wadsworth Longfellow, John Greenleaf Whittier, and W. E. Henley. Nor should one forget W. S. Gilbert's blandly absurd *Bab Ballads*, several of which furnished plots for the light operas by Gilbert and Sullivan.

Although the telling of tales has been taken over by the motion pictures, the television networks, the daily paper and, when he has a story to tell, the novelist, the ballad-maker persists. In America the pioneers and trailblazers repeated ballads from abroad, localized them, changed names, added incidents, and gave them a new home as well as new meanings. World wars showed that the ballad-maker was no anachronism. New and deeply disturbing events inspired new subjects, new rhythms, new oral communications. Folklore became poplore. Strange but immensely popular varieties of the old ballad form proliferated in "Country-

Western," "Rock-and-Roll," "Raga Rock," "Swinging Spiritual."
Ballad-like songs of protest raised echoes not only on campuses but
also across continents. Moreover, the balladist himself won honors.
In America, the younger generation of the 1960's knew Bob Dylan's
lines by heart. In France, Georges Brassens, ballad-maker and
ballad-singer, was rewarded with the sale of two hundred thousand
copies of his book and fifteen million records and, more surprisingly, was honored by the Académie Français which, in 1967,
gave him its highest award, the *Grand Prix de Poésie*.

The future possibilities of the ballad as a poetic form are endless.
The story-poem, whether read or sung, is always needed. It is
communally satisfying, for it is close to the heart of humanity and
vibrates with the beat of the everyday world.

BALLADE. The ballade, not to be confused with the ballad, is
a strict form established by French poets in the Middle Ages and
perfected by François Villon in the fifteenth century. Two hundred years later it was revived by Theodore de Banville, a virtuoso
performer, with intricate rhyme schemes. Although the ballade had
come to England with the late medievalists, it did not attract a
wide audience until the nineteenth century when Austin Dobson,
W. E. Henley, Andrew Lang, Edmund Gosse, and particularly
Algernon Charles Swinburne made the ballade almost as popular
as the sonnet. "Most of the French forms," wrote Austin Dobson,
"are not yet suited for, nor are they intended to rival, the more
approved natural rhythms in the treatment of grave and elevated
themes. What is modestly advanced for them is that they may
add a new charm of buoyancy, a lyric freshness, to amatory and
light verse."

It should be noted that Dobson spoke for his generation when
he said that the imports from France were not yet suited for grave
and elevated themes. Less than a century later, poets were giving
the French forms a new dignity by employing them not so much
for light verse as for the expression of serious and even somber
poetry.

The structure of the ballade is unusually strict. It consists of
three stanzas of eight (a very few examples have ten) lines and

another stanza (or half-stanza) of four lines called the *envoy* which, following the old custom, is generally addressed to some prince or imaginary power. The rhymes of the first stanza are arranged in the order *a-b-a-b-b-c-b-c*, and the rhymes as well as the arrangement are repeated in all the other stanzas, the envoy (or half-stanza) being rhymed *b-c-b-c*. No rhyme-word or rhyming sound may be repeated throughout the entire ballade. If the word *light* is used in the first stanza, it cannot be repeated (nor can the word *delight* be used) in any other stanza.

An outstanding feature of the ballade is its refrain. The refrain is the line which ends all the stanzas and the envoy. It is repeated *in its entirety* and gives a unity to the poem. The importance of the strictures as well as the restrictions of the form may be gleaned from the following rueful ballade by James Kenneth Stephen, poet and parodist, whose *Lapsus Calami* is a collection of inimitable take-offs.

BALLADE OF THE INCOMPETENT
BALLADE-MONGER

I am not ambitious at all;
I am not a poet, I know
(Though I do love to see a mere scrawl
To order and symmetry grow),
My muse is uncertain and slow,
I am not expert with my tools,
I lack the poetic argot,
But I hope I have kept to the rules.

When your brain is undoubtedly small,
'Tis hard, sir, to write in a row
Some five or six rhymes to Nepaul
And more than a dozen to Joe.
The meter is easier, though,
Three rhymes are sufficient for "ghouls,"
My lines are deficient in go,
But I hope I have kept to the rules.

Unable to fly, let me crawl;
Your patronage kindly bestow.

> *I am not the author of "Saul,"*
> *I am not Voltaire or Rousseau.*
> *I am not desirous, oh no,*
> *To rise from the ranks of the fools*
> *To shine with Gosse, Dobson, and Co.,*
> *But I hope I have kept to the rules.*
>
> *Dear Sir, though my language is low,*
> *Let me dip in Pierian pools.*
> *My verses are only so-so,*
> *But I hope I have kept to the rules.*

Many balladists ended their verses with a refrain which asked a large (and usually rhetorical) question. Again and again the singer inquired "Where are?" or "What has become of?"—the classic *ubi sunt* on which medieval Latin poets liked to hang their songs. Some of the refrains favored by the English poets were "Where are the ships of Tyre?" "Where are the cities of old time?" "Where are the gods of yesterday?" "And where are the galleons of Spain?" The most famous of those with a haunting interrogative refrain is Villon's *Mais où sont les neiges d'antan,* which Sainte-Beuve said transformed a hackneyed formula by the alchemy of genius. The best-known translation of this ballade is by Dante Gabriel Rossetti; however, since the rhyme scheme is not carried out as laid down in the first stanza, it does depart from the norm. Nevertheless, in the first stanza, it is a winning approximation of Villon. The "Ballade of Dead Ladies" begins:

> *Tell me now in what hidden way is*
> *Lady Flora the lovely Roman?*
> *Where's Hipparchia, and where is Thais,*
> *Neither of them the fairer woman?*
> *Where is Echo, beheld of no man,*
> *Only heard on river and mere,*
> *She whose beauty was more than human?*
> *But where are the snows of yester-year?*

Andrew Lang's translation of the same ballade is more exact, but, as a poem, it is something of a comedown after Rossetti's. Here, for comparison, is the first stanza:

Nay, tell me now in what strange air
The Roman Flora dwells to-day.
Where Archippiada hides, and where
Beautiful Thais has passed away?
Whence answers Echo, afield, astray,
By mere or stream, around, below?
Lovelier she than a woman of clay.
Nay, but where is the last year's snow?

A similar nostalgia pervades the nineteenth-century ballade-makers. An air of unhappy evanescence hangs over W. E. Henley's "Ballade of Dead Actors," in which the *ubi sunt* theme begins rather than ends the poem:

BALLADE OF DEAD ACTORS

Where are the passions they essayed,
And where the tears they made to flow?
Where the wild humors they portrayed
For laughing worlds to see and know?
Othello's wrath and Juliet's woe?
Sir Peter's whims and Timon's gall?
And Millamant and Romeo?
Into the night go one and all.

Where are the braveries, fresh or frayed?
The plumes, the armors—friend and foe?
The cloth of gold, the rare brocade,
The mantles glittering to and fro?
The pomp, the pride, the royal show?
The cries of war and festival?
The youth, the grace, the charm, the glow?
Into the night go one and all.

The curtain falls, the play is played:
The Beggar packs beside the Beau;
The Monarch troops, and troops the Maid;
The Thunder huddles with the Snow.
Where are the revellers high and low?
The clashing swords? The lover's call?
The dancers gleaming row on row?
Into the night go one and all.

Prince, in one common overthrow
The Hero tumbles with the Thrall:
As dust that drives, as straws that blow,
Into the night go one and all.

Among Henley's other virtuoso triumphs there is his "Villon's Straight Tip to All Cross Coves," a bravura ballade in thieves' argot with the refrain "Booze and the blowens cop the lot."

Another translation, this one from modern French, is my own rendering of an episode in Edmond Rostand's *Cyrano de Bergerac*. The Vicomte de Valvert has spoken contemptuously of Cyrano's enormous nose, and Cyrano has made a long speech apostrophizing the proboscis. This causes Valvert to call Cyrano a clown. Cyrano thereupon challenges Valvert to a duel and announces he will compose a ballade while fighting. Searching for appropriate rhymes, he engages his opponent and, during the combat, improvises the three standard verses with a challenging refrain and a triumphant envoy.

CYRANO'S IMPROVISED BALLADE

My hat is flung swiftly away;
My cloak is thrown off, if you please;
And my sword, always eager to play,
Flies out of the scabbard I seize.
My sword, I confess, is a tease,
With a nimble and mischievous brain;
And it knows, as the blade makes a breeze,
I shall strike as I end the refrain.

You should have kept quiet today.
I could carve you, my friend, by degrees.
But where? For a start, shall we say
In the side? Or the narrowest squeeze
'Twixt your ribs, while your arteries freeze,
And my point makes a sly meaning plain?
Guard that paunch! You're beginning to wheeze!
I shall strike as I end the refrain.

I need a word rhyming with a,
For, look, you turn paler than cheese
And whiter than—there's the word!—clay.
Your weak thrusts I parry with ease;
Too late now to pause or appease.
Hold on to your spit, though in pain,
For—if you'll permit the reprise—
I shall strike as I end the refrain.

Pray God, prince, to pardon all these
Poor efforts of yours, all in vain.
I thrust as you sink to your knees;
And I strike—as I end the refrain!

Here is a ballade presumably extemporized by a troubadour of
the old school, although actually it was written by the author of
this book as a burlesque of the medieval fantasies in James Branch
Cabell's *Jurgen.*

BALLADE OF THE MINSTREL

I offer you more than earthly riches
  In coin that none but the poet pays:
Freedom from all the stings and itches
  Of every annoying custom and craze;
  A cup of healing; a stirrup of praise;
A mood to match the liveliest pleasure;
  A lift to the feet of dragging days—
All in the heart of a minstrel's measure.

I offer you more. I offer you niches
  Where a sour world's grumbling never strays,
Where ripples a mirthful music which is
  An echo of man's first laughter that plays
  In various keys and secret ways.
There still is a land of Light and Leisure
  (If you will pardon so mouldy a phrase)
All in the heart of a minstrel's measure.

I offer all that ever bewitches
  The mind of man from its yeas and nays.
To the poet, immortal hemistitches;

To the soldier, conquest crowned with bays;
  To the lover, the breath of a thousand Mays;
To the boy, a jungle of buried treasure;
  To the cheated and broken, a merciful haze,
All in the heart of a minstrel's measure.

Master, I offer what never decays
Though all else wither. Master, what says your
  Will to the magics that quicken and raise
All in the heart of a minstrel's measure?

Modern ballades with particularly interesting and humorous refrains are Louis MacNeice's "Ballade for Mr. MacLeish" ("You need not tell us what we know") and "Ballade in a Bad Temper" ("You know what you can do with that!"), Rolfe Humphries' "Ballade of the Court Ladies" ("We've never seen a unicorn"), Richard Wilbur's "Ballade for the Duke of Orleans" ("I die of thirst here at the fountain-side"), James Branch Cabell's "The Hoidens" ("For the Fates are captious girls"), Hilaire Belloc's "A Ballade of Deep Gloom" ("I wish to God that I could pay my bills"), G. K. Chesterton's "Ballade d'une Grande Dame" ("It shall not be forgiven you") and his "A Ballade of Suicide" which follows:

A BALLADE OF SUICIDE

The gallows in my garden, people say,
Is new and neat and adequately tall.
I tie the noose on in a knowing way
As one that knots his necktie for a ball;
But just as all the neighbors—on the wall—
Are drawing a long breath to shout "Hurray!"
The strangest whim has seized me. . . . After all
I think I will not hang myself today.

To-morrow is the time I get my pay—
My uncle's sword is hanging in the hall—
I see a little cloud all pink and gray—
Perhaps the rector's mother will not call—
I fancy that I heard from Mr. Gall

That mushrooms could be cooked another way—
I never read the books of Juvenal—
I think I will not hang myself today.

The world will have another washing day;
The decadents decay; the pedants fall;
And H. G. Wells has found that children play,
And Bernard Shaw discovered that they squall;
Rationalists are growing rational—
And through thick woods one finds a stream astray,
So secret that the very sky seems small—
I think I will not hang myself today.

Prince, I can hear the trump of Germinal,
The tumbrils toiling up the terrible way;
Even today your royal head may fall—
I think I will not hang myself today.

BALLADE WITH DOUBLE REFRAIN.   As its name indicates, this is a ballade with two refrains, one of which occurs in the middle of each stanza, the other in the usual place at the end of each stanza. Both refrains are repeated in the envoy. To avoid monotony, the two refrains are usually opposite in nature, presenting either a contradiction in character or a sharp contrast in mood. A minor classic of its kind is Austin Dobson's "Ballade of Prose and Rhyme."

BALLADE OF PROSE AND RHYME

When the roads are heavy with mire and rut,
In November fogs, in December snows,
When the North Wind howls, and the doors are shut,
There is place and enough for the pains of prose;—
But whenever a scent from the whitethorn blows,
And the jasmine-stars to the casement climb,
And a Rosalind-face at the lattice shows,
Then hey!—for the ripple of laughing rhyme!

When the brain gets dry as an empty nut,
When the reason stands on its squarest toes,
When the mind (like a beard) has a "formal cut,"

There is place and enough for the pains of prose;—
But whenever the May-blood stirs and glows,
And the young year draws to the "golden prime,"—
And Sir Romeo sticks in his ear a rose,
Then hey!—for the ripple of laughing rhyme!

In a theme where the thoughts have a pedant-strut
In a changing quarrel of "Ayes" and "Noes,"
In a starched procession of "If" and "But,"
There is place and enough for the pains of prose;—
But whenever a soft glance softer grows,
And the light hours dance to the trysting-time,
And the secret is told "that no one knows,"
Then hey!—for the ripple of laughing rhyme!

In the work-a-day world,—for its needs and woes,
There is place and enough for the pains of prose;
But whenever the May-bells clash and chime,
Then hey!—for the ripple of laughing rhyme!

Another variant is the DOUBLE BALLADE which is not to
be confused with the Ballade with Double Refrain. The Double
Ballade is a ballade with double the usual number of stanzas ex-
cluding the envoy. The verses ordinarily consist of eight lines, although there are several instances (such as Henley's "Double
Ballade on the Nothingness of Things") which employ eleven
lines. Neither as flexible nor as popular as the conventional ballade, it was a lure only for expert technicians like Swinburne and
Henley, and good examples of it are rare. John Payne's melancholy "Double Ballade of the Singers of the Time" remains one
of the best of its genre.

DOUBLE BALLADE OF THE
SINGERS OF THE TIME

Why are our songs like the moan of the main,
When the wild winds buffet it to and fro,
(Our brothers ask us again and again)
A weary burden of hopes laid low?
Have birds ceased singing or flowers to blow?
Is Life cast down from its fair estate?

This I answer them—nothing mo'—
Songs and singers are out of date.

What shall we sing of? Our hearts are fain,
  Our bosoms burn with a sterile glow.
Shall we sing of the sordid strife for gain,
  For shameful honor, for wealth and woe,
  Hunger and luxury,—weeds that throw
Up from one seeding their flowers of hate?
  Can we tune our lutes to these themes? Ah no!
Songs and singers are out of date.

Our songs should be of Faith without stain,
  Of haughty honor and deaths that sow
The seeds of life on the battle-plain,
  Of loves unsullied and eyes that show
  The fair white soul in the deeps below.
Where are they, these that our songs await
  To wake to joyance? Doth any know?
Songs and singers are out of date.

What have we done with meadow and lane?
  Where are the flowers and hawthorn-snow?
Acres of brick in the pitiless rain,—
  These are our gardens for thorpe and stow!
  Summer has left us long ago,
Gone to the lands where the turtles mate
  And the crickets chirp in the wild-rose row.
Songs and singers are out of date.

We sit and sing to a world in pain;
  Our heartstrings quiver sadly and slow;
But aye and anon the murmurous strain
  Swells up to a clangor of strife and throe,
  And the folk that hearken, or friend or foe,
Are ware that the stress of the time is great
  And say to themselves, as they come and go,
Songs and singers are out of date.

Winter holds us, body and brain;
  Ice is over our being's flow;
Song is a flower that will droop and wane,
  If it have no heaven toward which to grow.

Faith and beauty are dead, I trow,
Nothing is left but fear and fate:
Men are weary of hope; And so
Songs and singers are out of date.

The wide range of the ballade's accomplishments is shown in Gleeson White's *Ballades and Rondeaus,* in *One Hundred and One Ballades* illustrated by John Nash, and in the more extended *Lyric Forms from France* edited with a scholarly account of their history and use by Helen Louise Cohen.

BATHOS is the opposite of pathos. Or, rather, it is a false exaggeration of pathos, for it is emotion overdone or rhetoric overblown and, hence, spurious. It is usually marked by a descent from the exalted to the banal in which the sublime plunges headlong into the ridiculous. In a sample speech by the Player in *Hamlet,* the Player King is both bombastic and bathetic as he declaims:

> *Pyrrhus at Priam drives; in rage strikes wide;*
> *But with the whiff and wind of his fell sword*
> *The unnerved father falls. Then senseless Ilium,*
> *Seeming to feel this blow, with flaming top*
> *Stoops to his base, and with a hideous crash*
> *Takes prisoner Pyrrhus' ear: for, lo! his sword,*
> *Which was declining on the milky head*
> *Of reverend Priam, seem'd i' the air to stick:*
> *So, as a painted tyrant, Pyrrhus stood,*
> *And like a neutral to his will and matter,*
> *Did nothing.*

A more obvious example of bathos is the mockery of Pyramus and Thisbe's sad romance in *A Midsummer Night's Dream.* Pyramus, played by Bottom, a weaver and one of Shakespeare's most grotesque clowns, stabs himself and soliloquizes:

> *Thus die I thus, thus, thus.*
> *Now I am dead,*
> *Now I am fled;*

My soul is in the sky.
Tongue, lose thy light;
Moon, take thy flight;
Now die, die, die, die, die.

BLANK VERSE is unrhymed verse, usually in iambic pentameter.
(See page 209). It is the form of most meditative poetry and
nearly all poetic drama. It is the medium of Milton's epics and of
Marlowe's and Shakespeare's plays. Its flexibility is great because
the rhythm of iambic pentameter is so close to speech. Scholars
have asserted that this meter is the most important in the literature of the western world. Shakespeare's lines constantly display
the variability of blank verse, from the plainly colloquial speech of:

Friends, Romans, countrymen, lend me your ears;
I come to bury Caesar, not to praise him.

to the lyric lift of:

If music be the food of love, play on;
Give me excess of it, that, surfeiting,
The appetite may sicken, and so die.
That strain again! It had a dying fall.
O, it came o'er my ear like the sweet sound
That breathes upon a bank of violets,
Stealing and giving odor.

Milton's blank verse is equally free and flexible. He considered
it the noblest medium, because as he wrote in a preface to *Paradise Lost*, "the sense is variously drawn out from one verse to another." Milton could fashion his ten-syllable lines as lightly as:

With thee conversing, I forget all time;
All seasons and their change, all please alike.
Sweet is the breath of Morn, her rising sweet
With charm of earliest birds; pleasant the sun,
When first on this delightful land he spreads
His orient beams on herb, tree, fruit, and flower . . .

And he could stress the ten syllables so heavily that they were weighted and expanded far beyond the usual beat of iambic pentameter. For example:

Rocks, caves, lakes, fens, bogs, dens, and shades of death

The poets of the Neo-classical period did not of course discard the iambic pentameter line. Dryden and Pope used it extensively, but usually with rhyme, chiefly in matched couplets. Unrhymed blank verse, however, except for James Thomson's *The Seasons*, was not popular in the eighteenth century. But the nineteenth century restored blank verse to its earlier grandeur with Wordsworth's *The Prelude*, Keats's *Hyperion*, Browning's *The Ring and the Book*, and Tennyson's *Idylls of the King*. The twentieth century again brought new freedom to blank verse in the long narratives of Edwin Arlington Robinson and the dramatic monologues of Robert Frost.

Although the term "blank verse" is customarily used to describe lines in iambic pentameter, it is not solely confined to the traditional unrhymed line of ten syllables and five accents. Any verse which is without end-rhyme and has a regular structure (as opposed to free verse which is irregular) might be considered blank verse. There are even blank verse lyrics, such as William Collins' "Ode to Evening":

> *Now air is hushed, save where the weak-eyed bat*
> *With short, shrill shriek flits by on leathern wing;*
> > *Or where the beetle winds*
> > *His small but sullen horn . . .*

The several poems in Tennyson's *The Princess* that constitute a small anthology of lyrics are actually blank verse songs, such as the one beginning:

> *Tears, idle tears, I know not what they mean,*
> *Tears from the depth of some divine despair*
> *Rise in the heart, and gather to the eyes,*

In looking on the happy autumn-fields,
And thinking of the days that are no more.

and the picturesque, passionate lyric which opens:

Now sleeps the crimson petal, now the white;
Nor waves the cypress in the palace walk;
Nor winks the gold fin in the porphyry font.
The firefly wakens. Waken thou with me.

Besides utilizing the traditional ten-syllable five-beat blank verse, Longfellow made the blank verse six-accented line (dactylic hexameter) familiar in *Evangeline*:

This is the forest primeval. The murmuring pines and the
hemlocks,
Bearded with moss, and in garments green, indistinct in the
twilight,
Stand like Druids of eld, with voices sad and prophetic . . .

Another blank verse variant is the four-accented unrhymed line with trochaic feet (TROCHAIC TETRAMETER, see page 299) made famous by Longfellow in *Hiawatha*:

As unto the bow the cord is,
So unto the man is woman;
Though she bends him, she obeys him;
Though she draws him, yet she follows;
Useless each without the other.

BLUES. A form originating with Negro musicians, the blues are individual creations that resemble folk-songs. They express in seemingly artless and often childishly simple verse the joys, griefs, and unfulfilled longings of a transplanted race. They are akin to the spirituals, but with major differences. The spirituals were originally sung *a cappella*, with no instrumental accompaniment; the blues are always sung (or recited) against a musical background. The spirituals, moreover, invoke a better world to come; the blues are bound to this troubled earth. Langston Hughes' first volume was entitled *The Weary Blues*; it contained this refrain:

I got the Weary Blues
And I can't be satisfied.
Got the weary blues
And can't be satisfied—
I ain't happy no mo'
And wish that I had died.

The melancholy of the blues is emphasized by the repetition of a line or a phrase, sometimes called a "burden." (See page 175.) The repeated phrase or (to resort to double meanings) "burden" was loosened in what became known as "Talking Blues." But the unhappiness was retained. One of the best current examples of this genre was composed by Adrian Henri, an English poet, painter, and teacher who worked in fairs and carnivals, designed "Events" or "Happenings," and, in the old manner, sang his songs to guitar accompaniment. Here is "Adrian Henri's Talking After Christmas Blues":

ADRIAN HENRI'S TALKING AFTER CHRISTMAS BLUES

Well I woke up this mornin' it was Christmas Day
And the birds were singing the night away
I saw my stocking lying on the chair
Looked right to the bottom but you weren't there
    there was
       apples
          oranges
             chocolates
               . . . aftershave
—but no you.

So I went downstairs and the dinner was fine
There was pudding and turkey and lots of wine
And I pulled those crackers with a laughing face
Till I saw there was no-one in your place
    there was
       mincepies
          brandy
             nuts and raisins
               . . . mashed potato
—but no you.

Now it's New Year and it's Auld Lang Syne
And it's 12 o'clock and I'm feeling fine
Should Auld Acquaintance be Forgot?
I don't know, girl, but it hurts a lot
   there was
     whisky
      vodka
        dry Martini (stirred
         but not shaken)
. . . and 12 New Year Resolutions
—all of them about you.

So it's all the best for the year ahead
As I stagger upstairs and into bed
Then I looked at the pillow by my side
. . . I tell you, baby, I almost cried
   there'll be
     Autumn
      Summer
       Spring
         . . . and Winter
—all of them without you.

BUCOLIC POETRY. See PASTORAL POETRY on page 246.

BURDEN. An old word (also spelled "burthen") for a chorus or refrain. A repeated central idea or set of syllables, often meaningless, it owes its name to the Old French *bourdon*, a humming or droning sound. It has come to mean a line or lines recurring during the progress of a poem.

The lines set in roman in the following verses are the "burden" or refrain. Repeated throughout the poem, they are first sung by an individual singer and then taken up by a chorus, often by the audience. They are found (as below) in ballads, Shakespearian lyrics, and folk songs.

Near the king's court was a young child born,
  With a hey lillylo and a how lo lan;
And his name it was called Young Hynd Horn,
  And the birk and the broom bloom bonnie.

* * *

O fairest lady ever seen,
   With a hey-ho and a lily gay,
Give your consent to be my queen,
   As the primrose spreads so sweetly.

* * *

She sat down below a thorn,
   Fine flowers in the valley;
And there she had her sweet babe born,
   And the green leaves they grow rarely.

* * *

It was a lover and his lass,
   With a hey and a ho and a hey nonino,
That o'er the green corn-field did pass,
   In the spring-time, the only pretty ring-time,
When birds do sing, hey ding a ding, ding,
Sweet lovers love the spring.

* * *

Fifteen men on the dead man's chest,
   Yo-ho-ho and a bottle of rum!
Drink and the devil had done for the rest,
   Yo-ho-ho and a bottle of rum!

* * *

A farmer was plowing his field one day,
   Riteful, riteful, titty fi day,
A farmer was plowing his field one day,
When the devil came up and to him he did say
   With a riteful, riteful, titty fi day.

* * *

As I went out one morning to take the pleasant air,
   Lolly too dum, too dum, lolly too dum day,
As I went out one morning to take the pleasant air,
I overheard a mother a-scolding her daughter fair,
   Lolly too dum, too dum, lolly too dum day.

C

CADENCE. A musical term denoting the close of a musical passage, cadence has come to mean the flow of rhythm and the fall of the voice toward the end of a line or a sentence. Amy Lowell said that free verse should really be called "cadenced verse, since it is built on 'organic rhythm,' the rhythm of the speaking voice." "Compose in the sequence of the musical phrase," said Ezra Pound, "not in the measure of a metronome." For further details see FREE VERSE on pages 201–202.

CAESURA. A caesura (sometimes spelled cesura) is a pause or break within the poetic line. It does not affect the metrical count, but it divides the line into more or less equal parts. When it occurs near the beginning of the line it is known as "initial caesura"; when it occurs toward the middle of the line it is called "medial caesura"; when the break comes near the end of the line it is "terminal caesura." Pope, who constantly used a ten-syllable line, held that the pause should come after the fourth or fifth syllable. Here, for example, are two couplets from Pope's *Essay on Man*, where the pause occurs after the fourth or fifth syllable.

> *Know then thyself: / presume not God to scan:*
> *The proper study / of mankind is Man.*

> *Honor and shame / from no condition rise;*
> *Act well your part, / there all the honor lies.*

Shakespeare's lines are rich in a variety of caesuras. For example:

> *He jests at scars / that never felt a wound.*

> *But soft! / What light from yonder window breaks?*
> *It is the East, / and Juliet is the sun.*

Multiple breaks within a single line are frequent in modern poetry. The effect is staccato, as in Henley's:

The gods are dead? / Perhaps they are. / Who knows?
Living / at least in Lemprière / undeleted,
The wise, the fair, / the awful, / the jocose,
Are one and all / I like to think / retreated
In some still land / of lilacs and the rose.

CHANSONS DE GESTE. Although the word "geste" means little more than a gesture today, in Old French it signified a deed, an historical event. The *Chansons de Geste* of the twelfth and thirteenth centuries glorified fabulous heroes and legendary romances. More than eighty of these epic poems spread through France and found their way by diffusion into England and Italy. The most famous is the *Chanson de Roland*, which tells of Charlemagne's army led by Count Roland, betrayed by the traitor Ganelon, disastrously defeated at Roncevaux, of another battle in which Charlemagne triumphed, and of the execution of Ganelon.

CHANT ROYAL. One of the rarer French forms, the chant royal got its name because it was supposed to be sung before kings and its composition was considered worthy of royal honors. Actually a larger form of the ballade, it consists of five stanzas of eleven lines and an envoy of seven. Its purpose as well as its purport is serious, even solemn. However, there have been occasional lighthearted royal chants, such as H. C. Bunner's burlesque "Behold the Deeds!"—a "Plaint of Adolphe Culpepper Ferguson, Salesman of Fancy Notions, held in durance of his Landlady for a failure to connect on Saturday Night."

The rhyme order of the chant royal varies somewhat with the different practitioners of the form. Usually it is as follows: *a-b-a-b-c-c-d-d-e-d-e*. The rhymes of the envoy follow in the same order as those in the last seven lines, namely *c-c-d-d-e-d-e*.

In spite of its difficulty, this form has found more favor than the double ballade to which it is related. With most of the poets, however, the chant royal begins as a virtuoso piece and remains little more than a tour de force. The most noted and by far the best chant royal in English is Austin Dobson's "The Dance of Death," inspired by Holbein, and prefaced with an epigraph: *Contra vim Mortis / Non est medicamen in hortis.*

THE DANCE OF DEATH

He is the despots' Despot. All must bide,
Later or soon, the message of his might;
Princes and potentates their heads must hide,
Touched by the awful sigil of his right;
Beside the Kaiser he at eve doth wait
And pours a potion in his cup of state;
The stately Queen his bidding must obey;
No keen-eyed Cardinal shall him affray;
And to the Dame that wantoneth he saith—
"Let be, Sweet-heart, to junket and to play."
There is no King more terrible than Death.

The lusty Lord, rejoicing in his pride,
He draweth down; before the armèd Knight
With jangling bridle-rein he still doth ride;
He crosseth the strong Captain in the fight;
The Burgher grave he beckons from debate;
He hales the Abbot by his shaven pate,
Nor for the Abbess' wailing will delay;
No bawling Mendicant shall say him nay;
E'en to the pyx the Priest he followeth,
Nor can the Leech his chilling finger stay.
There is no King more terrible than Death.

All things must bow to him. And woe betide
The Wine-bibber, the Roisterer by night;
Him the feast-master, many bouts defied,
Him 'twixt the pledging and the cup shall smite;
Woe to the Lender at usurious rate,
The hard Rich Man, the hireling Advocate;
Woe to the Judge that selleth right for pay;
Woe to the Thief that like a beast of prey
With creeping tread the traveller harryeth:—
These, in their sin, the sudden sword shall slay.
There is no King more terrible than Death.

He hath no pity,—nor will be denied.
When the low hearth is garnishèd and bright,
Grimly he flingeth the dim portal wide,

And steals the Infant in the Mother's sight;
He hath no pity for the scorned of fate:—
He spares not Lazarus lying at the gate,
Nay, nor the Blind that stumbleth as he may;
Nay, the tired Ploughman,—at the sinking ray,—
In the last furrow,—feels an icy breath,
And knows a hand hath turned the team astray.
There is no King more terrible than Death.

He hath no pity. For the new-made Bride,
Blithe with the promise of her life's delight,
That wanders gladly by her Husband's side,
He with the clatter of his drum doth fright;
He scares the Virgin at the convent grate;
The Maid half-won, the Lover passionate;
He hath no grace for weakness and decay:
The tender Wife, the Widow bent and gray,
The feeble Sire whose foostep faltereth,—
All these he leadeth by the lonely way.
There is no King more terrible than Death.

ENVOY

Youth, for whose ear and monishing of late,
I sang of prodigals and lost estate,
Have thou thy joy of living and be gay;
But know not less that there must come a day,—
Aye, and perchance e'en now it hasteneth,—
When thine own heart shall speak to thee and say,
There is no King more terrible than Death.

CHANTEY. The word chantey is said to come from the French *chantez,* sing! A chantey is a song sung by sailors while at work. There are short-haul chanteys like the one beginning "Oh, Shenandoah, I love your daughter," forecastle chanteys about whaling ships like "Blow Ye Winds," and capstan chanteys like:

> *Way, hay, up she rises,*
> *Way, hay, up she rises,*
> *Way, hay, up she rises,*
> *Earlye in the morning.*
> *What will we do with a drunken sailor?*

> *What will we do with a drunken sailor?*
> *What will we do with a drunken sailor*
> *Earlye in the morning?*

CHIASMUS. An inversion of parallel phrases. It is encountered in criss-cross prose, for example: "He was no good; no better was she." Pope sees man "destroying others, by himself destroyed." Shakespeare ends his 154th sonnet with this chiasmus: "Love's fire heats water; water cools not love."

CINQUAIN. A five-line stanza—the name comes from the French word *cinque*, five—the cinquain was invented by Adelaide Crapsey. The lines consist, respectively, of two, four, six, eight, and two syllables. The short, strictly structured result is reminiscent of the Japanese tanka. (See page 294.) Here are two of her fragile but precise poems. The first is entitled "November Night," the second "The Warning."

> *Listen . . .*
> *With faint dry sound,*
> *Like steps of passing ghosts,*
> *The leaves, frost-crisp'd, break from the trees*
> *And fall.*

$$* \quad * \quad *$$

> *Just now,*
> *Out of the strange*
> *Still dusk . . . as strange, as still . . .*
> *A white moth flew. Why am I grown*
> *So cold?*

Also see quintet on page 258.

CLASSICAL. The word "classical" means different things to different people. It is customarily applied to the kind of writing which endures, and, more specifically, refers to Greek and Roman literature. In general the word "classical" connotes careful restraint, balanced proportions, and purity of form. The critic Roger Fry expressed the difference between "romantic" and "classical" this way: "I call 'romantic' any work of art which to produce its effect counts on the association of ideas which it sets up in the mind of the spectator. I call 'classical' the work which to provoke emotion depends on its own formal organization."

In spite of Fry's reputation, his definition has been sharply challenged. The word "classical" has far wider implications than such a disposal would suggest, and the term "classical poetry" has produced a body of opinions that date from antiquity. In the fourth century B.C. Aristotle's *Poetics* announced an esthetic based on firm structure and strict unity of action. Three hundred years later, Horace's *Ars Poetica* argued for a more informal manner, a relaxed communication, direct and discursive, resembling an epistle. According to Horace, texture was preferable to structure. These two theories have each in turn dominated (and sometimes divided) concepts of classical poetry, and both have influenced the wavering course of criticism.

CLERIHEW.   The word clerihew owes its origin to the middle name of Edmund Clerihew Bentley, author of a perfect murder mystery, *Trent's Last Case*, as well as of several biographies; he is the inventor of this verse-form. A clerihew is composed of two rhymed couplets, one line of which (usually the first) incorporates the name of a famous person; the other lines deal with a characteristic of the person named or with an episode (usually fictitious) in his career. Bentley himself wrote more than a hundred clerihews and attracted many disciples, including the composer Constant Lambert and W. H. Auden.

The first three clerihews which follow are by Bentley; the next three are by Louis Untermeyer.

> *Edward the Confessor*
> *Slept under the dresser.*
> *When that began to pall,*
> *He slept in the hall.*

> *When Alexander Pope*
> *Accidentally trod on the soap*
> *And came down on the back of his head—*
> *Never mind what he said.*

George the Third
Ought never to have occurred.
One can only wonder
At so grotesque a blunder.

Although the Borgias
Were rather gorgeous,
They loved the absurder
Kinds of murder.

Alfred, Lord Tennyson,
Lived upon venison.
Not cheap, I fear,
Because venison's deer.

Francesca da Rimini
Lived in a chiminey,
Full of ghouls in the gloam—
But still, home is home!

CLICHÉ. A French word originally meaning an electrotype, or a die used hundreds of times for the same impression, the term has come to signify an expression so timeworn that it has lost its original vitality, a stock phrase that has been used and overused until it has become a blurred stereotype, so common that it no longer can surprise. "Fall of night," "break of day," "dark despair" once conveyed striking images, but they are now clichés, rubber-stamp expressions. They are like coins, once bright and clean-cut, that have been handled so often that they present nothing more than a flat blank surface. Only a lazy or incompetent poet would use such trite and wholly ineffective adjective-and-noun "poeticisms" as "azure sky," "silvery moon," "caressing winds," "golden gates," "modest violet," "playful breeze," "gentle night," et cetera.

Occasionally a poem triumphs over a hackneyed phrase or two, but when clichés are allowed to accumulate, the poem falls to pieces. What follows was written by William Lisle Bowles, a late-eighteenth-century writer who pleased many of his contemporaries.

> *Beautiful landscape! I could look on thee*
> *For hours, unmindful of the storm and strife*
> *And mingled murmurs of tumultuous life.*
> *Here, all is still as fair; the stream, the tree,*
> *The mellow sunshine on the bank: no tear,*
> *No thought of Time's swift wing, or gentle night,*
> *That comes to steal away the long sweet light—*
> *No sighs of sad humanity are here.*
> *Here is no hint of mortal change. The day—*
> *Beneath whose light the dog and peasant-boy*
> *Gambol, with look, and almost bark, of joy—*
> *Still seems, though centuries have past, to stay.*
> *Then gaze again, that shadowed scenes may teach*
> *Lessons of peace and love, beyond all speech.*

Apostrophizing the scene, Bowles takes all the beauty out of it by burying it under a mass of such dead accumulations as "storm and strife," "mingled murmurs," "tumultuous life," "mellow sunshine," "Time's swift wing," "gentle night," "sad humanity," "mortal change," "shadowed scenes." The poem fails to make any impression on the reader because it is nothing more than a string of threadbare tenth-hand items.

CONCEIT.   In the literary sense, a conceit is a witty conception, a fanciful image, an ingenious thought. Elizabethan and Metaphysical conceits are examined in the chapter entitled "The Conceits of Poetry" beginning on page 64.

CONCRETE POETRY.   See page 133 in the chapter "The Oddities of Poetry."

CONNOTATION is the association or implication suggested by a word as opposed to *denotation*, which is the explicit meaning. A word may connote entirely different things to different people, suggesting images completely alien to plain meaning. For illustration of how ambiguous connotation may become, see the discussion of Hart Crane's "logic of metaphor" in the chapter "The Images of Poetry" on page 62.

CONSONANCE. An unusual device of sound, consonance is the repetition of consonants in place of conventional rhyme. The repetition occurs at the beginning and also at the end of words, such as "hill-hall," "came-comb," "lean-lane." The repetition of consonant sounds at the end of words only is sometimes accepted as consonance; Emily Dickinson was fond of using consonance instead of rhyme in this way—"time-lamb," "man-noon," "wool-until." In any case, consonance matches the consonants; the vowel-sound is purposely designed *not* to rhyme.

Apart from its novelty, consonance (as the name implies) is the counterpart of assonance. Pairing *all* the consonants and un-matching all the vowels, the poet has a wide choice of effects—"post-past-pest," "mate-meet-moot," "leaves-lives-loves," "stars-stirs-stairs." Wilfred Owen mixed rhyme and consonance dramatically, as in his "Miners."

> *But the coals were murmuring of their* mine
> *And moans down there,*
> *Of boys that slept wry sleep, and* men
> *Writhing for air.*
>
> *I saw white bones in the cinder-shard,*
> *Bones without* number;
> *For many hearts with coal are charred,*
> *And few remember.*
>
> *I thought of all who worked dark* pits
> *Of war, and died*
> *Digging the rock where Death reputes*
> *Peace lies indeed.*

Rhymed consonants and unrhymed vowels further the poignant phantasma of Owen's war experience, "Strange Meeting," a tragic dream which ends:

> *"I am the enemy you killed, my* friend.
> *I knew you in this dark; for so you* frowned
> *Yesterday through me as you jabbed and* killed.
> *I parried, but my hands were loath and* cold.
> *Let us sleep now . . ."*

Two-syllable consonance adds suspense to Archibald MacLeish's *Conquistador* with such pairs as "laughing-leafing," "trouble-treble," "barley-barely," "gather-together," "marrow-tomorrow," "having-heaving."

A variation of consonance is found in a rather odd method of binding lines together. It is called ANALYZED RHYME and consists of varying the same consonants with shifting vowels. For example, in the following poem, "Dark Flower," by the author, the consonants in each quatrain are paired in couplet form (*a-a-b-b*) while the vowels are rhymed (*a-b-b-a*) thus:

> *Intangibly the intricate vein*
> *Perfects its traceries of vine.*
> *The hand is taught, the heart is tried*
> *Whenever the body can be betrayed.*

> *Obedient to an ancient rune,*
> *It flowers without sun or rain.*
> *No branch has borne a richer freight*
> *But let none sever the sanguine fruit.*

COUPLET.   Formerly called a distich, a couplet, as the name implies, is a pair of rhymes matched in immediate succession. The two lines may be matched in length or they may differ in length. The deceptive ease of the couplet, the dexterity and definiteness of the two matching lines reached its perfection in the eighteenth-century couplets of Pope. With the most meticulous craftsmanship and the most deceptive grace, Pope united brilliance and malevolence, polish and passion—"those fine shades," as Lytton Strachey wrote, "and delicate gradations of sound." Some of Pope's finest couplets are poems in themselves, rhymed aphorisms packed into two memorable lines. There is, for example, the inscription on the collar of a dog which Pope gave to his Royal Highness:

> *I am his Highness' dog at Kew.*
> *Pray tell me, sir, whose dog are you?*

There is the dig at his fellow-poets in which Pope mockingly combined alliteration and sarcasm:

> *Pensive poets painful vigils keep,*
> *Sleepless themselves to give their readers sleep.*

There are the clinched couplets which Pope used with savage incision to cut down the character of the Duchess of Marlborough:

> *Who, with herself, or others, from her birth*
> *Finds all her life one warfare upon earth:*
> *Shines in exposing knaves, and painting fools,*
> *Yet is whate'er she hates and ridicules. . . .*
> *From loveless youth to unrespected age,*
> *No passion gratified except her rage.*

Equally bitter is the sixteenth-century Sir John Harington's two-line disposal of treason:

> *Treason doth never prosper. What's the reason?*
> *Why, when it prospers, none dare call it treason.*

A couplet served Hilaire Belloc to write his own light-hearted, punning epitaph:

> *When I am dead, I hope it may be said:*
> *"His sins were scarlet, but his books were read."*

There are also mixed, or uneven, couplets, in which the paired lines differ in length. The first of the two following examples is from Robert Herrick's "Thanksgiving to God, for His House"; the second is the opening of Robert Browning's "Love Among the Ruins."

> *Lord, Thou hast given me a cell*
> *Wherein to dwell,*
> *A little house, whose humble roof*
> *Is weather-proof;*
> *Under the spars of which I lie*
> *Both soft and dry;*
> *Where Thou my chamber for to ward*
> *Hast set a guard*
> *Of harmless thoughts to watch and keep*
> *Me, while I sleep.*

* * *

Where the quiet-colored end of evening smiles
  Miles and miles
On the solitary pastures where our sheep
  Half-asleep
Tinkle homeward thro' the twilight, stray or stop
  As they crop—

See also HEROIC COUPLET on page 206.

D

DACTYL. A dactyl is a metrical unit of one accented syllable followed by two unaccented syllables: ′ ◡ ◡ . It is sometimes called a "waltzing" foot and is found in such words as "happiness," "century," "merriment," "joyfully." Frequently the three-syllable dactyl and the three-syllable anapest slide into each other; few lines of verse can maintain so pronounced a beat without variation. Here are two examples of poems of different line lengths built on dactylic feet. The first is from Thomas Hood's "The Bridge of Sighs"; the second is from Longfellow's "Evangeline," recalling the *Aeneid* which Longfellow was imitating rhythmically.

Touch her not scornfully;
Think of her mournfully,
  Gently and humanly;
Not of the stains of her.
All that remains of her
  Now is pure womanly.

This is the forest primeval; but where are the hearts that beneath it
Leaped like the roe when he hears in the woodland the voice of the huntsman?

An ingenious diversion of dactyls was invented by two poets, Anthony Hecht and John Hollander. Their appropriately entitled *Jiggery-Pokery* (1967) is a compendium of DOUBLE DACTYLS. The form, according to the ultra-scholarly introduction, "is composed of two quatrains, of which the last line of the first rhymes with the last line of the second. All the lines except the rhyming ones, which are truncated, are composed of two dactylic feet. The first line of the poem must be a double dactylic nonsense line like 'Higgledy-Piggledy' or 'Pocketa-Pocketa.' The second line must be a double dactylic name"—the blurb mentions such double dactylic notables as Marcus Antonius, Josephine Bonaparte, and Pico Mirandola. "Then, somewhere in the poem, preferably in the second stanza, there must be at least one double dactylic line which is one word long."

Since double dactyls are more easily exemplified than defined, here are three: The first is by the music critic Harold Schonberg; the second is by the poet-essayist David McCord; the third is by a consultant in physics and electronics, John Moore.

> *Higgledy-Piggledy*
> *Sergei Rachmaninoff*
> *Sat at the concert grand,*
> *Much like a mouse.*
>
> *Playing his Beethoven*
> *Superpianistically,*
> *Also his Schumann, and*
> *Counting the house.*

* * *

> *Dirigo-Hereigo*
> *Edwin A. Robinson,*
> *Born at Head Tide, was a*
> *Sad, lonely man.*
>
> *Dark but agreeable*
> *Prosopopoeiable*
> *Verse that he wrote. How the*
> *Fellow could scan!*

* * *

Rockety-Jockey
Lemuel Gulliver
Messaged from space in a
Horrified blurt:

"Hyper-dimensional
Extraterrestrials'
Bodies are weak. It's their
Shadows that hurt!"

DIMETER. A line of verse which has two metrical feet is called a dimeter. It shapes a dramatically short and abruptly accented line, as in Walter de la Mare's "All but Blind," which begins:

All but blind
   In his chambered hole
Gropes for worms
   The four-clawed mole.

James Stephens' "The Main-Deep" achieves the effect of a heavy surf with its two-footed lines:

The long, rolling,
Steady pouring,
Deep-trenchéd
Green billow . . .

DISTICH. Two lines of joined verse. See COUPLET on page 186.

DISTRIBUTED STRESS. It is sometimes difficult to determine which of two consecutive syllables should be accented. In this case, when the emphasis appears to hover uncertainly above the two syllables, it is known as "hovering accent" or "distributed stress." A languid effect is achieved by Tennyson in "The Lotus Eaters" with its wavering distributed stresses:

There is sweet music here that softer falls
Than petals from blown roses on the grass,
Or night-dews on still waters between walls
Of shadowy granite in a gleaming pass.

DITHYRAMB. The Greek ritual dances in honor of Dionysus were climaxed by a dithyramb, an ecstatic outburst in a wild choric hymn. Today the word signifies a passionate and usually overemotional speech or poem.

DIZAIN. A ten-line poem with a strict rhyme scheme: *a-b-a-b-b-c-c-d-c-d* favored by sixteenth-century French poets. Several dizains were sometimes brought together to form a kind of ballade or chant royal. Examples in English poetry are rare.

DOGGEREL. Poorly conceived, badly written, and generally inane verse is known as doggerel. Its effect is that of a tasteless and unintentionally humorous jingle. Choice examples of doggerel are to be found in *The Stuffed Owl: An Anthology of Bad Verse*, selected by D. B. Wyndham Lewis and Charles Lee, and *The Worst English Poets*, compiled by Christopher Adams, a pseudonym of the poet-essayist Kenneth Hopkins. Lines of abysmal badness have been written not only by third-rate poetasters but also by poet laureates. Dryden, Shadwell, Cibber, Southey, Wordsworth, and Tennyson have been guilty of the most lamentable lapses. It is almost impossible to believe, but it is nevertheless true that Tennyson wrote a three-stanza poem beginning:

> *O darling room, my heart's delight,*
> *Dear room, the apple of my sight*
> *With thy two couches soft and white,*
> *There is no room so exquisite,*
> *No little room so warm and bright,*
> *Wherein to read, wherein to write.*

This early Tennysonian banality (which he later suppressed) vies with the appalling—yet somehow appealing—crudities of Julia Moore, "The Sweet Singer of Michigan." Her critical survey of Byron begins:

> *"Lord Byron" was an Englishman,*
> *A poet I believe;*

His first works in old England
Was poorly received.
Perhaps it was "Lord Byron's" fault,
And perhaps it was not.
His life was full of misfortunes,
Ah, sad was his lot.

Even more funereally comic is Julia Moore's elegy on the death of "Little Libbie."

While eating dinner, this dear child
Was choked on a piece of beef.
Doctors came, tried their skill awhile,
But none could give relief . . .
Her friends and schoolmates will not forget
Little Libbie that is no more.
She is waiting on the shining step
To welcome home friends once more.

DOUBLE BALLADE. SEE BALLADE on page 168.

DOUBLE DACTYLS. SEE DACTYL on page 188.

Ɛ

ECHO VERSE. See "The Oddities of Poetry" on page 125.

ECLOGUE. Originally a short bucolic poem in the form of a dialogue between two shepherds. Its prime exemplar in Greece was the pastoral poet Theocritus. In Rome, Virgil, greatest of Latin poets, surpassed all idyllic poetry with the sweetness of his *Eclogues*. In English poetry the term was extended to mean any poem on a rural theme, such as Spenser's *The Shepherd's Calendar*. The word was further amplified to allow for urban and controversial commentary, as in Louis MacNeice's "Eclogue from Iceland," W. H. Auden's "The Age of Anxiety," Allen Tate's "Eclogue of the Liberal and the Poet," and Robert Frost's "Build Soil," which he subtitled "A Political Pastoral."

ELEGY. The word "elegy" means exactly what the Greek word *elegos* meant: a lament, a song of mourning, a sorrowful meditation. An elegy may be a poem on the death of an intimate friend— Milton's "Lycidas," Tennyson's "In Memoriam," Arnold's "Thyrsis"; a grieving tribute to a great poet—Shelley's "Adonais," Auden's "In Memory of W. B. Yeats"; or a solemn meditation on humanity—Gray's "Elegy Written in a Country Churchyard." Whitman's "When Lilacs Last in the Dooryard Bloom'd" is a classic example of an elegy in free verse. Rilke's *Duino Elegies,* sensitively translated by J. B. Leishman and Stephen Spender, are "elegies" in that, as Leishman tells us in his commentary, their theme is a lament for "great lovers and, also, those who have died young, through reflexion on whose destiny we shall achieve an intuition . . . into the unity of life and death." Nor should one forget the tongue-in-cheek "Elegy on the Death of a Mad Dog" and "An Elegy on the Glory of Her Sex, Mrs. Mary Blaine" by Oliver Goldsmith.

ELISION. The omission of a vowel when it precedes another vowel is sometimes called synalepha but usually elision. For example: "The sun is down and th'evening's nightingales" or "Th'uncertain times oft varying in their course."

ENJAMBMENT. When the sense of a line of verse demands another line to complete the meaning, we say that the line runs on, or that there is enjambment. The word comes from the French *enjamber,* "to stride over." A much-quoted example is the opening of Keats's *Endymion* with its run-on lines:

> *A thing of beauty is a joy forever:*
> *Its loveliness increases; it will never*
> *Pass into nothingness; but still will keep*
> *A bower quiet for us, and a sleep*
> *Full of sweet dreams, and health, and quiet breathing.*

The opposite of a run-on line is a line which has a distinct pause at the end and is therefore called "end-stopped." When pairs of lines are, in themselves, little epigrams or short statements, as in most eighteenth-century couplets, the lines are end-stopped. Witness these "closed" couplets from Goldsmith's *The Deserted Village*:

> *There, in his noisy mansion, skilled to rule,*
> *The village master taught his little school; . . .*
> *The village all declared how much he knew—*
> *'Twas certain he could write, and cipher too; . . .*
> *And still they gazed, and still the wonder grew*
> *That one small head could carry all he knew.*

ENVOY. From the French *envoi*, a "sending" or "dispatching." As the concluding half-stanza of the ballade, the envoy sums up or "dispatches" the idea inherent in the preceding stanzas. (See BALLADE on page 160.)

EPIC. A long narrative poem written with great sweep, the epic is characterized by the scope and amplitude of its theme. It is a story which sums up an epoch. Heroes emerge, adventures ensue, nations are embattled, but they are all merely parts of a larger design, noble in its conception. The figures and events are often mythical, versions and revisions of oral legends. Though epics have no fixed form, the European epic usually follows the pattern established by Homer's *Odyssey* and *Iliad*. The poet begins by stating his subject. "Arms and the man I sing," opens the *Aeneid*. "Achilles' wrath, to Greece the direful spring/Of woes unnumbered, Heavenly Goddess, sing!" declares the *Iliad* in Pope's version. The first lines of Milton's *Paradise Lost* promise that the epic will tell

> *Of man's first disobedience, and the fruit*
> *Of that forbidden tree, whose mortal taste*
> *Brought death into the world, and all our woe . . .*

After invoking the Muse, the poet plunges into the action *in medias res* and we are in the middle of the tale—Odysseus wandering toward Ithaca, Aeneas landing near Carthage, Satan plotting in Hell. There ensues either a physical conflict (Greeks versus Trojans, God versus Satan, Beowulf versus Grendel) or a wearisome search—Aeneas struggling to find a site for future empire, Odysseus traveling homeward for years—a quest interrupted by countless digressions.

Dante's *The Divine Comedy*, Tasso's *Jerusalem Delivered*, Spenser's *The Faerie Queene*, Hardy's *The Dynasts*, Benét's *John Brown's Body* are epics that depart from the Homeric formula.

Pope satirized the epic tradition and especially epic battles in *The Rape of the Lock:*

> *While through the press enraged Thalestris flies,*
> *And scatters death around from both her eyes,*
> *A beau and witling perished in the throng,*
> *One died in metaphor, and one in song.*

Byron went even further than Pope in mocking the epic tradition in his irreverent *Don Juan.*

> *My poem's epic, and is meant to be*
> *   Divided in twelve books; each book containing,*
> *With love and war, a heavy gale at sea,*
> *   A list of ships and captains and kings reigning,*
> *New characters; the episodes are three.*
> *   A panoramic view of hell's in training,*
> *After the style of Virgil and of Homer,*
> *So that my name of Epic's no misnomer.*

EPIGRAM.   Coleridge defined the word by asking and answering a question.

> *What is an epigram? A dwarfish whole;*
> *Its body brevity, and wit its soul.*

Being brief, an epigram is limited to a single idea tightened by an ingenious turn of thought. Sometimes it is nothing more than a clever saying; sometimes it holds a large thought in its small compass. When the epigram is expressed in verse, it attains an added shape and sharpness. The eighteenth-century poets, with their love of pointed wit and barbed finesse, excelled in epigrammatic deftness. Pope's rhymed essays, epistles, and miscellaneous poems are studded with epigrams as keen as these:

> *Get place and wealth—if possible with grace;*
> *If not, by any means, get wealth and place.*

> *Chaste to her husband, frank to all beside,*
> *A teeming mistress, but a barren bride.*

> *What dire offence from amorous causes springs;*
> *What mighty contests rise from trivial things!*

Blake put more than wit into his epigrams. He packed them with profound understanding as well as with mystical suggestiveness.

> *Great things are done when men and mountains meet;*
> *This is not done by jostling in the street.*

> *Terror in the house does roar,*
> *But Pity stands before the door.*

> *Do what you will, this life's a fiction,*
> *And is made up of contradiction.*

Most verse epigrams are in couplets, as above, but many are slightly more extended, as in the following quatrains. The first two are by Blake; the third, entitled "Beethoven and Michelangelo," is by John Banister Tabb; the fourth is by Hilaire Belloc; the fifth by Edwin Markham.

> *To see a World in a grain of sand,*
> *And a Heaven in a wild flower,*
> *Hold Infinity in the palm of your hand,*
> *And Eternity in an hour.*

* * *

What is it men in women do require?
The lineaments of gratified desire.
What is it women do in men require?
The lineaments of gratified desire.

* * *

One made the surging sea of tone
*   Subservient to his rod;*
One, from the sterile womb of stone,
*   Raised children up to God.*

* * *

The Devil, having nothing else to do,
Went off to tempt My Lady Poltagrue.
My Lady, tempted by a private whim,
To his extreme annoyance, tempted him.

* * *

He drew a circle that shut me out—
Heretic, rebel, a thing to flout.
But Love and I had the wit to win:
We drew a circle that took him in.

EPITAPH. Originally an epitaph was an inscription cut into a tombstone. Necessarily almost as brief as an epigram, it differed from the ELEGY (see page 193) by being a particular rather than a general and usually lengthy expression of grief. Although most epitaphs honor the dead, some are cynical and plainly scurrilous. Even before his wife died, Dryden wrote a savage little couplet:

Here lies my wife. Here let her lie.
Now she's at peace. And so am I.

The Greek Anthology is full of epitaphs which are not only touching but also blithe, bitter, and downright bawdy. Here are two:

This portrait painter boasted twenty sons,
But never got a likeness—no, not once.

> *My name is Dion. Here I lie,*
> *Beaten by life, a silly game.*
> *I had no wife nor child, and I*
> *Wish that my father had said the same.*

John Gay's own epitaph is a disillusioned epigram, a shrug one might have expected from the author of *The Beggar's Opera.*

> *Life is a jest, and all things show it.*
> *I thought so once. But now I know it.*

The best epitaphs, however, are serious, pitiful, and sometimes moving. The first of these which follow was written by Pope upon the death of Isaac Newton; the second, by Robert Herrick, was occasioned by the death of a child; the third, by Hilaire Belloc, is a tribute to a dead hostess; the fourth is an anonymous appeal.

> *Nature and Nature's laws lay hid in night:*
> *God said, "Let Newton be!" and all was light.*
>
>   *   *   *

> *Here a pretty baby lies*
> *Sung asleep with lullabies.*
> *Pray be silent, and not stir*
> *Th' easy earth that covers her.*
>
>   *   *   *

> *On this bad world the loveliest and the best*
> *Has smiled and said "Good Night" and gone to rest.*
>
>   *   *   *

> *Here lie I, Martin Elginbrodde,*
> *Ha' mercy on my soul, Lord God,*
> *As I wad do, were I Lord God,*
> *An' Thou wert Martin Elginbrodde.*

EPITHALAMION. Sometimes spelled "Epithalamium," the Greek word means "at the bridal chamber." An epithalamion was the song sung after the wedding ceremonies had been completed.

Sometimes it assumed a ribald character, playing variations on jests about the first night. In most cases, however, it is solemn with religious overtones, as in the Biblical "Song of Songs," or idyllic, as in Spenser's "Epithalamion," a poem of more than four hundred lines which plays changes on the murmurous refrain: "That all the woods shall answer, and their echo ring." Years later, Spenser wrote another nuptial song, coining the word "Prothalamion," presumably sung before the wedding ceremony, with this refrain: "Sweet Thames! run softly, till I end my song."

EPITHET. An epithet is a word (usually an adjective) which expresses some salient or especially revealing quality of the thing or person to which it is applied. The difference between "a yellow topaz" and "a sun-bright topaz" is the difference between an ordinary adjective and an epithet. At its best, an epithet can disclose the unsuspected character of a familiar object. Homer spoke of the "wine-dark sea," "rosy-fingered Dawn," "crocus-clad Morn," "laughter-loving Aphrodite," and "swift-footed Achilles." Blake summoned the tiger's "fearful symmetry." Whitman evoked the "mad, naked summer night" and "lovely and soothing death." Emily Dickinson wrote about "the accent of a coming foot" and feeling "zero at the bone." Rupert Brooke appreciated "the cool kindliness of sheets."

Keats's poems are a treasury of epithets. His "Ode to a Nightingale" alone yields such magically descriptive phrases as "full-throated ease," "deep-delved earth," "sunburnt mirth," "beaded bubbles," "leaden-eyed despairs," "lustrous eyes," "viewless wings of Poesy," "verdurous glooms," "embalmed darkness," "dewy wine," "murmurous haunt of flies," "easeful death," "alien corn," and two lines which every poet has envied for their rich suggestiveness:

> *Charmed magic casements, opening on the foam*
> *Of perilous seas, in faery lands forlorn.*

It was the change of a single word that lifted those lines from a pretty picture into an unearthly one. In the first draft Keats had written "keelless seas," but he altered the adjective to the haunting "perilous," an epithet which now seems inevitable.

EPODE.   An epode is part of a long ode, literally an "additional song." The epodes of Horace are poems in which long verses are followed by short ones.

EUPHUISM.   An ornate and overrefined style is euphuistic. The term derives from the name of Euphues, a highly affected character in John Lyly's sixteenth-century prose romance of the same name. Euphuism is often an elaborate effort to avoid the simple phrase. Instead of calling a spade a spade, the Euphuist refers to it as "a sharpened tongue of iron, hungering to taste the earth." The use of high-flown comparisons and lavish constructions was imitated by many of Lyly's contemporaries and, in its very extravagance, extended the possibilities—and dangers—of poetic diction.

EYE RHYME.   See RHYME on page 260.

F

FABLIAU.   The fabliau is one of the oldest types of versified story-telling; it existed long before the twelfth century, when it became popular in France. Its range is short, its character earthy and frequently obscene. Many fabliaux are animal tales, little fables to which morals were often but not always attached. Most fabliaux, however, are comic and coarse—three of the roughest and most ribald are Chaucer's "The Miller's Tale," "The Reeve's Tale," and "The Summoner's Tale."

FIGURES OF SPEECH.   Figures of speech are devices that enrich language so that it conveys more than the literal meaning. Colorful effects have always been achieved by direct comparison or indirect suggestion, by finding a likeness in things that are unlike each other. The chief figures of speech are defined under

HYPERBOLE (page 208), METAPHOR (page 225), SIMILE (page 225), METONOMY (page 227), PERSONIFICATION (page 248), and SYNECDOCHE (page 293).

FOOT. A foot, so called because it used to be (and often still is) the practice to keep time to rhythms by tapping with the foot, is a group of syllables which constitutes a metrical unit. There are about thirty combinations of long and short, or accented and unaccented, syllables, most of them being found in Greek and Latin versification where the syllables are measured by quantity rather than by stress or accent. The most common feet (or measures) in English are five. They are the IAMB or IAMBUS (see page 209), the TROCHEE (see page 298), the ANAPEST (see page 150), the DACTYL (see page 188), and the SPONDEE (see page 291). Less common are the AMPHIBRACH (see page 149) and the practically unused AMPHIMACER (see page 149). All these are cited and cleverly illustrated by Coleridge in a set of definitions, "Metrical Feet."

> *Trochee trips from long to short.*
> *From long to long in solemn sort*
> *Slow Spondee stalks; strong foot! yet ill able*
> *Ever to come up with Dactyl trisyllable.*
> *Iambics march from short to long.*
> *With a leap and a bound the swift Anapests throng.*
> *One syllable long, with one short at each side,*
> *Amphibrachys haste with a stately stride.*
> *First and last being long, middle short, Amphimacer*
> *Strikes his thundering hoofs like a proud high-bred racer.*

FOUND POETRY. See the chapter "The Oddities of Poetry" on page 132.

FOUR-LINE STANZA. See QUATRAIN on page 255.

FREE VERSE. Free verse or, as it is sometimes called, using the French equivalent, *vers libre*, is based on a broad and usually irregular movement rather than any fixed form or precise meter. Its proponents claim that it is superior to formal verse on account of its reliance on the spontaneous rhythms of speech. Amy Lowell, a pioneer in and a champion of free verse, contended that the best name for the form in English should be "cadenced verse, for it is based upon cadence rather than upon actual meter. Metrical verse seeks its effects chiefly through definite lilt of meter and the magic and satisfaction of chime. 'Cadenced verse' gets its effects through subtle shades of changing rhythms and through a delicate sense of balance. . . . The unit of *vers libre* is not the foot, the number of syllables, the quantity, or the line. The unit is the *strophe*, the desire of verse to return upon itself."

The strophe in Greek drama was the full circle made by the chorus while walking about the altar, chanting, and returning upon itself. The length of time varied, but the movement was always one completed movement. Therefore, the word strophe, as applied to modern verse, indicates a complete round, or cadence. This application is anything but new. In *Convention and Revolt in Poetry* John Livingston Lowes points out that regular verse at its best is essentially strophic. "The great strophic rhythms of *Paradise Lost*, for example, are as free as the strophic rhythms of any poem in *vers libre* . . . What the modern unrhymed cadences abandon is the recurrent beat of the line."

Unrhymed cadences are at least as old as the Bible. Hebrew poetry is built on cadence and balance; the King James version of *Job, The Song of Songs*, and the *Psalms* is free verse at its most magnificent. After writing nothing but lyrics, Heinrich Heine indulged himself in the free verse liberty of *The North Sea* cycles. Matthew Arnold abandoned his usually strict meters for the irregular rhythms of *The Strayed Reveller*, W. E. Henley found new flexibilities in his unorthodox *Echoes* and *London Voluntaries*, Walt Whitman established hitherto undiscovered frontiers of American poetry in the resounding speech rhythms of *Leaves of Grass*.

FRENCH FORMS. The French forms are intricate and often elaborate forms of verse which were high fashion in fourteenth-century France. Among those who gave rich expression to earlier troubadour verse were Oton de Granson, Christine de Pisan, and

Eustache Deschamps, who alone wrote more than one thousand ballades and almost two hundred rondeaus. Chaucer wrote several ballades which are assumed to be the earliest English examples of the form, but it was not until the middle of the nineteenth century, when the difficult constructions were revived in England, that they became a vogue and were used mainly to turn a pert phrase or play with a pretty refrain.

In the twentieth century, however, the forms took on a new and vitalizing character. The artificial structures were strengthened by serious concerns and deep feeling. Among the more notable examples are Elizabeth Bishop's "Sestina" in *Questions of Travel*; Barbara Howes' trio of triolets, "Early Supper," in *Light and Dark*; and those remarkable villanelles "Time will say nothing but I told you so" in *The Collected Poetry of W. H. Auden*, "The Waking" in Roethke's *Collected Poems* and "Do not go gentle into that good night" in Dylan Thomas' *Collected Poems*.

The principal French forms are the BALLADE (see page 160), the RONDEAU (see page 268), the TRIOLET (see page 296), and the VILLANELLE (see page 301). Although each of these has different rules governing its formation, all have at least one rule in common: No word or syllable once used as a rhyme can be used again throughout the poem, not even if it is spelled differently. That rule has been violated from time to time, but the strict pattern demands that the rhyming syllable in every case must be a new sound.

G

GEORGIAN POETRY. Between 1912 and 1922 there appeared a series of anthologies which aimed to introduce younger and little known poets in the hope of creating a less apathetic audience for poetry. The first collection, assembled by Edward Marsh, included Lascelles Abercrombie, Rupert Brooke, W. H. Davies, Walter de la Mare, D. H. Lawrence, John Masefield, James Stephens, and others who had little in common except a love of the English countryside and a dislike of anything deeply distressing

(Lawrence was an exception here), and subsequent volumes widened the scope of Marsh's original group. But the gentle note continued to predominate as weaker poets were admitted and eventually "Georgian Poetry" became a disparaging term. Its neatness and oversimplifications were critically examined in a pejorative study, *The Georgian Revolt*, by Robert H. Ross in 1967.

GEORGIC. Originally a poem about country living. The outstanding work of this genre is Virgil's *Georgics*. Virgil's celebration of rustic life differed from most pastoral poetry by adding purpose to the poetry, the purpose being to incite the farmer to greater industry. William Cowper's *The Task* and James Thomson's *The Seasons* are English Georgics.

GLEEMAN. In the Middle Ages, wandering minstrels were often known as gleemen. They were so called because their songs were usually merry and spread joy.

GOLIARD POETRY. The word Goliard seems to have been derived from *gula*, glutton. In the Middle Ages Golias became a hero of the *Scholares Vagrantes*, the motley society of renegade clerics, student vagabonds, defrocked priests, jongleurs, and others who were the displaced bohemians of their day. Their irreverent songs celebrated the wicked pleasures of the flesh, the carnal delights of eating, wining, wooing, and wenching. John Addington Symonds issued a collection of translated medieval students' ballads, *Wine, Women, and Song*, in 1884. George F. Whicher published his translations, *The Goliard Poets*, in 1949. In 1937 Carl Orff set several of the Latin texts to lusty music in a "scenic secular cantata" entitled *Carmina Burana*.

GRAVEYARD VERSE. A term applied to the quaint and often crude rhymes found on tombstones in country cemeteries. The term also characterizes the poetry of certain eighteenth-century poets who, in contrast to the fastidious elegance of Dryden, Pope, and other classicists, cultivated thoughts that were melancholy and themes that dwelt gloomily upon mortality. Representative of the Graveyard School are Thomas Parnell's "Night-Piece on Death," Edward Young's "Night-Thoughts," Robert Blair's "The Grave," which Blake illustrated, and, most famous of them all, Thomas Gray's "Elegy Written in a Country Churchyard."

ℋ

HAIKU. A haiku—the word is sometimes spelled hokku—is a poem of seventeen syllables arranged in three lines. The first and third lines contain five syllables, the second line seven. In spite of its extreme brevity, a haiku not only makes a clear statement and presents a sharp picture but is also highly suggestive, rich in allusiveness and double meanings. Dating from the thirteenth century in Japan, the haiku has remained immensely popular there through the ages. In *An Introduction to Haiku* Harold Henderson explains that "most haiku are composed primarily for the pleasure of the author and his friends and not for publication." Nevertheless, he estimates that in Japan hundreds of thousands of new haiku, probably a million, are published every year. The seventeenth-century Basho is often named as the supreme master of haiku, chiefly for his Zen philosophy, but almost equal claims have been made for the more sophisticated Buson and the tender Issa.

The Imagists (see page 59) adapted and imitated the technique of the haiku and the slightly longer tanka (see page 294); Adelaide Crapsey approximated the form in her cinquains (see page 181).

Four examples follow. The first two are original concepts from *Seventeen Chirps* by Gerald Robert Vizenor; the third and fourth, respectively entitled "Silence" and "Peace," are adaptations from the Japanese by Louis Untermeyer.

> October sunflowers
> Rows of defeated soldiers
> Leaning in the frost.

* * *

Did the old gray stump
Remember its strength today
Raising the moon vines?

* * *

Dusk enters the streets;
The tongue of the temple bell
Has nothing to say.

* * *

On the mouth of a
Cannon half-buried in grass
A butterfly sleeps.

HENDECASYLLABIC. This word comes from a Greek word meaning "eleven-syllable." Hendecasyllabic verse is verse written in lines of eleven syllables. Catullus used it in some forty of his poems. Tennyson and Swinburne attempted it without conspicuous success.

HEPTAMETER. A line of verse with seven metrical feet sometimes called a septenary, a heptameter verse usually has fourteen syllables and is therefore often known as a fourteener. Southwell's short allegory, "The Burning Babe," is composed in rhymed heptameters.

My faultless breast the furnace is; the fuel, wounding thorns;
Love is the fire, and sighs the smoke; the ashes, shame and scorns;
The fuel justice layeth on, and mercy blows the coals;
The metal in this furnace wrought are men's defiléd souls . . .

HEROIC COUPLET. The "heroic line" (i.e. iambic pentameter) was indeed originally used for heroic or noble themes, but the term "heroic couplet" signifies nothing more than a pair of rhymed iambic pentameter (five-foot) lines. Usually the heroic couplet is end-stopped, each line having a logical pause at its end. Chaucer used the form with vigor and humor; Dryden gave it added firmness; Keats varied it with run-on flexibility; Pope surpassed all with a combination of swiftness and incisiveness. Apart from their poetic brilliance, Pope's "Moral Essays," his "Essay on Man" and "Essay on Criticism" are a glittering galaxy of heroic couplets. Here are four instances:

> *One science only will one genius fit;*
> *So vast is art, so narrow human wit.*
>
> *All are but parts of one stupendous whole,*
> *Whose body Nature is, and God the soul.*
>
> *Whoever thinks a faultless piece to see,*
> *Thinks what ne'er was, nor is, nor e'er shall be.*
>
> *A little learning is a dangerous thing;*
> *Drink deep, or taste not the Pierian spring.*

Frederic Prokosch's *The Missolonghi Manuscript* has Byron contend that Pope deliberately restricted himself in clinging slavishly to the heroic couplet. But Samuel Rogers, who refused the laureateship upon the death of William Wordsworth, disagrees. He not only defends but exalts the precise pairing of rhymed iambic pentameter lines. "The heroic couplet," says Rogers, "what a blessing it is! The grave becomes graceful, the tragic becomes ironical, the witty becomes incisive, the wise becomes supple. All passion grows civilized in the cool embrace of the heroic couplet . . . Nothing will ever take its place for spice and variety."

It has been argued that the only true "heroic line" is the hexameter in Greek and Latin, and that the English heroic couplet is heroic only when it is used on a heroic subject, as in Pope's renderings of Homer's *Odyssey* and *Iliad*; whereas Pope's couplets in his non-narrative *Essays* are not so much "heroic" as "dogmatic."

HEXAMETER. A six-foot line. The classical hexameter was strictly measured. Its first four feet might be either dactylic or spondaic, the fifth was dactylic, and the sixth was spondaic. English equivalents are not so exact; any line of six feet is considered a hexameter. Homer's *Iliad* and Virgil's *Aeneid* are prime examples of epics written in the classical measure. William Benjamin Smith and Walter Miller translated the *Iliad* in English dactylic hexameters beginning:

Sing, O Goddess, the wrath of Achilles, scion of Peleus,
Ruinous wrath, that afflicted with numberless woes the Achaeans.

HOMONYM. Homonyms are words which are pronounced the same but which are spelled differently and have entirely different meanings. "Sight-site-cite," "write-right-rite," "wait-weight," "lone-loan," "pain-pane," "mien-mean" are so-called homonymic rhymes. They are not "true rhymes," of course, for, though they are spelled differently, they have identical vowel and consonant sounds. Nevertheless, they sometimes qualify as eye-rhymes if not as ear-rhymes. In French verse, homonyms are not only permitted but qualify as perfect rhymes.

HYPERBOLE. An exaggeration employed to give force or intensity to a statement is a hyperbole. Everyday examples are "I've been waiting for hours and hours," "I'm dying of thirst," "She's as old as the hills." Marlowe's invocation of Helen is magnificent hyperbole:

> *Was this the face that launched a thousand ships,*
> *And burnt the topless towers of Ilium?*

Shakespeare emphasizes horror with hyperbole when he has Lady Macbeth cry "All the perfumes of Arabia will not sweeten this little hand!" Wit sharpens the cumulative hyperbole of Marvell's ironic adoration in "To His Coy Mistress" (see page 121), especially in the lines beginning:

> *My vegetable love should grow*
> *Vaster than empires, and more slow.*
> *An hundred years should go to praise*
> *Thine eyes, and on thy forehead gaze:*
> *Two hundred to adore each breast:*
> *But thirty thousand to the rest . . .*

J

IAMB. The iamb (or iambus) consists of an unaccented syllable followed by an accented one. It is sometimes called the skipping foot—the light touch of the toe followed by the firm planting of the sole—and is noted thus: ˘ /. Such words as "delight," "begin," "again," "hello," and "arise" are, in themselves, iambic feet. The iamb is the most natural and the most predominant foot in the language; it might be said that English verse is founded on it. The line of five iambic feet (iambic pentameter) is the keystone of English poetry. It is the basis of blank verse, but it is not used exclusively in blank verse, for the five-foot iambic line is also used in the heroic couplet, the sonnet, and a variety of other rhymed units. Here are two iambic couplets:

> Thĕ gráve's ă fíne ănd prívătĕ plácĕ
> But none, I think, do there embrace.

*   *   *

> And once, in some swamp forest, all of these,
> My child, were trees.

ICTUS. The word *ictus* is a Latin word meaning a stroke or a blow; in literary use it refers to the heavy stress placed on certain syllables. In classical poetry, that stress usually falls on the long syllable of the foot. The opposite of ictus is arsis, which is the unstressed syllable of a metrical foot.

IDYLL. A short lyrical poem celebrating the charm of country life. In its praise of tranquillity it is related to the PASTORAL (see page 246) and tends toward conventionalized and usually idealized descriptions of nature. The *Idylls* of Theocritus are the most famous of the classical models. Tennyson's *Idylls of the King* is a Victorian adaptation which substitutes a chivalric ideal for the pastoral element, and Browning's *Dramatic Idylls* justify

their title only because the idyll has no set form. The most idyllic
as well as one of the most famous of English lyrics is Christopher
Marlowe's "The Passionate Shepherd to his Love" which begins:

> *Come live with me and be my love,*
> *And we will all the pleasures prove*
> *That hills and valleys, dales and fields,*
> *Or woods or steepy mountain yields.*

IMAGISM. See the chapter "The Images of Poetry" on page
56.

INCREMENTAL REPETITION. In *The Popular Ballad*
Francis B. Gummere used this term to describe a device common
to ancient ballads: a phrase or a line repeated, not as a refrain but
as key words that with slight changes add to the suspense of the
poem. Incremental repetition is used to particularly good effect in
such ballads as "Edward, Edward," "Lord Randal," "Young
Hunting," and "Mary Hamilton." Two examples:

> *He's courted her in the kitchen,*
> *He's courted her in the hall,*
> *He's courted her in the lowest cellar,*
> *And that was worst of all.*

*   *   *

> *O fare thee well, my wedded wife,*
> *O fare you well, my children five,*
> *And fare thee well, my daughter Jane,*
> *That I love best that's born alive.*

INITIAL RHYME. There are two kinds of initial rhyme. The
first is ALLITERATION (see page 145). The second is a variation of internal rhyme where the rhymes occur at the very beginning instead
of the end of the lines. Sheer trickery, the device was practiced
by that prodigious craftsman, Thomas Hood, notably in "The
Double Knock," beginning:

Rat-tat *it went upon the lion's chin.*
"That hat! *I know it!" cried the joyful girl.*
"Summer's *it is. I know him by his knock;*
Comers *like him are welcome as the day!*
Lizzy! *go down and open the street-door;*
Busy *I am to anyone but him.*
Know him *you must—he has been here before;*
Show him *upstairs, and tell him I'm alone."*

INTERNAL RHYME is the repetition of rhyme-sounds within the line, or woven inside the structure of the poem itself. Variously employed for serious and comic effects, its permutations are endless. In its simplest form, it is, perhaps, best known by way of Coleridge's *The Rime of the Ancient Mariner:*

> *And through the* drifts *the snowy* clifts
> *Did send a dismal sheen:*
> *Nor shapes of* men *nor beasts we* ken—
> *The ice was all between.*

Kipling popularized internal rhyme in lines like:

The sin they do *by* two *and* two *they must* pay *for one* by
one—
And . . . the god that you *took* from a *printed* book *be with*
you, Tomlinson!

I. A. Richards used a more subtle variation in his "Waking Thoughts," whose first stanza runs:

> *Turn the mind then to that*
> *Which being won all's done.*
> *Stable it there*
> *To take that rest as best.*
> *Too many the mind's roads,*
> *Their throngs too beat, too fleet,*
> *Too unaware.*
> *Mind is its bonds*
> *And they'll not break.*
> > *How wake?*

An equally adroit use of internal rhyme occurs in T. S. Eliot's little-known minor poem, "Virginia":

> Red *river, red river,*
> Slow flow *heat is silence*
> *No* will *is* still *as a river*
> Still. Will *heat move*
> *Only through the mocking*-bird
> Heard *once?* Still hills
> Wait. Gates wait. *Purple trees,*
> *White trees,* wait, wait,
> Delay, decay. . . .

Poe's "The Raven" is built on a veritable concatenation of internal rhyming which Poe felt was a "novel effect, arising from an extension of the application of the principles of rhyme and al-literation."

Ah, distinctly I remember *it was in the bleak* December;
And each separate dying ember *wrought its ghost upon the floor.*
Eagerly I wished the morrow;—*vainly I had sought to* borrow
From my books surcease of sorrow—*sorrow for the lost Lenore*—
For the rare and radiant maiden *whom the angels name Lenore*—
                    Nameless here for evermore.

The ingenious Thomas Hood, already cited in connection with initial rhyme, surpassed all other verbal jugglers in "A Nocturnal Sketch" with its trio of rhymes at the end of every line:

> *Evening is come; and from the* dark park, hark,
> *The signal of the setting* sun: one gun!
> *And six is sounding from the* chime, prime time
> *To go and see the Drury* Lane Dane slain,
> *Or hear Othello's jealous* doubt spout out,
> *Or Macbeth raving at the* shade-made blade. . . .

A more complicated system of intertwining rhymes is in my own "Roast Leviathan" and "Boy and Tadpoles," where the rhymes occur in the middle, beginning, and end of the lines, making a tapestrylike pattern of sound. An excerpt from the latter:

A sea *of lapis* lazuli,
With casual *sunbeams* lacing gold
On light skiffs facing *the* west, *on* old
Bright cliffs, *the* crest *of some mythical* story,
On clouds that rest *on the promontory,*
On waves that reach white *arms to the* beach.
Sparkle *and* shimmer . . . glimmer *and* shine . . .
The sea grows dimmer, *and* darkens *like* wine.
Who is that swimmer, *untiring,* returning,
Churning *the* brine?
Is it Leander, that daring boy?
*Those skiffs, the sea*faring Ulysses'?
And this is—Troy?

For other variants see RHYME on page 260.

INVERSION. Although the word is sometimes used to denote an inverted foot (a turning-about by substituting a stressed for an unstressed syllable and vice versa), the word inversion usually refers to a reversal of the normal word order. It is often resorted to by poor versifiers and is generally regarded as a slipshod way of fitting words to the rhyme or rhythm. For example:

Out on the broad Atlantic rises an island fair,
Her beacons gleaming brightly, guarding the waters there.
Proudly on the horizon she rears her cliffs sublime,
Their rugged sides deep with scars dealt by the storms of time.

Nevertheless, inversion—the reversing of the natural order of certain words—has been used for the sake of emphasis in poems as profound as many of Emily Dickinson's. For example:

I never saw a moor,
I never saw the sea;
Yet know I how the heather looks,
And what a wave must be.

I never spoke with God,
Nor visited in heaven;
Yet certain am I of the spot
As if the chart were given.

Here the inversions—"Yet know I" and "Yet certain am I"—
make the reader feel the strength of Emily Dickinson's convictions
even more than if she had put the phrases in the usual way.

IRONY is a dissembling, an expression of double meaning, a statement in which the words suggest the opposite of their literal sense.
Shakespeare used irony to devastating effect when Ophelia reminds
Hamlet that his father has been dead "twice two months" and
Hamlet replies, "O heavens! Die two months ago and not forgotten yet! Then there's hope a great man's memory may outlive his
life half a year." Mark Antony's funeral oration is pointed in its
irony as he refers to Caesar's assassins:

> *For Brutus is an honorable man—*
> *So are they all, all honorable men.*

Shelley is sweepingly ironic when his supposed traveler en-
counters a shattered head, two trunkless stone legs sunk in desert
sand, and a pedestal inscribed with these words:

> *My name is Ozymandias, King of Kings:*
> *Look on my works, ye Mighty, and despair!*

Byron uses irony in a romantic rather than a tragic sense when,
in *Childe Harold's Pilgrimage* and *Don Juan*, he prepares well-
planned sentimental or sensual situations and then topples them
with mockery. In *Satires of Circumstance* Thomas Hardy builds
little masterpieces of irony with cool precision. An example:

> *"And now to God the Father," he ends,*
> *And his voice thrills up to the topmost tiles,*
> *Each listener chokes as he bows and bends,*
> *And emotion pervades the crowded aisles.*
> *Then the preacher glides to the vestry-door,*
> *And shuts it, and thinks he is seen no more.*
>
> *The door swings softly ajar meanwhile,*
> *And a pupil of his in the Bible class,*
> *Who adores him as one without gloss or guile,*

Sees her idol stand with a satisfied smile
And reenact at the vestry-glass
Each pulpit gesture in deft dumb-show
That had moved the congregation so.

𝒦

KENNING is an interesting, almost forgotten device employed in Anglo-Saxon poetry. A curious archaic figure of speech, kenning is part epithet and part metaphor. An object is not named but referred to by a word or phrase describing its quality or characteristic. The sea is "the whale's road" or "the swan's bath," a ship is "wave-floater" or "ocean steed" or "sea wood," a king is "ring-giver," man is "earth-dweller" and his body is "flesh-coat" or "bone-house," the sun is "sky candle" or "rapture of heaven," a harp is "glee-wood," and a wife is idealized as "weaver of peace." Metaphor, the heart of poetry, lives in such epithets, picture-names which are both quaint and appropriate.

𝓛

LAMENT. Poems expressing grief either for a person or for a disaster are, generally speaking, laments. David's *Lament for Jonathan* and Jeremiah's *Lamentations* are Biblical examples. The Anglo-Saxon *Deor's Lament* is a recital of sorrow, with a refrain of resignation: "That went by; this, too, will pass." The *ubi sunt* theme—where are the snows, or the gods, or the loves, of yesteryear?—so prevalent in ballades prompted formal and stylized laments. Shelley's dirge-like "A Lament" is a variant of the *ubi sunt* motif expressed in ten short lines.

O world! O life! O time!
On whose last steps I climb,
  Trembling at that where I had stood before;
When will return the glory of your prime?
No more—Oh, never more!

> *Out of the day and night*
> *A joy has taken flight;*
> *Fresh spring, and summer, and winter hoar,*
> *Move my faint heart with grief, but with delight*
> *No more—Oh, never more!*

LAY. A medieval term (formerly spelled *lai*) for a brief narrative or a short lyrical poem. Lyrical *lais* flourished in twelfth-century France, and romantic tales were rhymed in the folklore of Brittany. When the form was imported into England, it was known as the "Breton lay." Chaucer adapted it for his *Canterbury Tales* in "The Franklin's Tale," the prologue of which begins:

> *The old and noble Bretons in their days*
> *Turned their adventures into divers lays,*
> *Rhymed them according to their ancient tongue,*
> *Which lays, with their own instruments, were sung.*

Macaulay's *Lays of Ancient Rome* and Scott's *Lay of the Last Minstrel* are nineteenth-century narratives which extend the appellation to poems of some length.

LIGHT VERSE. Variously known as Vers de Société, Familiar Verse, and Occasional Verse, Light Verse is written chiefly to entertain. Its characteristic is a nimble ease, a light and even elegant touch—Locker-Lampson called his collection *Lyra Elegantiarum*. Carolyn Wells suggested Gentle Verse, saying that the term implied pieces composed by and for gentlefolk. There are, nevertheless, examples of light verse which are far from gentle, being barbed and rude; some of them, like Swift's savage couplets and Eliot's early poems, contain deeply satiric thrusts. However, most light verse lives up to its name. It is not only light but low-pitched, playful, tightly and sometimes trickily rhymed. It is, as Locker-Lampson wrote, a kind of verse "where sentiment never surges into passion and where humor never overflows into boisterous merriment." The theme may be trivial, but there is a crispness and often an unexpected twist to the lines, as in David McCord's "Epitaph to a Waiter":

> *By and by*
> *God caught his eye.*

And in McCord's tersely mocking "History of Education":

> *The decent docent doesn't doze:*
> *He teaches standing on his toes.*
> *His student dassn't doze—and does.*
> *And that's what teaching is and was.*

Other of McCord's contemporaries who blend light verse and serious thought are John Betjeman, A. P. Herbert, Phyllis McGinley, Morris Bishop, Richard Armour, William Jay Smith, Melville Cane and, preeminently, Ogden Nash, whose virtuosity has been said (by Nash) to fill a *Golden Trashery of Ogden Nashery*. This is the final verse of his "A Man Can Complain, Can't He" with its take-off of Dunbar's lamenting line *Timor mortis conturbat me* and the familiar phrase "Another day, another dollar."

> *Between the dotard and the brat*
> *My disaffection veers and varies;*
> *Sometimes I'm sick of clamoring youth,*
> *Sometimes of my contemporaries.*
> *I'm old too soon, yet young too long:*
> *Could Swift himself have planned it droller?*
> *Timor vitae conturbat me;*
> *Another day, another dolor.*

Paul Dehn is both grave and gay in *For Love and Money* which, he says, like Shelley's dome of many-colored glass, "is intended to stain the white radiance of the reader's leisure"; and his *Quake, Quake, Quake*, a set of mordant parodies on familiar poems, confronts man with the madness of his course toward self-destruction. Here is Dehn's twist on the famous "O western wind":

> *O nuclear wind, when wilt thou blow*
> *That the small rain down can rain?*
> *Christ, that my love were in my arms,*
> *And I had my arms again.*

The poetry of the past is accompanied and enriched by the dazzle of light verse. Pope's lighthearted *Rape of the Lock* is more rewarding, less weighty and more witty than his *Moral Essays*. Literature would be dull indeed without the scintillating contributions of Robert Herrick, Matthew Prior, Thomas Moore, Thomas Hood, W. S. Landor, W. M. Praed, Edward Lear, Lewis Carroll, Frederick Locker-Lampson, C. S. Calverley, Austin Dobson, G. K. Chesterton, Hilaire Belloc, W. S. Gilbert and George Gordon Byron—the last oddly paired couple being two superb satirists whose iron fists were concealed in the finest of velvet gloves.

No one has summed up the charm of light verse more neatly than Austin Dobson in "Jocosa Lyra," a dexterous tribute enhanced by the supple feminine rhymes:

> *In our hearts is the Great One of Avon*
> > *Engraven,*
> *And we climb the cold summits once built on*
> > *By Milton,*
>
> *But at times not the air that is rarest*
> > *Is fairest,*
> *And we long in the valley to follow*
> > *Apollo.*
>
> *Then we drop from the heights atmospheric*
> > *To Herrick,*
> *Or we pour the Greek honey, grown blander,*
> > *Of Landor;*
>
> *Or our cosiest nook in the shade is*
> > *Where Praed is,*
> *Or we toss the light bells of the mocker*
> > *With Locker.*
>
> *Oh, the song where not one of the Graces*
> > *Tight-laces—*
> *Where we woo the sweet Muses not starchly,*
> > *But archly—*
>
> *Where the verse, like a piper a-Maying,*
> > *Comes playing,*
> *And the rhyme is as gay as a dancer*
> > *In answer.*

> *It will last till men weary of pleasure*
> > *In measure.*
> *It will last till men weary of laughter . . .*
> > > *And after!*

In Dobson's time the line between prose and verse was strictly drawn, but, as "Jocosa Lyra" implies, the line between light verse and serious poetry was already thinning. Today light verse and serious poetry have become almost inseparable. The fusion is apparent not only in the Sweeney poems, "The Hippopotamus," "Mr. Eliot's Sunday Morning Service," and other early Eliot acerbities, but in the mixture of sly and solemn in the lines of Robert Frost, E. E. Cummings, W. H. Auden, William Empson, and a generation of their followers.

For other forms of LIGHT VERSE see CLERIHEW (page 182), DOUBLE DACTYLS (page 189), LIMERICK (below), and SYMMETRICS (page 292).

LIMERICK. The career of the limerick has been strange and scandalous. Beginning as an innocent little five-line stanza, it has become the only kind of poetry exchanged at cocktail parties, unprintable though not unspeakable. The origin of the name is uncertain; it has been asserted, without evidence, that it emanates from an Irish song, each verse of which ends "We'll all come up, come up, to Limerick." However, long before the limerick grew into censurable metamorphoses, it appeared in books for children. Its first appearance was among nursery rhymes as exemplary as:

> *There was an old lady of Leeds*
> *Who spent all her time in good deeds.*
> > *She worked for the poor*
> > *Till her fingers were sore,*
> *This pious old lady of Leeds.*

The simplicity of the form may account for its subsequent popularity. The five lines are always built on no more (and no less) than two rhymes—the rhymes being expressed by the symbol *a-a-b-b-a*—with the third and fourth lines one foot shorter than

the other three. One of Mother Goose's jingles is a perfect limerick
and probably one of the oldest.

> *Hickory, dickory, dock,*
> *The mouse ran up the clock.*
> *The clock struck one—*
> *The mouse ran down—*
> *Hickory, dickory, dock.*

The formula caught the fancy of Edward Lear. He composed
more than two hundred limericks because, as he said, they lend
themselves to "limitless varieties for rhymes." In spite of the "limitless varieties" Lear took little advantage of the possibilities. Part
of the charm of the limerick as we know it today is the surprise of
the last line, the sudden swoop and unexpected twist of the climax.
Lear ignored this. He rarely introduced a new rhyme as a conclusion; practically all Lear's last lines are repetitions or slight variations of the first line. For example:

> *There was an Old Man on the Border,*
> *Who lived in the utmost disorder.*
> *He danced with the Cat*
> *And made tea in his Hat,*
> *Which vexed all the folks on the Border.*

Toward the end of the nineteenth century the limerick was
accepted as an established poetic form. Versifiers and even such
famous poets as Rudyard Kipling and Robert Louis Stevenson tried
their hands at variations on the model. They found the repetition
of the same word in the first and last lines monotonous and un-
necessary. They came up with unpredictable rhymes and astonishing, sometimes reprehensible, non sequiturs. Even novelists like
John Galsworthy and Arnold Bennett vied to extend the range
and tone of the limerick. The next two limericks illustrate the
change in technique. The first, by Kipling, follows the Lear formula of repeating the first line with but slight variation at the conclusion; the second, by Galsworthy, avoids the repetition.

> *A very small boy in Quebec*
> *Stood buried in snow to his neck.*
>   *When asked, "Are you friz?"*
>   *He said, "Yes, I is.*
>   *But we don't call this cold in Quebec."*

*   *   *

> *An angry young husband named Bickett*
> *Said, "Turn yourself round and I'll kick it.*
>   *You have painted my wife*
>   *In the nude to the life.*
>   *Do you think, Mr. Greene, that was cricket?"*

Lear had written a limerick about a man who was, in both senses, bored by a bee. It ran:

> *There was an old man in a tree,*
> *Who was horrible bored by a bee.*
>   *When they said, "Does it buzz?"*
>   *He replied, "Yes, it does!*
>   *It's a horrible brute of a bee!"*

Burlesquing Lear's lines, W. S. Gilbert, who rollicked in rhyme and outrhymed any poet of his day, wrote a limerick which had no rhyme at all:

> *There was an old man of St. Bees,*
> *Who was stung in the arm by a wasp.*
>   *When asked, "Does it hurt?"*
>   *He replied, "No, it doesn't.*
>   *I'm so glad it wasn't a hornet."*

Oliver Wendell Holmes could never resist a pun—at the beginning of his medical career he said he would be grateful for small fevers. His punning limerick is one of the most often quoted.

> *The Reverend Henry Ward Beecher*
> *Called a hen a most elegant creature.*

The hen, pleased with that,
Laid an egg in his hat.
And thus did the hen reward Beecher.

There are also the puzzlers—those that take advantage of pecu-
liarities in spelling and pronunciation—as well as the tongue-
twisters. Here are three anonymous examples:

A bright little girl in St. Thomas
Discovered a suit of pajhomas.
Said the maiden, "Well, well!
Whose they are I can't tell.
But I'm sure that those garments St. Mhomas."

The principal food of the Siouxs
Is Indian maize, which they briouxs.
And then, failing that,
They'll eat any old hat,
A glove, or a pair of old shiouxs.

There was a young fellow named Tate,
Who dined with his girl at 8:08.
But I'd hate to relate
What that fellow named Tate
And his tête-à-tête ate at 8:08!

LYRIC.   As the name suggests, a lyric was a song sung to the
accompaniment of a lyre. Shaped to no particular form, the lyric
outgrew that original meaning and referred to any short, metrical,
and usually rhymed poem—"usually," for there are blank verse
and even free verse lyrics. (See page 172.) Flexible and varied, the
lyric's chief characteristic is its singing tone. Musical and emotional, it sometimes illumines a narrative, as in the *Lyrical Ballads*
of Wordsworth and Coleridge. In its purest form the lyric achieves
folk-like simplicity in the songs of Burns and attains magnificence
in the lyrics of Blake.

The term also refers to words written for popular songs—Ira
Gershwin, for example, wrote "lyrics" to his brother George's
music.

M

MADRIGAL. A short poem, usually set to music, the madrigal was popular in Italy as early as the fourteenth century—Petrarch composed madrigals as well as sonnets. Its vogue spread eventually to England, where the Elizabethans, like the Italians and the Dutch, elaborated it into contrapuntal songs for mixed voices. Part-singing was a passion in the late sixteenth century; unaccompanied madrigals were the delight of the court. The Elizabethans were natural musicians; if a man could not invent a three-part madrigal, at least he was expected to lend his voice to one. Thomas Morley issued several volumes of madrigals, including some set to Shakespeare's words. More than two hundred years later, Gilbert and Sullivan introduced mock madrigals into their light operas, notably in *The Mikado*, when four of the principals tearfully join in a pre-nuptial song.

> *Brightly dawns our wedding day.*
> *Joyous hour, we give thee greeting!*
> *Whither, whither, art thou fleeting?*
> *Fickle moment, prithee stay!*
> *What though mortal joys be hollow,*
> *Pleasures come if sorrows follow,*
> *Though the tocsin sound ere long,*
> *Ding dong! Ding dong!*
> *Yet until the shadows fall*
> *Over one and over all,*
> *Sing a merry madrigal—*
> *A madrigal!*

The most comprehensive collection of its kind, one which includes the repertory of verse set by the lutenist composers, is *English Madrigal Verse, 1588–1632* by E. H. Fellows, revised and enlarged in 1968 and published by Oxford University Press.

MASQUE. One of the most favored English entertainments during the sixteenth and seventeenth centuries was the masque. Masques were based on mythical or allegorical subjects and called for a combination of all the theatrical devices: music, drama, dance, lavish costumes, and magnificent scenery. The Elizabethan poets invested the masque with glamor, but their poetry was subordinated to the spectacle. The best masques were created by Ben Jonson abetted by Inigo Jones, who originated such remarkable stage effects as moving clouds, thunderstorms, erupting volcanoes, and gods descending from the skies. Masques enlivened several of Shakespeare's plays, briefly in *Romeo and Juliet*, elaborately in *The Tempest* and *The Winter's Tale*. One of Shakespeare's imitators, Francis Beaumont, pleased the nobility with his *Masque of the Inner Temple*, from which lyrics continue to be quoted. Milton's *Arcades* and *Comus* are masques which played variations on Milton's favorite theme: the struggle between Good and Evil.

Stripped of its trappings, the masque-form has survived the centuries. It attained elevation in Shelley's impassioned *The Masque of Anarchy* and in Robert Frost's ruminative, riddling *A Masque of Reason* and *A Masque of Mercy*.

MEASURE. Measure is another name for foot. The measure, or foot, corresponds to a beat in a bar of music; it "measures" the syllables or accents in a line of verse.

MEIOSIS. From the Greek, meaning "less" or "to make smaller," meiosis is a term denoting understatement, frequently ironic. Housman uses meiosis dramatically in *A Shropshire Lad* when the soliloquy of a murderer ends:

> *Long for me the rick will wait,*
> *And long will wait the fold,*
> *And long will stand the empty plate,*
> *And dinner will be cold.*

One of Siegfried Sassoon's anti-war poems begins: "Does it matter?—losing your leg? . . . Does it matter?—losing your sight?" and ends with bitter meiosis:

> *Do they matter?—those dreams from the pit?* . . .
> *You can drink and forget and be glad,*
> *And people won't say that you're mad;*
> *For they'll know that you've fought for your country,*
> *And no one will worry a bit.*

METAPHOR. Aristotle declared that what a poet needs beyond everything else is a command of metaphor, the ability to see similarity in things dissimilar. Metaphor and its close relation, simile, are poetry's most constant properties; theirs is the power of illuminating and establishing a kinship between objects wholly unlike each other. "Poetry begins in metaphor, in trivial metaphors," said Robert Frost, "and goes on to the profoundest thinking that we have."

Both metaphor and simile are devices of comparison. When the comparison is stated it is a simile. The statement is made by the use of "as" or "like." Christina Rossetti's "My heart is *like* a singing bird," John Gould Fletcher's comparison of Lincoln "*like* a gaunt, scraggy pine," and Phyllis McGinley's picture of pigeons "pompous *as* bankers" are similes. When the comparison, omitting "as" and "like," is implied, we have a metaphor. When Macbeth says "Life's but a walking shadow" he is uttering a metaphor. When Herrick tells his mistress "You are a tulip seen today," his metaphor is more arresting than Burns's simile, "O my love is *like* a red, red rose." A metaphor is usually more effective than a simile because it makes an instant comparison and an imaginative fusion of two objects without the use of explanatory prepositions. Christina Rossetti's pretty simile about her heart being *like* a singing bird is surpassed by Drayton's metaphor about the same organ: "My heart the anvil where my thoughts do beat."

Mixed metaphors are frowned on because they create a confusion instead of a fusion of effects, like the "Irish bull" about the man who, whenever he opened his mouth, put his foot in it.

In poetry mixed metaphors are often as provocative as Hart Crane's (see page 62) or as powerful as Milton's castigation of "pastors" in "Lycidas" as "Blind mouths! that scarce themselves know how to hold/A sheephook. . . ."

In a lecture entitled "Metaphor as Pure Adventure," given at the Library of Congress (December 4, 1967), James Dickey said: "The making of poetic metaphors is an intrinsic process, a continual process of transfiguring reality. . . . I would also say that metaphor permits one to experience at the same time the perpetual and the instantaneous, the paired objects both in the world they came from and in their linguistic relationship in the poem. . . . It is in the language of metaphor charged with specific emotions that the poet makes his statement and creates, out of the world as it is, the world that he must (because he is what he is) bring to birth."

METER. From the Greek *metron*, "measure," the word meter denotes measured rhythm, a regular succession of beats arranged according to a particular pattern. Greek and Latin poetry were governed by "quantity" which divided syllables into long or short, the length and shortness depending usually upon the length of the vowel, although some syllables might be considered either long or short depending on their position in the line. English poetry, however, is based on ACCENT (see page 141), and "meter" in English refers to the pattern of accented and unaccented syllables. However, the syllable count should not be too precise; the charm of irregularity saves the strictest meters from monotony. Robert Frost put it quizzically; meter, he said, is what allows the poet to move easily in harness. I. A. Richards wrote that "verse in which we constantly get exactly what we are ready for and no more is merely toilsome and tedious." C. Day Lewis confirms the appeal of inexactness: "One of the things that please the ear when we listen to a poem being read aloud is the contrast, the sort of friendly wrestle between its meter and its speech-rhythm. The meter is like a tide pulsing regularly underneath, the speech-rhythm is a less regular movement, like ripples on the surface." Meter, in short, has a decidedly regular accent while rhythm is variable. (See page 265 for RHYTHM.)

"You can write a grammar of the meter," say W. K. Wimsatt and Monroe C. Beardsley in *The Concept of Meter: An Exercise in Abstraction*, "but you cannot write a grammar of the meter's interaction with the sense, any more than you can write a grammar of the arrangement of metaphors." The pulse of meter makes the listener receptive to what it conveys. Coleridge declared that meter tends "to increase the vivacity and susceptibility both of the general feeling and of the attention." The poet's task is to choose the meter which is most fitting to the matter and which will "increase the vivacity and susceptibility" of the reader.

The name of a meter is determined by the number of feet in the line. The terms are: Monometer (one foot), Dimeter (two feet), Trimeter (three feet), Tetrameter (four feet), Pentameter (five feet), Hexameter (six feet), Heptameter (seven feet), Octameter (eight feet).

It should be added that metrical feet were once called "numbers." In his "Epistle to Dr. Arbuthnot" Pope wrote:

> *As yet a child, nor yet a fool to fame,*
> *I lisped in numbers, for the numbers came.*

METONOMY. Metonomy and synecdoche are related to metaphor and simile, being forms of comparison. Metonomy (literally "name change") is the substitution of one thing to represent another, a kind of transposed epithet. We say "the kettle is boiling" when we mean that the water in the kettle is boiling. Byron describes the night before the battle of Waterloo by saying:

> *And Belgium's capital had gathered then*
> *Her beauty and her chivalry . . .*

By "beauty" and "chivalry" he implies lovely women and gallant men. James Shirley begins a seventeenth-century dirge with these lines:

> *The glories of our blood and state*
>   *Are shadows, not substantial things;*
> *There is no armor against fate;*
>   *Death lays his icy hand on kings.*

Sceptre and Crown
Must tumble down,
And in the dust be equal made
With the poor crooked scythe and spade.

By metonomy Shirley here indicates that—just as Shakespeare's "Golden lads and girls all must/Like chimney-sweepers, come to dust"—so kings ("Sceptre and Crown") and farmers ("scythe and spade") are equal in death. (See SYNECDOCHE on page 293.)

MONOMETER. Shortest of all measures, monometer ("single foot") is so difficult to sustain throughout a poem that it is rarely used. However, Robert Herrick's "Upon His Departure Hence" transcends its iambic brevity in staccato but graceful three-line stanzas.

Thus I
Pass by
And die:

As one
Unknown
And gone

I'm made
A shade
And laid

I' th'grave:
There have
My cave,

Where tell
I dwell.
Farewell.

MUSE. In Greek mythology the nine daughters of Zeus and Mnemosyne (Memory) were in charge of the arts and sciences. They were called the Muses, and four of them were responsible for the various types of poetry: Erato, for love poetry; Euterpe, for lyric poetry; Calliope, for epic poetry; Polyhymnia, for sacred poetry. The ancients made appeals to the individual Muses for

particular purposes. Later, poets invoked a more abstract figure
to give them inspiration. Milton began *Paradise Lost* with this
entreaty:

> *Of man's first disobedience, and the fruit*
> *Of that forbidden tree, whose mortal taste*
> *Brought death into the world and all our woe,*
> *With loss of Eden, till one greater Man*
> *Restore us, and regain the blissful seat,*
> *Sing, Heavenly Muse . . .*

Shakespeare invoked the aid of the divinity at the very beginning of *King Henry* V:

> *O! for a Muse of fire, that would ascend*
> *The brightest heaven of invention . . .*

Pausing amidst such light lyrics as "Go, lovely rose" and "That
which her slender waist confined," Edmund Waller indited a
heavy panegyric to the Lord Protector. In it he remarked:

> *Illustrious acts high raptures do infuse,*
> *And every conqueror creates a Muse.*

Sidney, having trouble composing a love poem to Stella, "studying inventions fine" and "turning others' leaves to see if thence
would flow/Some fresh and fruitful showers," was rebuked by the
goddess.

> *Biting my truant pen, beating myself for spite—*
> *"Fool!" said my Muse to me, "look in thy heart and write."*

The last line is one which might serve as a motto for any writer.

N

NARRATIVE VERSE. Narrative verse is poetry which tells a
story. It may contain lyrical or philosophical passages, but its chief
purpose is to relate a tale. Since the time of the gleemen, the

troubadours, and the balladists, poets have found that a story is enhanced by the addition of rhythm and, more often than not, of alliteration and rhyme. Narrative poetry requires no single particular form. It ranges from Homer's epic *Odyssey* and *Iliad* through Chaucer's *The Canterbury Tales,* Scott's *Marmion,* Coleridge's *The Rime of the Ancient Mariner,* Keats's *The Eve of St. Agnes,* and Browning's *Dramatis Personae* to such modern transcripts of realism as Masefield's *The Everlasting Mercy* and Robert Frost's *North of Boston,* and includes as well that favorite of romantic youth, Noyes's "The Highwayman."

NUMBERS.   Another name for measure or metrical foot. (See last paragraph on METER on page 227.) Thomas Dekker laughs at the fools who "add to golden numbers, golden numbers." Longfellow moralizes at the start of "A Psalm of Life":

> *Tell me not in mournful numbers,*
> *"Life is but an empty dream!"*
> *For the soul is dead that slumbers,*
> *And things are not what they seem.*

Pope extolls the power of numbers with not displeasing inversions:

> *Hark! the numbers soft and clear*
> *Gently steal upon the ear;*
> *Now louder and yet louder rise,*
> *And fill with spreading sounds the skies.*

O

OCCASIONAL POETRY.   In its more limited sense, Occasional Poetry is another name for Light Verse or *Vers de Société.* In general, however, the term is applied to poems celebrating a birthday, a marriage, a victory, the founding of an institution, or any other (presumably notable) occasion. According to tradition, England's poet laureate is expected to hail the occasion of the queen's birthday with a commemorative poem. But Cecil Day

Lewis, who was appointed poet laureate in 1968, said he did not expect to confine his poetry to the royal family. "If he can, a poet laureate should, from time to time, write a public poem, one that would be of interest to everyone, a poem based on a national triumph or tragedy."

Among tragedy-based poems which have outlasted their occasions are Milton's "On the Late Massacre in Piedmont," Hopkins' "The Wreck of the Deutschland," Hardy's "The Convergence of the Twain," Yeats's "Easter 1916," and Auden's "In Memory of W. B. Yeats."

OCTAVE. In its particular application, the octave is the eight-line unit of the sonnet as contrasted with the six-line unit which follows. (See SONNET on page 285.)

In a general sense, an octave is any eight-line stanza. Its variety of structure is almost endless. It is often composed of a pair of quatrains—*a-b-a-b-c-d-c-d*—as in Frost's "The Trial by Existence."

> *Even the bravest that are slain*
>   *Shall not dissemble their surprise*
> *On waking to find valor reign,*
>   *Even as on earth, in paradise;*
> *And where they sought without the sword*
>   *Wide fields of asphodel fore'er,*
> *To find that the utmost reward*
>   *Of daring should be still to dare.*

Another popular form of the octave has a rhyme-scheme of two tercets linked by a pair of rhymes—*a-a-a-b-c-c-c-b*—as in Drayton's "Agincourt":

> *Fair stood the wind for France*
> *When we our sails advance,*
> *Nor now to prove our chance*
>   *Longer will tarry;*
> *But, putting to the main,*
> *At Caux, the mouth of Seine,*
> *With all his martial train*
>   *Landed King Harry.*

The ever-dexterous Swinburne gave the form a languorous music by mixing feminine and masculine rhymes in the formula of a quatrain, a tercet, and an added line which repeats the rhyme of the two *b*'s in the quatrain—*a-b-a-b-c-c-c-b*—as in "The Garden of Proserpine," and a variant—*a-b-a-b-c-c-a-b*—as in the chorus from "Atalanta in Calydon," which follows:

> *Come with bows bent and with emptying of quivers,*
> * Maiden most perfect, lady of light,*
> *With a noise of winds and many rivers,*
> * With a clamor of waters, and with might;*
> *Bind on thy sandals, O thou most fleet,*
> *Over the splendor and speed of thy feet;*
> *For the faint east quickens, the wan west shivers,*
> * Round the feet of the day and the feet of the night.*

A special form of the octave is known as *ottava rima*, so called because it was originally used by Boccaccio, Tasso, and other Italian poets. Its form is *a-b-a-b-a-b-c-c*. Byron employed it amusingly in "Don Juan," mockingly in "The Vision of Judgment":

> *The angels were all singing out of tune,*
> * And hoarse with having little else to do*
> *Excepting to wind up the sun and moon,*
> * Or curb a runaway young star or two,*
> *Or wild colt of a comet, which too soon*
> * Broke out of bonds o'er the ethereal blue,*
> *Splitting some planet with its powerful tail,*
> *As boats are sometimes by a wanton whale.*

Yeats made use of *ottava rima* with psychological penetration in "Among School Children" and "Sailing to Byzantium." Keats gave it sensuousness in "Isabella, or the Pot of Basil," founded on a story from Boccaccio. Here is a typical stanza:

> *Parting they seemed to tread upon the air,*
> * Twin roses by the zephyr blown apart,*
> *Only to meet again more close, and share*
> * The inward fragrance of each other's heart.*

> *She, to her chamber gone, a ditty fair*
> *Sang, of delicious love and honeyed dart;*
> *He, with light steps went up a western hill*
> *And bade the sun farewell, and joyed his fill.*

OCTOMETER: Verses made of eight metrical feet are comparatively rare. In spite of their unwieldy length Poe favored them. The eighteen stanzas of "The Raven" are built on octometer.

> *Open here I flung the shutter, when, with many a flirt and flutter,*
> *In there stepped a stately Raven of the saintly days of yore;*
> *Not the least obeisance made he; not a minute stopped or stayed*
> *   he;*
> *But, with mien of lord or lady, perched above my chamber door—*
> *Perched upon a bust of Pallas just above my chamber door—*
> *   Perched, and sat, and nothing more.*

In "A Blot in the 'Scutcheon," Browning accentuated the tragedy with a lyric in perfect trochaic octometer. It begins:

> *There's a woman like a dewdrop, she's so purer than the purest;*
> *And her noble heart's the noblest, yes, and her sure faith's the*
> *   surest.*

ODE. In Greece the ode grew out of a choric song, stately and solemn. Built on a set of themes and responses, the ode was sung by divided choirs; half the singers intoned the strophe (turn), the other half replied with the antistrophe (counter-turn), while both united in the epode (after-song). Because of their ingenuity Pindar's odes attained the greatest fame and served as models for the early English expressions of the form. Abraham Cowley was the first to pattern his odes after what he believed to be the Pindaric style, but Cowley failed to comprehend that, although Pindar varied the arrangement of verses, each verse was strictly patterned. Cowley's inconsistencies were remedied by Thomas Gray who, in "The Progress of Poesy," restored the form.

The odes of Horace, in which each stanza followed the same metrical pattern, served as another and better model. The best-known example of this type is Andrew Marvell's "An Horatian Ode upon Cromwell's Return from Ireland."

Most English odes are irregular. Differing with the times and the temperament of the poet, the odes of Dryden, Coleridge, Wordsworth, Shelley, and Keats are so free as to assume the character of improvisations—some of them are actually extended and sustained lyrics. Nevertheless, they preserve the original spirit of exaltation, the reaching toward sublimity.

Among the greatest odes of the past are Milton's "On the Morning of Christ's Nativity," Gray's "Ode on a Distant Prospect of Eton College," Collins' "Ode to Evening," Wordsworth's "Intimations of Immortality," Shelley's "Ode to the West Wind" and his "Ode to Liberty," and Keats's rapturous odes, each of which dictates its own pattern and presents the stanzaic ode at its highest. (See page 49 in the chapter "The Sound and Sense of Poetry.")

Although the ode is met less frequently in modern poetry, the traditional notes of elevation and intensity are heard in William Vaughn Moody's "An Ode in Time of Hesitation," Stephen Vincent Benét's "Ode to Walt Whitman," Elinor Wylie's "Hymn to Earth," Edna St. Vincent Millay's "Ode to Silence," Allen Tate's "Ode to the Confederate Dead," and W. H. Auden's "Ode: To my Pupils."

ONOMATOPOEIA.   The making or forming of a word by imitating a sound is the simplest and probably the oldest of language devices—the Greek word literally means "to make a name." Some of the most common words not only imitate the sound they represent but also suggest the sense and action of the word. The child knows that "bow-wow" is a dog, "ding-dong" is a bell, "buzz-buzz" is a fly, "choo-choo" is a locomotive, "moo-moo" is a cow. The writer relies on the device when he uses such onomatopoetic words as "bubble," "twitter," "crunch," "crackle," "clang," "crash," "smash," "squeak," "creak," "hiss," "fizz," "honk," "howl," "hush," "mew," and "mumble."

Perhaps the most quoted example of the poetic use of onomatopoeia is Tennyson's alliterative:

> *The moan of doves in immemorial elms*
> *And murmuring of innumerable bees.*

Tennyson himself preferred the line which suggested the liquid tones of a singing bird:

> *The mellow ouzel fluting in the elm.*

And W. S. Gilbert exulted in the comic effect of:

> *As he squirmed and struggled*
> *and gurgled and guggled,*
> *I drew my snickersnee!*

Vachel Lindsay delighted to play with words as sounds. His "The Kallyope Yell" attempted to express the boisterousness of the United States in the strident tones of the street calliope:

> *Music of the mob am I,*
> *Circus day's tremendous cry:—*
> *I am the Kallyope, Kallyope, Kallyope!*
> *Tooting hope, tooting hope, tooting hope;*
> *Hoot toot, hoot toot, hoot toot, hoot toot!*
> *Willy willy willy wah Hoo!*

OTTAVA RIMA. See under OCTAVE on page 232.

OXYMORON. An apparent contradiction in terms, a surprising paradox, the oxymoron is frequently encountered in daily speech. Examples: "artful artlessness," "thundering silence," "enjoying one's grief," "a raging calm," "sweet discords," "an honest villain," "conspicuous by his absence." The Greek word means "pointedly foolish," and Shakespeare not only played with the device in *The Rape of Lucrece* ("O modest wanton, wanton modesty") but forced oxymoron to the limit when Romeo mockingly described his feeling for Rosalind:

> *. . . O brawling love! O loving hate!*
> *O anything of nothing first create!*

O heavy lightness! serious vanity!
Misshapen chaos of well-seeming forms!
Feather of lead, bright smoke, cold fire, sick health!
Still-waking sleep, that is not what it is!
This love feel I, that feel no love in this!

P

PAEAN. A paean is a song of joy or thanksgiving. Originally it was a hymn of praise to the gods, particularly to Apollo, who was identified with Paian (Healer), the gods' physician.

PAEON. In Greek and Latin prosody, the paeon is a metrical foot of one long and three short syllables. The syllables are combined in various arrangements.

PALINODE. As the name suggests, a palinode is a kind of ode, but (*palin* meaning "again") one which is a correction, a retraction. Palinodes were fairly common in love poetry after Ovid, whose reasonable *Remedia Amoris* was a recantation of his unreservedly erotic *Ars Amatoria*. The classic example of an English palinode is Chaucer's *Legend of Good Women* written to offset his portrait of the faithless Criseyde in *Troilus and Criseyde*.

PANEGYRIC. A speech or poem of superlative praise. It is usually rhetorical and often excessive. Wordsworth's "Ode to Duty" is a panegyric glorifying the "stern Daughter of the Voice of God." The laudations are often so extreme that they lend themselves to burlesque. James "Byron" Elmore's "Ode to Sassafras" is not only a medicinal lyric but also a fine instance of the panegyric at its most laughable.

> *In the spring of the year*
> *When the blood is too thick,*
> *There's nothing so good*
> *As a sassafras stick.*

It *regulates the liver,*
    It *livens up the heart,*
And *to the whole system*
    New *life doth impart.*

O *sassafras! Sweet sassafras!*
    Thou *art the stuff for me!*
And *in the spring I love to sing,*
    Sweet *sassafras, of thee!*

PANTOUM. Although the pantoum is found in most collections of French forms, it is not at all a French form. It is a form of Malay origin and was first popularized by Victor Hugo in his *Orientales.* A poem of indeterminate length, it is composed of four-line stanzas, in which each verse repeats two lines from the preceding verse. To be precise, the second and fourth lines of each stanza become the first and third lines of the succeeding stanza, and so on until the end. At the close, the second and fourth lines of the last stanza are the same as the first and third lines of the opening stanza, but in reverse order.

A modern example of a pantoum by the author employs the reiterated lines in an attempt to reproduce the chatter of a group of new-rich at an opera.

"Looks like a big night to-night."
    "Here is the rest of the ghetto."
"There she is—there, to the right."
    "Heavens! I've lost my libretto!"

"Here is the rest of the ghetto."
    "How did they ever get in?"
"Heavens! I've lost my libretto!"
    "Hush! It's about to begin!"

"How did they ever get in?"
    "Why do they clap for the leader?"
"Hush! It's about to begin!"
    "Who sings the part of Aida?"

"Why do they clap for the leader?"
"Reginald, can't you keep still?"
"Who sings the part of Aida?"
   "I know that I'm going to be ill."

"Reginald, can't you keep still?"
   "I doubt if they're real; they don't glisten."
"I know that I'm going to be ill."
   "—She said, then I said, 'Now, listen—!' "

"I doubt if they're real; they don't glisten."
   "That Rossiter's girl's a disgrace!"
"—She said, then I said, 'Now listen—!' "
   "—and just a suggestion of lace."

"That Rossiter's girl's a disgrace,"
   "Oh, no, Wagner never is boring!"
"—and just a suggestion of lace."
   "Fred, will you kindly stop snoring."

"Oh, no, Wagner never is boring!"
   "There she is—there, to the right."
"Fred, will you kindly stop snoring."
   "Looks like a big night to-night!"

PARADOX. Webster defines paradox as something unbelievable, self-contradictory, absurd, yet, somehow, true. Erasmus' sixteenth-century *Praise of Folly* is a series of paradoxical arguments. In their juggling of balance and antithesis, Dryden and Pope created a poetry of paradox, which Donne and Marvell had already sounded with ironic effectiveness.

The term is amplified dramatically in Michael Drayton's sonnet "The Paradox" which is not only a paradoxical triumph but also a skillful assembly of oxymorons. (See page 235.)

> *When first I ended, then I first began;*
> *Then more I travelled further from my rest.*
> *Where most I lost, there most of all I won;*
> *Pinèd with hunger, rising from a feast.*
> *Methinks I fly, yet want I legs to go;*
> *Wise in conceit, in act a very sot;*

> *Ravished with joy amidst a hell of woe;*
> *What most I seem, that surest I am not.*
>
> *I build my hopes a world above the sky,*
> *Yet with the mole I creep into the earth;*
> *In plenty, I am starved with penury,*
> *And yet I surfeit in the greatest dearth.*
> *I have, I want; despair, and yet desire;*
> *Burned in a sea of ice, and drowned amidst a fire.*

In a lighter vein W. S. Gilbert explored the possibilities of paradox through several of his operettas. In *The Pirates of Penzance*,
the pirate king informs Frederic, the pirate apprentice, that, although Frederic has lived twenty-one years, he was born on the
twenty-ninth of February, which comes only every fourth year, and
so, counting by birthdays, he's only a little over five. More amused
than anyone else, Frederic sings:

> *How quaint the ways of paradox,*
> *At common sense she gaily mocks!*
> *Though counting in the usual way,*
> * Years twenty-one I've been alive,*
> *Yet, reckoning by my natal day,*
> * I am a little boy of five!*
> *A paradox, a paradox,*
> *A most ingenious paradox!*

PARALLELISM. From the Greek meaning "side by side,"
parallelism is the setting up of counterparts of phrasing or the
matching of ideas. In poetry parallelism is accomplished by balance
and repetition. The King James version of the Bible derives much
of its rhetorical and rhythmical power from accumulating parallel
structures. Here are two excerpts, the first from Job, the second
from Ecclesiastes:

Let the day perish wherein I was born,
And the night in which it was said, There is a man child conceived.
Let that day be darkness;
Let not God regard it from above,
Neither let the light shine upon it.

Let darkness and the shadow of death stain it;
Let a cloud dwell upon it;
Let the blackness of the day terrify it.
As for that night, let darkness seize upon it;
Let it not be joined unto the days of the year,
Let it not come into the number of the months.
Lo, let that night be solitary,
Let no joyful voice come therein.
Let them curse it that curse the day,

*   *   *

To everything there is a season,
And a time to every purpose under the heaven:
A time to be born, and a time to die;
A time to plant, and a time to pluck up that which is planted;
A time to kill, and a time to heal;
A time to break down, and a time to build up;
A time to weep, and a time to laugh;
A time to mourn, and a time to dance;
A time to cast away stones, and a time to gather stones together;
A time to embrace, and a time to refrain from embracing;
A time to get, and a time to lose;
A time to keep, and a time to cast away;
A time to rend, and a time to sew;
A time to keep silence, and a time to speak;
A time to love, and a time to hate;
A time of war, and a time of peace.

English poetry is rich in parallelisms. Here are three disparate examples from three different periods. The first ("Of Human Life") is by the seventeenth-century Henry King; the second (from "A Song to David") is by the eighteenth-century Christopher Smart; the third (from "Song of Myself") is by the nineteenth-century Walt Whitman.

> *Like to the falling of a star,*
> *Or as the flights of eagles are,*
> *Or like the fresh spring's gaudy hue,*
> *Or silver drops of morning dew.*

Or like a wind that chafes the flood,
Or bubbles which on water stood:
Even such is man, whose borrowed light
Is straight called in, and paid to night.
The wind blows out, the bubble dies;
The spring entombed in autumn lies;
The dew dries up, the star is shot;
The flight is past—and man forgot.

* * *

Strong is the lion—like a coal
His eyeball—like a bastion's mole
His chest against the foes:
Strong the gier-eagle on his sail,
Strong against tide, the enormous whale
Emerges, as he goes.

But stronger still, in earth and air,
And in the sea, the man of prayer;
And far beneath the tide;
And in the seat to faith assigned,
Where ask is have, where seek is find,
Where knock is open wide.

* * *

Press close bare-bosom'd night—press close magnetic nourishing
night!
Night of south winds—night of the large few stars!
Still nodding night—mad naked summer night.

Smile O voluptuous cool-breath'd earth!
Earth of the slumbering and liquid trees!
Earth of departed sunset—earth of the mountains misty-topt!
Earth of the vitreous pour of the full moon tinged with blue!
Earth of shine and dark mottling the tide of the river!
Earth of the limpid gray of clouds brighter and clearer for my sake!
Far-swooping elbow'd earth—rich apple-blossom'd earth!
Smile, for your lover comes.

PARNASSIAN. A term applied to a type of poetry which originated with a group of mid-nineteenth-century French poets centering about Leconte de Lisle. Although Parnassian poetry is lyrical, it is curiously objective. Since Mount Parnassus was sacred to the Muses, Parnassian poetry devoted itself largely to a thoughtful creation of Art, though not exclusively to Art for Art's sake. Craftsmanship was the great desideratum; Gautier said that a poet was essentially a sculptor, and the Parnassians adopted the designation as a credo. The assumption that a poem should be "carved" accounts for the lapidary style manifested in the Parnassian preoccupation with hard surfaces, stone, marble, monuments, tombs, raw gems, engraved jewels, and what Austin Dobson (an English Parnassian) called "the resisting mass." Dobson's paraphrase of Gautier's "L'Art" (another version of which is the Epilogue on page 305) ends with these two stanzas:

> *Even the gods must go:*
> *Only the lofty Rhyme*
> *Not countless years o'erthrow,*
> *Nor long array of time.*
>
> *Paint, chisel, then, or write;*
> *But, that the work surpass,*
> *With the hard fashion fight,*
> *With the resisting mass.*

PARODY. In the broadest sense, parody is a mock imitation of a piece of writing or of a particular style, an imitation twisted or exaggerated to be humorous. When it is merely a ridiculing of an author's words or a distortion of his phrases, it degenerates into burlesque. A striking example is Catherine Fanshawe's mockery of two famous lines by Pope. Pope's couplet runs:

> *Here shall the Spring its earliest sweets bestow.*
> *Here the first roses of the year shall blow.*

Changing only one word and one letter, Catherine Fanshawe achieved this ludicrous burlesque:

> *Here shall the Spring its earliest colds bestow.*
> *Here the first noses of the year shall blow!*

True parody is more than comic mimicry; it is a satirical travesty and sometimes a critical showing-up of a writer's mannerisms. Many parodies have outlived the poem parodied, most notably the verses written by Lewis Carroll for the two Alice books. Almost all his masterpieces of nonsense are also masterpieces of parody. For example the theologian Dr. Isaac Watts had written an uplifting poem, "Against Idleness and Mischief," which begins:

> *How doth the little busy bee*
> *Improve each shining hour,*
> *And gather honey all the day*
> *From every opening flower.*

Alice recited it this way:

> *How doth the little crocodile*
> *Improve his shining tail,*
> *And pour the waters of the Nile*
> *On every golden scale.*

Robert Southey's didactic "The Old Man's Comforts and How He Gained Them" opens:

> *"You are old, Father William," the young man cried,*
> *"The few locks which are left you are gray;*
> *You are hale, Father William, a hearty old man.*
> *Now tell me the reason, I pray."*

> *"In the days of my youth," Father William replied,*
> *"I remembered that youth would fly fast,*
> *And abused not my health, and my vigor at first,*
> *That I never might need them at last."*

Carroll's old man bears no relation to Southey's sanctimonious babbler except by way of a rhythmic response.

"You are old, Father William," the young man said,
  "And your hair has become very white;
And yet you incessantly stand on your head—
  Do you think, at your age, it is right?"

"In my youth," Father William replied to his son,
  "I feared it might injure the brain;
But, now that I'm perfectly sure I have none,
  Why, I do it again and again."

Mary Howitt's once-popular moralizing "The Spider and the Fly" begins:

"Will you walk into my parlor?" said the spider to the fly.
" 'Tis the prettiest little parlor that ever you did spy."

The Mock Turtle sings it this way in *Alice's Adventures in Wonderland:*

"Will you walk a little faster?" said a whiting to a snail.
"There's a porpoise close behind us and he's treading on my tail."

In the Alice books Wordsworth's "Resolution and Independence," a poem about an aged leech-gatherer, turns into the lachrymose White Knight's tale, "I'll tell thee everything I can: There's little to relate"; G. W. Langford's sweet homily, "Speak gently; it is better far/ To rule by love than fear" becomes the Duchess' lullaby: "Speak roughly to your little boy/ And beat him when he sneezes"; while the style of Thomas Hood's melodramatic "Dream of Eugene Aram" is satirized by Tweedledee's nonsense:

The sun was shining on the sea,
  Shining with all his might:
He did his very best to make
  The billows smooth and bright—
And this was odd, because it was
  The middle of the night.

Apart from Carroll, some of the most serious authors have been notable parodists. Among the best are Thackeray, Swinburne, Bret Harte, C. S. Calverley, Phoebe Cary (surprisingly enough!), Bayard Taylor, Owen Seaman, Anthony C. Deane, and, though his work in this vein is practically unknown, Rudyard Kipling.

Kipling himself is neatly parodied by Deane as Deane rewrites the jingle of Jack and Jill in the style of one of Kipling's *Barrack-Room Ballads*. It begins:

Now Jack looked up—it was time to sup and the bucket was
yet to fill—
And Jack looked around for a space and frowned, then beckoned
his sister Jill.
And twice he pulled his sister's hair, and thrice he smote her
side.
"Ha' done, ha' done with your impudent fun. Ha' done with
your games!" she cried.
"You have made mud pies of a marvelous size—finger and face
are black.
You have trodden the Way of Mire and Clay. Now up and wash
you, Jack!
Or else, if ever we reach our home, there waiteth an angry dame.
Well you know the weight of her blow—the supperless open
shame!
Wash, if you will, on yonder hill. Wash, if you will, at the
spring.
Or keep your dirt to your certain hurt, and an imminent
walloping!"

That the nature of parody adapts itself to the changing character of the times is proved by Paul Dehn's *Quake, Quake, Quake*, a bitter counterblast to Tennyson's tenderly mournful "Break, break, break." Written during (and for) the age of the atomic bomb, Dehn lampoons the classics with "A Leaden Treasury of English Verse," rewrites a hymnal with terrifying prophecies, paraphrases the most cherished parts of Stevenson's *Child's Garden of Verses* with black comedy, and turns Mother Goose rhymes into up-to-date horrors like:

Jack and Jill went up the hill
To fetch some heavy water.
They mixed it with the dairy milk
And killed my youngest daughter.

Among the more interesting collections of this genre are *A Parody Anthology* edited by Carolyn Wells, *Apes and Parrots* collected by J. C. Squire, *The Echo Club* by Bayard Taylor, *Rejected Addresses* by Horace and James Smith, *New Rhymes for Old* by Anthony C. Deane, *In Cap and Bells* by Owen Seaman, *The Moxford Book of English Verse* by A. Stodart-Walker, *The Antic Muse* edited by Robert P. Falk, *Parodies from Chaucer to Beerbohm, and After* edited by Dwight Macdonald, and *Collected Parodies* by Louis Untermeyer.

PASTORAL.   Originally a pastoral poem was one which portrayed the life and customs of shepherds, in Latin "pastores," leaders of the flock who lived close to the soil. Theocritus' *Idylls* and Virgil's *Eclogues* are the classic models. Later writers transferred the shepherds to a world of sylvan streams, whispering woods, rest-inducing fields, and no labor. The Elizabethans further prettified the pastoral scene; their shepherdesses were standardized; they dressed in fancy costumes and were wooed with the most elegant phrases in the most artificial styles. The lyrics of the period are densely populated with ardent Strephons and coy Chloes, handsome Corydons and garlanded Phillidas, with an occasional wanton Amaryllis.

The pastoral convention was both upheld and altered by Milton's "Lycidas," Shelley's "Adonais," and Arnold's "Thyrsis," which, though cast in the classic mode, registered genuine emotion and created their own patterns. Although modern poetry does not attempt to revive the peace and simplicity of the Virgilian note, such a poem as Frost's "Build Soil" is a dialogue between two suspiciously intellectual peasants: Meliboeus, "the potato man," and Tityrus, who lives by writing poems on a farm and therefore calls himself a farmer. Frost subtitled the ten-page poem "A Political Pastoral"; it turned into a dialectical discussion wittily revolving around an Eclogue. (See page 192 for ECLOGUE.)

PATHETIC FALLACY. The device of giving inanimate objects distinctly human emotions is called "pathetic fallacy," a phrase invented by Ruskin. A fallacy it may be, but there is nothing particularly pathetic about calling the air "kindly," the cold "cruel," the sea "angry," the storm "pitiless," or the sun "benevolent." Ruskin, however, spoke for other purists when he insisted that endowing nature with the feelings of men and women creates an excitement, "making us, for the time, more or less irrational . . . There is no greater baseness in literature than the habit of using these metaphorical expressions in cold blood."

Ruskin to the contrary, poets all the way from Donne to Dylan Thomas have delighted in such keen and spontaneous "metaphorical expressions." Wordsworth informs us that nature could never find its way into Peter Bell's heart because Peter could see things only as they appeared to be.

> *In vain, through every changeful year,*
> *Did Nature lead him as before;*
> *A primrose by a river's brim*
> *A yellow primrose was to him,*
> *And it was nothing more.*

"Every Thing" by Harold Monro whimsically expatiates on the comforting camaraderie of ordinary household articles—the candle that bows "in a smoky argument" before it goes out, the kettle puffing "its tentacle of breath," the copper basin that tumbles from the shelf because it knows "the lean and poise of gravitable land," the impetuous gas that begins "irascibly to flare and fret, wheezing into its epileptic jet," the "ruminating" clock that stirs its body and begins to rock, "warning the waiting presence of the night" . . . The poet concludes by thanking all these "kind Reposeful Teraphim"—

> *Remain my friends: I feel, though I don't speak,*
> *Your touch grow kindlier from week to week.*
> *It well becomes our mutual happiness*
> *To go toward the same end more or less.*

There is not much dissimilarity,
Not much to choose, I know it well, in fine,
Between the purposes of you and me,
And your eventual Rubbish Heap, and mine.

PENTAMETER. A line of verse which has five metrical feet is not only the norm of blank verse but is also the most frequently encountered form in English poetry. Practically all of Shakespeare's plays are written in this measure:

How far this little candle throws his beams!
So shines a good deed in a naughty world.

The alternation of unaccented and accented syllables shows these to be iambic lines, and since there are five beats, the verse is an example of iambic pentameter. The sonnet, the heroic couplet, and many lyrics are also based on pentameter.

PERSONIFICATION. Related to metaphor and "pathetic fallacy," personification (pedantically called "prosopopeia") is a form of comparison which attributes human characteristics to abstractions or things which are not human. When Milton says that "the floods clap their hands" and "Confusion heard his voice," he is individualizing the floods as if they were people and endowing Confusion with personal life. Happiness is a vague emotion, but Shelley gives it human shape when he cries:

Rarely, rarely, comest thou,
Spirit of Delight!

Drayton's sonnet beginning "Since there's no help, come let us kiss and part" vividly personifies Passion, Faith, and Innocence in the last six lines:

Now in the last gasp of Love's latest breath,
When, his pulse failing, Passion speechless lies,
When Faith is kneeling by his bed of death,
And Innocence is closing up his eyes,
Now if thou wouldst, when all have given him over;
From death to life, thou might'st him yet recover.

Though personification was largely used to animate mythological figures and forces, modern poetry does not disdain the device. Francis Thompson gives the wind the power of a plunging stallion when he writes that he "clung to the whistling mane of every wind." Robinson Jeffers feels that "the mountains pasture with their heads down," Carl Sandburg sees Chicago as "stormy, husky, brawling, City of the Big Shoulders," Dylan Thomas says that "the lips of time leech to the fountain head," and Léonie Adams "humanizes" twilight in her "Homecoming":

> When I stepped homeward to my hill,
> Dusk went before with quiet tread . . .

PETRARCHAN SONNET.   See SONNET on page 285.

POETIC DICTION.   Dryden defined poetic diction as the choice of fine words and the harmony of numbers. This was in line with Aristotle's pronouncement that a writer should aim at a diction which should be elevated, full of allusive rather than ordinary terms, rare words and stylistic comparisons—all of which lift literature, and especially poetry, above the level of the commonplace. As a result, most poetry is embellished with unusual metaphors and picturesque epithets. Anglo-Saxon kennings (see page 215) show how much poetic diction went into Old English poems; we see too how far the making of epithets characterizes the work of Chaucer, Spenser, and Shakespeare, as well as the romantic creations of Byron, Shelley, and Keats.

Those who believed in poetic diction went to great lengths to avoid common expressions. Cows were "the lowing kine," fish were "finny prey," fog was "an empurpled shroud," the sky was "the vaulted empyrean."

Sunrise is a common phenomenon, yet poets described it in their own highly colored poetic diction. Shakespeare gave it active personification:

> Night's candles are burnt out, and jocund day
> Stands tiptoe on the misty mountain tops.

Keats, out of his own sensuous love of sheer color, described sunrise thus:

Now morning from her orient chambers came,
And her first footsteps touched a verdant hill:
Crowning its lawny crest with amber flame,
Silvering the untainted gushes of its rill.

William Drummond, the Scottish poet and mathematical genius, called up the dawn in the diction of the classics:

Phoebus, arise,
And paint the sable skies
With azure, white, and red.

Omar Khayyám, according to Fitzgerald, saw dawn as an armed warrior triumphing over darkness:

Wake! For the Sun who scattered into flight
The Stars before him from the field of Night,
*   Drives Night along with them from Heaven, and strikes*
The Sultan's turret with a shaft of light.

A. E. Housman captured the phenomenon in a striking marine metaphor:

Wake! The silver dusk returning
*   Up the beach of darkness brims,*
And the ship of sunrise burning
*   Strands upon the eastern rims.*

Kipling vigorously asserted that, on the road to Mandalay:

. . . . the Dawn comes up like thunder outer China 'crost the Bay!

Quite an opposite effect was achieved by Oscar Wilde when, along a dark and silent street:

The dawn, with silver-sandalled feet,
Crept like a frightened girl.

Emerson began his "Concord Ode" with a figure of speech which describes a visual as well as a spiritual sunrise:

> *O tenderly the haughty day*
> *Fills his blue urn with fire;*
> *One morn is in the mighty heaven,*
> *And one in our desire.*

Emily Dickinson depicted both sunrise and sunset in her inimitable blend of personification, wonder, and whimsicality:

> *I'll tell you how the sun rose,—*
> *A ribbon at a time.*
> *The steeples swam in amethyst,*
> *The news like squirrels ran.*
>
> *The hills untied their bonnets,*
> *The bobolinks begun.*
> *Then I said softly to myself,*
> *"That must have been the sun!"*
>
> *But how he set, I know not.*
> *There seemed a purple stile*
> *Which little yellow boys and girls*
> *Were climbing all the while,*
>
> *Till when they reached the other side,*
> *A dominie in gray*
> *Put gently up the evening bars,*
> *And led the flock away.*

Poetic diction has been a matter of dispute for years. Wordsworth was one of those who protested most vehemently against the substitution of fancy periphrases for plain words. The poet, he claimed, was a man speaking to men, a man using the language of everyday conversation. Wordsworth scorned overdecorated phrases and advocated not only a return to nature but also a return to expressing things in a natural way.

Whitman also held out against poetic diction. To Whitman the cosmic and the commonplace were synonymous. No circumlocution, no matter how poetically framed, was as powerful as colloquial speech. His blunt idiom (sometimes marred by odd affectations) glorified homely images. Something like a credo was announced when, in "Song of Myself," he wrote the simplest and most profound of statements:

I believe a leaf of grass is no less than the journeywork of the stars,
And the pismire is equally perfect, and a grain of sand, and the egg
*   of the wren . . .*
And the narrowest hinge in my hand puts to scorn all machinery,
And the cow crunching with depressed head surpasses any statue.
And a mouse is miracle enough to stagger sextillions of infidels.

J. M. Synge was another who preferred the vernacular to the elaborations of poetic diction. In an introduction to *The Playboy of the Western World* he wrote: "I got more aid than any learning could have given us from a chink in the floor of an old Wicklow house that let me hear what was being said by the servant girls in the kitchen." He enlarged the theme in a preface to his *Poems:*

> I have often thought that at the side of the poetic diction, which every one condemns, modern verse contains a great deal of material, using poetic in the same special sense. The poetry of exaltation will always be the highest; but when men lose their poetic feeling for ordinary life and cannot write poetry of ordinary things their exalted poetry is likely to lose its strength of exaltation. . . . Even if we grant that exalted poetry can be kept successful by itself, the strong things of life are needed in poetry also, to show that what is exalted or tender is not made by feeble blood. It may almost be said that before verse can be human it must learn to be brutal.

POLYPHONIC PROSE.   See pages 101–102 in the chapter "The Prose of Poetry."

PROJECTIVE VERSE.   Projective verse is another manifestation of the modern resistance to poetic diction. Initiated and strongly proclaimed by Ezra Pound and William Carlos Williams, it calls for a language of mixed imagism and unrelieved colloquialism, a language devoted to particulars instead of generalities—"no ideas but in things"—a compulsive energy, and a poetry derived from impulse rather than from plan. It also places more importance on the syllable than on the phrase or line. In a much-quoted essay on projective verse Charles Olson wrote: "It is by their syllables that words juxtapose in beauty, by these particles of

sound as clearly as by the sense of the words which they compose."
Furthermore Olson, an acknowledged leader of the Projectivists,
stressed continual dynamic activity—"one perception must immediately and directly lead to a further perception . . . Keep
it moving as fast as you can." Little was said about form and
content, although Robert Creeley, the poet who edited Olson's
Selected Writings, maintained that the idea shaped the form and
that "form is never more than an extension of content."

The beginning of Olson's *Maximus Poems* exemplifies the projectivist manner:

> *The thing you're after*
> *may lie around the bend*
> *of the nest (second) time slain, the bird! the bird!*
>
> *After there! (strong) thrust, the mast! flight*
> > *of the bird*
> > *o kylix, o*
> > *Antony of Padua*
> > *sweep low, o bless*
>
> *the roofs, the old ones, the gentle steep ones*
> *on whose ridge-poles the gulls sit, from which they depart,*
>
> > > *and the flake-racks*
> *of my city!*

The Projectivists met with considerable opposition. It was objected that their work was spasmodic and shapeless with scarcely
a memorable thought or an arresting line, that the contents were
vague and the poetry itself so arbitrary and often so empty that the
reader had to "project" himself into it. As innovators the Projectivists were accused of being literary anarchists, the assumption
being that the predetermined anti-traditionalist usually turns into
the determined anti-poet. The repudiation of emotion as old-
fashioned and eloquence as outdated tended to become a vogue of
inverted academism. "The whole theory of projective verse, where
the form is tailored to the pulse-rate and breathing of the poet,"
wrote A. Alvarez in the London *Times Literary Supplement,*
March 23, 1967, "seems to ensure only a kind of psychic myopia."

In spite of technical advances, the only thing that matters and has always mattered (to rephrase a remark of Stravinsky's) is content. Nothing dates so quickly as the fashionable innovator who is an hour or so ahead of his times.

PROSODY. Whether prosody is, as Webster defines it, the science or the art of versification, including the study of metrical patterns and stanza forms, prosody is the general term applied to the structure of verse. This includes the matter of accent, the rules for the treatment of syllables, whether they are to be considered long or short, and the measurement of sounds and stresses. In his introduction to *The Structure of Verse* Harvey Gross utters a warning. He writes: "The politics of prosodical study might well dismay the student anxious to discover necessary facts and basic principles. Bitter feuding between rival schools of prosodists—the linguists versus the aestheticians, the 'timers' versus the 'stressers,' the quantifiers versus the strict foot-and-syllable scanners—has done little to clarify the issues or even to furnish a simple map of the terrain."

Agreeing with this, poets have gone further in expressing their dissatisfaction with the scholarly structures of prosody. Robert Graves maintained that the canons of prosody are artificial as well as academic—"the laws of prosody are, to verse, very much as copperplate models are to natural writing." In his cantankerous but cogent *ABC of Reading* Ezra Pound contended that "prosody and melody are attained by the listening ear, not by an index of nomenclatures, or by learning that such and such a foot is called a spondee. . . . Hence the extreme boredom caused by the usual professorial documentation or the aspiring thesis on prosody. The answer is: Listen to the sound it makes."

Only a pedant reads poetry according to prosodic rules. Even a reader who knows nothing about scansion and structural linguistics knows that the recognition of poetry and the response to it is not a mathematical exercise but an emotional experience.

PROSOPOPEIA.   See PERSONIFICATION on page 248.

PROTHALAMION.   See EPITHALAMION on page 198.

Q

QUANTITY. Quantity, the time required for the pronunciation of a syllable, was the basis of Greek and Latin poetry. In classical prosody, quantity rather than stress, which is the basis of English poetry, determined that a long syllable was one which contained a long vowel, or a short vowel plus two or more consonants, and was equal to two short syllables.

QUATRAIN. The quatrain is the most prevalent unit of English verse. It consists of only four lines, yet it is almost endless in its variety. The most familiar arrangement is the one in which the rhymes occur in the second and fourth lines, an arrangement expressed by the letters *x-a-y-a*—*x* and *y* representing the first and third unrhymed lines. This quatrain is often called the ballad stanza since practically all ballads are made of quatrains on this order.

> *Saint Stephen was a clerk*   x
>   *In King Herod's hall.*   a
> *And servéd him of bread and cloth*   y
>   *As every king befall.*   a

*   *   *

> *There lived a wife at Usher's Well,*   x
>   *And a wealthy wife was she;*   a
> *She had three stout and stalwart sons,*   y
>   *And sent them o'er the sea.*   a

Almost as common is the quatrain which rhymes the first and third as well as the second and fourth lines—*a-b-a-b*. Here are five examples varying in beat and length of line.

> *Lifting my eyes from Hesiod's book,*
> *I saw young Pyrrha pass and nod,*

Linger, and give another look . . .
Goodbye to dull old Hesiod.

ADAPTED BY L. U. FROM THE GREEK
ANTHOLOGY

Happy the man whose wish and care
A few paternal acres bound,
Content to breathe his native air
In his own ground.

ALEXANDER POPE

I strove with none, for none was worth my strife.
Nature I loved and, next to Nature, Art.
I warmed both hands before the fire of life;
It sinks, and I am ready to depart.

WALTER SAVAGE LANDOR

"What's your most vexing parasite,"
Said Mars to Earth, "since life began?"
Earth roared an answer through the night
In emphasis of thunder, "Man!"

NORMAN GALE

A noble, nasty course he ran,
Superbly filthy and fastidious.
He was the world's first gentleman,
And made the appellation hideous.

WINTHROP MACKWORTH PRAED

Another type of quatrain is composed of two couplets—*a-a-b-b*. Here are three examples differing not only in length of line but in mixture of meters.

As sap foretastes the spring,
As earth ere blossoming
Thrills
With far daffodils . . .

FRANCIS THOMPSON

I would live for a day and a night
In the rigorous land where everything's right.
Then I would sit and make a song
In the leisurely land where everything's wrong.

ANNA WICKHAM

Presentiment is that long shadow on the lawn
Indicative that suns go down,
The notice to the startled grass
That darkness is about to pass.

EMILY DICKINSON

A less familiar but effective variety is the quatrain in which the first and last lines rhyme together and the two middle lines form a couplet—*a-b-b-a*—sometimes called an envelope stanza.

Calm is the morn without a sound,
Calm as to suit a calmer grief,
And only through the faded leaf
The chestnut pattering to the ground.

ALFRED TENNYSON

You come in the year when promises are broken,
And petals fear the late, as fruit the early frost-fall;
When the young expect little, and the old endure total recall,
But discover no logic to justify what they had taken, or forsaken.

ROBERT PENN WARREN

Sometimes quatrains are composed entirely on a single rhyme: *a-a-a-a*. This example is by Dante Gabriel Rossetti:

The wind flapped loose, the wind was still,
Shaken out dead from tree to hill;
I had walked on at the wind's will—
I sat now, for the wind was still.

There is also the "Omar stanza," so called because it was popularized by Fitzgerald in his adaptation of the *Rubáiyát of Omar*

Khayyám, a form which Swinburne borrowed for his "Laus Veneris." The first, second, and fourth lines are rhymed, while the third line is unrhymed: *a-a-x-a:*

> *Some for the glories of this world; and some*
> *Sigh for the Prophet's Paradise to come;*
>   *Ah, take the cash, and let the credit go,*
> *Nor heed the rumble of a distant drum!*

Quatrains are often complete poems, such as those under EPI-GRAM and EPITAPH on pages 195 and 197. Many have an epigrammatic disposal, like the following.

> *For all your days prepare,*
>   *And meet them ever alike:*
> *When you are the anvil, bear—*
>   *When you are the hammer, strike.*

EDWIN MARKHAM

QUINTET.   Rhymed in a variety of ways, the quintet is a five-line stanza. There are many rhyme patterns; the division of rhymes seems to be mainly three and two, either *a-b-a-b-b* or *a-b-a-b-a*. The first formula is illustrated by a much-quoted stanza.

>   *Go, lovely rose!*
> *Tell her, that wastes her time and me*
>   *That now she knows,*
> *When I resemble her to thee,*
> *How sweet and fair she seems to be.*

EDMUND WALLER

Robert Browning's "The Patriot" conforms to the second pattern of rhymes: *a-b-a-b-a*. This is its first stanza:

> *It was roses, roses, all the way,*
>   *With myrtle mixed in my path like mad:*
> *The house-roofs seemed to heave and sway,*
>   *The church-spires flamed, such flags they had,*
> *A year ago on this very day!*

There is also a five-line stanza with an odd, unrhymed last line, as in George Herbert's "Denial":

> *My bent thoughts, like a brittle bow,*
> *Did fly asunder;*
> *Each took its way. Some would to pleasure go,*
> *Some to the wars and thunder*
> *Of alarms.*

An altogether unrhymed form of the five-line stanza is the CINQUAIN invented by Adelaide Crapsey. (See page 181.)

R

REALISTIC POETRY. Realistic poetry is the result of a naturalistic approach, a manner of writing about life as it is, or seems to be, without imposing a philosophy upon it. In contradistinction to the classical writers, the realist concentrates on objectivity, on what appears to be the unglamorous truth of a situation, and he dwells upon such details as may emphasize complete truthfulness. He is not concerned with making the world brighter or better—he leaves that to the romanticist. He is satisfied with telling the truth, the whole truth, and (sometimes too repetitively) nothing but the truth. Realism, a quality usually associated with fiction, sinews the narrative poems of John Masefield, W. W. Gibson, and other celebrators of the workaday world.

REFRAIN. The refrain—sometimes called BURDEN (see page 175)—is a line or lines repeated at intervals throughout a poem. The word may also refer to the line which ends each stanza of the BALLADE. (See page 161.) A feature of primitive poetry, it is found in ritual dances, songs of labor such as sailors' CHANTEYS (see page 180), and folk-tunes, as well as in works of literary art like Tennyson's "Lady of Shalott," Rossetti's "Sister Helen," and Poe's "The Raven."

RHYME. What constitutes rhyme has always been a matter of dispute. The English language is not as rich in rhyme as several other tongues, and so many liberties have been taken that it is difficult to draw a line between what has been regarded as "pure" and "impure" rhyme. It is interesting to compare Henry Lanz's laboratory-conducted *The Physical Basis of Rime* with Burges Johnson's *New Rhyming Dictionary* and glimpse the vast gulf between philosophic theory and ordinary practice. Most of the poets of the past have been content to rely on the "pure" or "perfect" rhyme, but the twentieth century has witnessed all sorts of phonetic experiments to enrich the scant array of rhymes. Some of these innovations have been given names; others are still unacknowledged. There is, however, growing agreement about the following categories.

PURE or PERFECT RHYME. This is the norm of English verse. According to the accepted principle, the words intended to rhyme must be identical in sound from the vowel of the accented syllable to the end, but the consonants *pre*ceding the accented syllable must be *un*like in sound. In less technical terms, pure or perfect rhyme is the familiar, roundly satisfying rhyme, the rhyme which hits the bell with ringing (and sometimes damnable) certainty. It is the worn-out union of "June-moon-tune," and it is also the less obvious double rhyming of "daughter-water-slaughter" and the triple rhyming of "teachable-reachable-impeachable." It is not the combination of "days" and "daze" or "plain" and "plane." These are eye rhymes or HOMONYMS (see page 208); they are identical in sound and have none of the little unlikeness which complies with the definition (and constitutes the charm) of pure rhyme.

Another kind of eye rhyme occurs in words that are spelled so as to seem alike in pronunciation but are pronounced differently. "Love" and "move," "dies" and "eternities" are eye rhymes fancied by the Elizabethans. In lyrics for Sullivan's music, Gilbert often achieved comic effects with eye rhymes like:

> *A shepherd I*
> *From Arcady,*

Whereupon the chorus corrects the singer with:

> *A shepherd he*
> *From Arcady.*

POPULAR or IMPERFECT RHYME.   Popular or Imperfect rhyme is only a little less common than perfect rhyme. Frowned on by perfectionists, it has an ancient if not honorable lineage. Perfect rhyme matches "late" with "fate" and "done" with "one," but the old ballads do not hesitate to rhyme "late" with "fade" and "done" with "long." Imperfect rhyme matches the vowels but ignores the rule of following them with matching consonants. Here is an example from "Childe Maurice":

> *I got him in my mother's bower*
> *Wi' mickle sin and shame;*
> *I brought him up in the good greenwood*
> *Under the shower and rain.*

And here are two stanzas from America's brief saga of John Henry, the indomitable steel-driver:

> *John Henry said to his captain,*
> *"A man ain't nothin' but a man.*
> *Before I'd be beaten by an old steam-drill*
> *I'd die with my hammer in my hand."*
>
> *John Henry started at the right-hand side;*
> *The steam-drill started at the left.*
> *"Before I'd let that steam-drill beat me down,*
> *Lord, I'd hammer my fool self to death.*

Also see ASSONANCE on page 152.

SUSPENDED RHYME.   This is often regarded (suspiciously in some quarters) as a daring modern departure, although the

Elizabethans sometimes indulged in it and nineteenth-century New Englanders were not above pairing "earth" with "forth" and "poll" with "full." It is related to perfect rhyme inasmuch as it, too, follows the rule of unlike preceding consonants (if any) and identical final consonant sounds, but—and in this difference lies its novelty—the vowel sounds are quite different. Suspended rhyme, as the term indicates, is like a suspension in music, a holding back of the cadence. A light dissonance is created which is a surprising and, to most ears, a pleasing change from perfect rhyme. If it creates a slightly acrid tone, it adds spiciness to a succession of bland and anticipated sounds. Conrad Aiken, Archibald MacLeish, Elinor Wylie, Humbert Wolfe (see his "Iliad" on page 41), and (with particular deftness) John Crowe Ransom vary perfect rhymes with such suspensions as "false-else," "little-beetle," "lady-study," "clergy-orgy," "women-famine," "have-grave," "death-faith." Here is part of Ransom's "Husband Betrayed":

> *But there was heavy* dudgeon
> *When he that should have married him a* woman
> *To sit and drudge and serve him as was* common
> *Discovered he had wived a* pidgeon.

And here is a fragment from Louis MacNeice's "Prognosis":

> *Goodbye, Winter,*
> *The days are getting* longer,
> *The tea-leaf in the cup*
> *Is herald to a* stranger . . .
>
> *Will his name be Love*
> *And all his talk be* crazy,
> *Or will his name be Death*
> *And his message* easy?

As in music, the suspended rhyme, hesitating before resolution, is a momentary tension, a slight but piquant verbal surprise.

CONSONANTAL RHYME. Examples of consonance are given on pages 185–186. Similar to those of Wilfred Owen, where both preceding *and* concluding consonants are identical while the vowel-sounds are *un*matched, are the consonantal rhymes favored by Archibald MacLeish in "Weather" (lake-like, far-for, west-waste, stirs-stars, gather-together) and by Conrad Aiken in "Annihilation," which ends:

> *Rock meeting rock can know love* better
> *Than eyes that stare or lips that touch,*
> *All that we know of love is* bitter,
> *And it is not much.*

TANGENTIAL RHYME. As the term implies, tangential rhyme is a sidelong sort of rhyme, a light pairing of accented and unaccented syllables. Marianne Moore is an expert in this difficult manipulation. Witness "The Jerboa":

> *. . . one would not be* he
> *who has nothing but plen*ty.

> *. . . closed upper paws seeming one with the* fur
> *in its flight from a dan*ger.

> *. . . propped on hind legs, and tail as a third* toe
> *between leaps to its bur*row.

HALF-RHYME or APOCOPATED RHYME. From "apocope," literally "a cutting-off," apocopated rhyme is a half-rhyme, one where the second syllable of a double rhyme is cut off and only the first syllable rhymes. Examples: *fill-pillow, gun-money, mind-finding, breeze-freezing*. MacLeish makes constant use of such half-rhyming in "Conquistador," "Landscape as Nude," and "American Letter":

> *The wind is east but the hot weather continues,*
> *Blue and no clouds, the sound of the leaves thin . . .*

> *It is a strange thing—to be an American.*
> *Neither an old house it is with the air*

Tasting of hung herbs and the sun returning
Year after year to the same door and the churn
Making the same sound in the cool of the kitchen
Mother to son's wife, and the place to sit . . .

RUNOVER RHYME.   Another tour de force, a runover rhyme
pairs the last word of one line with the first word of another. This
rhyme is used mostly for comic effect. Eliot occasionally played
with runover rhymes, as did MacNeice in:

> . . . *not expecting* pardon,
> Harden*ed in heart anew,*
> *But glad to have sat* under
> Thunder *and rain with you.*

PURPOSES OF RHYME.   In English verse the *masculine*
(single) rhyme prevails and is the basis for most serious poetry,
while the *feminine* (double or triple) rhyme is used chiefly for
light or comic purposes. Together, however, they not only add
discipline to the line but make the thought more pointed and
concise, where unrhymed verse is often likely to plod on or lose
control.

For most poets, rhyme is a natural way of writing, a musical
punctuation. One cannot imagine Herrick, Keats, or Shelley without it; nor, to suggest the full gamut, can one think of such ex-
tremely differently pitched poets as Chaucer and Pope without
their matched rhyming. On the other hand there are poets, like
Whitman, to whom (in spite of "O Captain! My Captain!")
rhyme was an artificial device, a restriction that would have kept
them from saying things that only they could say. Milton rejected
rhyme for the colossal *Paradise Lost;* he felt he needed the roll
and thunder of blank verse for his epic. He inveighed against the
"jingling sound of like endings," rhyme being no necessary adjunct
or true ornament of poem or good verse, of longer works especially.
And, although Robert Bridges wrote many delicately rhymed
lyrics, he considered rhyme "so trammeled, its effects so cloying,
and its worthiest resources so quickly exhausted . . . that a
prosody which was good enough to do without it would immedi-

ately discard it in spite of its almost unparalleled achievements."

It is one of the glories of English poetry that the achievements of rhyme are truly unparalleled, that the music of rhyme adds allure to its lighter moments and strength to its flow of passionate speech.

Also see ALLITERATION on page 145, ASSONANCE on page 152, CONSONANCE on page 185, INITIAL RHYME on page 210, and INTERNAL RHYME on page 211.

RHYME ROYAL. See SEPTET on page 279.

RHYTHM. Since the expression of strong feeling tends to fall into a strong beat, the language of emotion is almost always rhythmical. Rhythm is organic; it is embedded in the blood. Man moved in rhythm before he was conscious of it. He did not understand the reasons for the rotation of light and dark, the pound of tide-heaving seas, the swing of the seasons, but he responded to them in his savage chants shaped by the insistent stamping of his feet. When language developed, he probably was as delighted as a child with reiterated sounds, with the clapping of hands and the repetition of alliterative syllables.

The child is father to the man not only in the Wordsworthian sense but also in the sense that he anticipates the intricate rhythms of maturity by beginning with simple ones. He bounces up and down in his crib, bangs his spoon on the table, drums his heels on the high-chair, and reacts instantly to the game of "pat-a-cake, pat-a-cake." His early talk is rhythmical with rhyming sounds; he cries "bow-wow" to the dog and "moo-moo" to the cow; the train is a "choo-choo." He likes to repeat "quack-quack," which describes the duck with onomatopoetic accuracy.

We grow up in rhythm. We feel it physically—in the breath, the pulse and the heartbeat; we measure it in our walking stride; we quicken to it in the sway of the dance. We feel it psychologically—we are lulled by the swing of a hammock; we are excited by the beat of a drum; what Emily Dickinson called "the accent of a coming foot" fills us with anticipation or apprehension.

The word "rhythm" derives from a Greek word meaning "to

flow." We live by this flow, by the flow which governs the inhalation and exhalation of the breath, the hours of waking and sleeping, the repetitions of appetite, of ingestion and elimination. Rhythm is not only in the elements which surround us but also in the very flow of our blood.

When rhythm is governed by (or reduced to) strict laws, it cannot be called simply rhythm but METER. (See page 226.) Hopkins spoke of the standard metrical pattern as Common or Running Rhythm. To this he opposed what he called Sprung Rhythm, which was largely based on the heavy-footed SPONDEE (see page 291), and for which Hopkins claimed that it conformed closely to actual speech and ranged from the stresses found in nursery rhymes to emotional intensities. To some, Hopkins' theory of Sprung Rhythm is a discovery which challenges the orthodox rules of prosody. To others, it is an aberration, a pedantic formula which is interesting as a term but invalid as a rule. Robert Bridges, Hopkins' mentor and editor, wrote that "poetic rhythm derives its beauty from the very conflict between meter, which makes us more or less expect a certain regular rhythm of accent corresponding with a typical metrical structure, and, on the other hand, a speech-rhythm which gives it all manner of variety by overriding it."

It cannot be stated too often that Rhythm is not Meter, although the two are related. In an unpublished book on music, Henry W. Simon emphasizes the difference. He points to Shakespeare's alternately stressed and unstressed pentameter lines and says: "Iambic meter is the numerical measure, the set-up expectancy, the strait-jacket from which the poet escapes by making infinite rhythmical variations while retaining the ten-syllable pattern. The art of doing it well—or superbly, as Shakespeare usually did—is the art of making those rhythmical variations express the idea or emotion that the words imply and implicitly carry."

The making of rhythmical variations is an indefinable art. Efforts to chart the varying effects of rhythm have had little success. A certain amount of regularity is pleasing and even therapeutic, while unrelieved repetition (the ticking of a clock, the beating of surf, the blow of a hammer) is likely to become irritating. But at what point? And to whom? Since the effect of rhythm is both physical and psychological, rhythm's "flow" will be different with different people, and particularly with poets. Alexander Pope's precise rhythmical beat is the very opposite of Gerard Manley Hopkins' disjointed or "sprung" rhythm; the mystical movement of William Blake has nothing in common with the loosely rhapsodical "yawp" of Walt Whitman. Poets find themselves in their rhythms—rhythms which shape what they have to say and individualize their ways of saying it.

RISPETTO. The rispetto is an Italian form which consists of two or more stanzas with different rhyme-schemes. It is short, usually amatory, and, though variations do exist, its length is almost always eight lines divided into two quatrains. As a rule, the first quatrain is built on the rhyme-scheme *a-b-a-b* and the second on *c-c-d-d*. The form never became popular in English, although examples of it may be found here and there, as in the following poem by A. Mary F. Robinson.

> *What good is there, ah me, what good is love?*
> *Since even if you love me, we must part;*
> *And since in either, if you cared enough,*
> *There's but division and a broken heart.*
>
> *And yet, God knows, to hear you say, "My dear,"*
> *I would lie down and stretch me on my bier.*
> *And yet would I, to hear you say, "My own,"*
> *With my own hands drag down the burial stone.*

ROMANTIC POETRY. The term is so vague that no definition is sufficiently comprehensive. Nevertheless it has been maintained that the Classical poet severely disciplined his material and was always in control of it, whereas the Romantic poet was at the mercy of his emotions. If this is true, every poet in every age may be said to be Romantic—Chaucer, Spenser, and the more violent Elizabethans such as Marlowe and Webster were no less Romantic than, say, Keats and Shelley.

As a rule, however, the term "poets of the Romantic Period" refers to those nineteenth-century poets who lived in two worlds: the world of actuality, with all its sordidness, and the world of the imagination, a world dominated by goodness, beauty and truth, for it is characteristic of the Romantic nature to believe in man's innate sense of goodness and his striving toward a state of beatific rectitude. The aim of Romanticism, wrote Stephen Spender, "is the creation of an ideal world . . . The peculiarity of this world is its impulsiveness, its waywardness, the extent to which it is personal to the poet himself . . . But the Romantics were seeking another experience. Theirs was the shaping spirit of the poet moving in emptiness over the universe and imagining that it was in contact with other shaping forces—Nature in Wordsworth, Beauty in Keats, Humanity in Shelley."

Wordsworth, Keats, and Shelley are conceded to be the three major figures of the Romantic Movement. Some critics increase the number to five by adding Coleridge and Byron, while others, anthologically minded, swell the list by including such interesting minor poets as Walter Savage Landor, Thomas Lovell Beddoes, and Sir Walter Scott. Whatever their differences in tone and technique, the various nineteenth-century exponents of the Romantic spirit are responsible for some of the finest achievements in English literature.

RONDEAU.   Next to the ballade, the rondeau is the most popular of the French forms. It consists of thirteen lines broken into three stanzas and has only two rhymes, not counting the fixed refrain. The refrain differs from that of the ballade by occurring always at the beginning of the poem as well as at the conclusion of the second and the last stanzas—it is usually the first half of the first line. Designating R as the refrain, the formula would be: Ra-a-b-b-a a-a-b-R a-a-b-b-a-R.

Most rondeaus are sprightly rather than serious; their characteristic note is an adroit and often affected charm. Austin Dobson, Edmund Gosse, W. E. Henley, and Justin Huntley McCarthy were prime nineteenth-century exponents of the manner. Here is McCarthy's unreservedly romantic rondeau "If I Were King":

> *If I were king—ah, love, if I were king!*
> *What tributary nations would I bring*
> *   To stoop before your sceptre and to swear*

Allegiance to your lips and eyes and hair.
Beneath your feet what treasures I would fling!

The stars should be your pearls upon a string,
The world a ruby for your finger ring,
    And you should have the sun and moon to wear
        If I were king.

Let then wild dreams and wilder words take wing,
Deep in the woods I hear a shepherd sing
    A simple ballad to a sylvan air
    Of love that ever finds your face more fair.
I could not give you any goodlier thing
        If I were king.

Although Austin Dobson excelled in pseudo-pastoral prettiness, a few of his rondeaus rose above piping and fluting. "In After Days" is one of them.

In after days when grasses high
O'ertop the stone where I shall lie,
    Though ill or well the world adjust
    My slender claim to honored dust,
I shall not question nor reply.

I shall not see the morning sky;
I shall not hear the night-wind sigh;
    I shall be mute, as all men must
        In after days!

But yet, now living, fain would I
That some one then should testify,
    Saying—He held his pen in trust
    To Art, not serving shame or lust.
Will none?—Then let my memory die
        In after days!

Recent rondeaus tend to dispense with affectations. Barbara Howes' "Death of a Vermont Farm Woman" and Celeste Turner Wright's "The Paper Flowers" are straightforward genre pieces, while John McCrae's "In Flanders Fields," one of the most quoted

poems of World War I, is macabre, and Charlotte Perkins Gilman's "A Man Must Live" is a bitterly ironic use of an artificial
form.

> *A man must live! We justify*
> *Low shift and trick to treason high,*
> *A little vote for a little gold,*
> *To a whole senate bought and sold,*
> *With this self-evident reply.*
>
> *But is it so? Pray tell me why*
> *Life at such cost you have to buy?*
> *In what religion were you told*
> *"A man must live"?*
>
> *There are times when a man must die.*
> *Imagine for a battle-cry*
> *From soldier with a sword to hold—*
> *From soldiers with the flag unrolled—*
> *This coward's whine, this liar's lie,*
> *"A man must live"!*

The insistence of the rondeau's refrain has tempted many poets
to avoid its plain repetition by twisting it to take on additional
meanings, or to play on the words in a series of puns. In such instances the spelling may be changed, but the sound of the refrain
must be identical each time it is repeated. Strict rondeaus have
been built on refrains that change their implications when they
appear first as (for example) "Immortal eyes," then as "Immortalize," and finally as "Immortal lies," or "If few are won" . . .
"If you are one" . . . "If you are won," or "A Roman knows" . . .
"A Roman owes" . . . "A Roman nose," or "My lady's eyes" . . .
"My lady sighs" . . . "My lady's size!" Here is a sample of the
kind which combines sentiment, internal rhymes, and a cautionary
pun. It is by Michael Lewis.

> *Do write, my love, for just the sight*
> *Of your so-cherished hand brings light*
> *Into each dull, disheartening day*
> *That darkens when you are away.*
> *You burn a beacon in the night.*

> Do not delay for brisk or bright
> Appraisals of the hour. Be trite,
>   Be trivial. But somewhere, pray,
>   Do write, "My love."
>
> My heart is like a quivering kite
> Straining toward some too perilous height,
>   While your heart plays serenely gay.
>   Play, then, awhile; but do not stay
> Away too long. Knowing my plight,
>   Do right, my love.

A more intricate set of word-plays by John Moore turns into a triple pun in a facetious narrative entitled "Ground Round":

> The sons raise meat out in the West,
> And by success they both seem blessed;
>   Their ranch, suspicious neighbors say,
>   Was named and financed in a way
> That fiction writers might suggest.
>
> Their father, feathering their nest,
> Doubled their wages. Now the quest-
>   ion is: was all that extra pay
>   (the sons' raise) meet?
>
> He then wrote, "Focus would be best
> To call your ranch." They thought and guessed.
>   "Why such a name? Oh, tell us, pray!"
>   A terse reply came the next day,
> Four words to answer their behest:
>   "The sun's rays meet."

RONDEAU REDOUBLÉ. The rondeau redoublé is not, as its name suggests, a double rondeau. It is so wide a departure from the rondeau that it scarcely resembles it except for the strictness of the rhyming pattern. It consists of six stanzas (quatrains) and a final refrain, all on two rhymes. The distinguishing feature is this: Each line of the first stanza becomes, in turn, the last line of the four succeeding stanzas. The last line of the sixth stanza is a new line, but it is followed by the first phrase of the first line.

The opening quatrain, therefore, is a kind of text on which the poem is built.

Here are two different treatments of the form. The first is a set of free variations on Horace's Twenty-Sixth Ode in Book One; the second ("The Passionate Poet to His Love") is a jesting elaboration of an old nursery rhyme. Both are by Louis Untermeyer.

> The Muses love me and I am content.
>   What are these cares and frets that I should fear?
> The wind will sweep them into banishment;
>   The sea will cover them and be their bier.
>
> Let others quail who fail to persevere,
>   And cringe, with looks that on the ground are bent,
> Let all the frightful powers of earth appear,
>   The Muses love me and I am content.
>
> What though no joy is given but only lent?
>   What though the skies are often dull and drear?
> What though the very dome of heaven be rent?
>   What are these cares and frets that I should fear?
>
> Then come, flute-playing Muse, come from the clear
>   Pierian spring. Come quickly, and present
> Your blessing on these lines, lest (so I hear)
>   The wind will sweep them into banishment.
>
> Euterpe, come, with mirth and music sent
>   To give the poet confidence and cheer.
> No doleful thoughts will mar our merriment;
>   The sea will cover them and be their bier.
>
> Attune my strings. And so, for many a year,
>   Singing of thee I will be diligent.
> And even when this life grows sad and sere,
>   One thought will gladden when all else is spent:
>   The Muses love me.

*   *   *

> Curly-locks, Curly-locks, wilt thou be mine?
> Thou shalt not wash dishes nor yet feed the swine,
> But sit on a cushion and sew a fine seam,
> And feast upon strawberries, sugar, and cream.

Curly-locks, Curly-locks, brighten and beam
Joyous assent with a rapturous sign.
Hasten the vision, quicken the dream—
Curly-locks, Curly-locks, wilt thou be mine?

Curly-locks, Curly-locks, come; do not deem
Thou needest be mindful of sheep or of kine.
Thou shalt not peel onions nor cook them in steam;
Thou shalt not wash dishes nor yet feed the swine.

Curly-locks, Curly-locks, thou shalt recline
Lovely and lithe by a languorous stream;
Thou shalt not grieve though the world is malign,
But sit on a cushion and sew a fine seam.

Curly-locks, Curly-locks, oft as we dine
I shall read verse of mine—ream upon ream—
And thou shalt applaud me with, "Ah, that is fine,"
And feast upon strawberries, sugar, and cream.

Come, while the days are all laughter and shine.
Come, while the nights are all glamour and gleam.
Youth is a goblet, Love is the wine,
And Life is a lyric that has but one theme:
"Curly-locks, Curly-locks!"

RONDEL.   Lavishly employed in fourteenth-century France, the early form of the rondeau was known as "rondel." It has no refrain but, to compensate for the lack, the rondel repeats two of its lines in their entirety. Representing the repeated lines with capital letters, the rhyming formula for the rondel would be: A-B-b-a a-b-A-B a-b-b-a-A-B. An example by John Payne:

Kiss me, sweetheart, the Spring is here,
And Love is lord of you and me!
The bluebells beckon each passing bee;
The wild wood laughs to the flowered year.

There is no bird in brake or brere
But to his little mate sings he,
"Kiss me, sweetheart, the Spring is here,
And Love is lord of you and me."

The blue sky laughs out sweet and clear;
The missel-thrush upon the tree
Pipes for sheer gladness loud and free;
And I go singing to my dear,
"Kiss me, sweetheart, the Spring is here,
And Love is lord of you and me!"

ROUNDEL.   Unlike the rondel, the roundel may claim to be an English invention, for it was designed by an English poet. Swinburne shortened the rondeau, called his adaptation a "roundel" or "little round," and wrote a hundred sentimental versions of the form. The roundel has eleven lines, two of which serve as the refrain. With R denoting the refrain, the formula is: *Ra-b-a-R b-a-b a-b-a-R.* In every case the refrain (R) rhymes with the *b* lines. Swinburne described its form poetically in one of his *Century of Roundels:*

A roundel is wrought as a ring or a star-bright sphere,
With craft of delight and with cunning of sound unsought,
That the heart of the hearer may smile if to pleasure his ear
                    A roundel is wrought.

Its jewel of music is carven of all or of aught—
Love, laughter or mourning—remembrance of rapture or fear—
That fancy may fashion to hang in the ear of thought.

As a bird's quick song runs round, and the hearts in us hear
Pause answer to pause, and again the same strain caught,
So moves the device whence, round as a pearl or a tear,
                    A roundel is wrought.

Swinburne's contemporaries were quick to try their hands at variations of the roundel. Here is one which Lytton Strachey wrote at eighteen.

A Roundel is a thing that's not
   So very irksome to compose.
It's something that one throws off hot,
   A Roundel is.
The first thing needful, I suppose,

> *Is some slight sentiment or plot;*
> *Then start off with a fitting close,*
> *Add rhymes (with luck you'll find a lot)*
> *And, my inquiring friend—who knows?—*
> *Perhaps you may have here just what*
> *A Roundel is.*

The parodist James Kenneth Stephens—see his "Ballade of the Incompetent Ballade-Monger" on page 161—added his mocking voice to a "Roundel of Regrets":

> *You would not hear me speak; you never knew,*
> *Will never know, the eloquence unique*
> *It was my purpose to bestow on you.*
> *You would not hear me speak.*
>
> *Dear, it was caprice or idle freak;*
> *Perhaps I did not even mean to woo;*
> *My meaning was not very far to seek.*
> *I might have gained the end I had in view;*
> *I might have failed, since words are often weak.*
> *It never can be settled now. Adieu!*
> *You would not hear me speak.*

RUNE. A rune—"rune" is an Anglo-Saxon word meaning "mystery"—was a dark and secret saying. The Scandinavians believed runes had magic power and incised them on their weapons and drinking horns. The term is also applied to ancient Scandinavian poetry; it is sometimes used as an archaic designation for a verse or song. In "The Bells" Poe imagined the King of the Ghouls tolling the bells, dancing and yelling, and

> *Keeping time, time, time,*
> *In a sort of runic rhyme . . .*

RUN-ON LINES are lines which, to complete their meaning, run over to the next line without a break. See ENJAMBMENT on page 193.

S

SAGA. A saga—the word is Anglo-Saxon for "a saying"—was once a tale of legends and battle-lore. Such tales were orally transmitted for centuries, sometimes in prose, sometimes in verse, until they were written down by the scribes—after which the word came to mean any long story of adventure. Longfellow's "The Saga of King Olaf" is a twenty-two-part poem beginning with "The Challenge of Thor" and concluding with "The Nun of Nidaros."

> *A strain of music closed the tale,*
> *A low, monotonous funeral wail,*
> *That with its cadence, wild and sweet,*
> *Made the long saga more complete.*

SAPPHICS. Whether or not Sappho invented it, the stanzaic form which bears her name is indeed derived from the work of the poet of Lesbos. The unrhymed metrical pattern is an intricate variation of long and short syllables. The form is exemplified in Swinburne's "Sapphics" and, more recently, in Edgar Pangborn's "Sapphics for Icarus," with the traditional short line at the end of each stanza.

> *We who stood down here on the empty headland*
> *knew the glow. We shrank from the heat and splendor*
> *fearing, called him back when a crimson cloudway*
> *   opened to take him.*
>
> *Nothing he would hear, as the light consuming*
> *overshone day's end, and the fierce limbs striving*
> *drove his mad wings deep in the surge of evening.*
> *   What do we wait for?*
>
> *Mild the slow night streams through a blur of quiet—*
> *early star, full dark, and his idle pinions*

> *ache for light no more. They are stirred and lifted,*
>   *cool in the long waves.*

As poet laureate, Southey experimented in various classical meters. "The Widow," written in Sapphics, begins:

> *Cold was the night-wind; drifting fast the snow fell;*
> *Wide were the downs, and shelterless and naked,*
> *When a poor wanderer struggled on her journey,*
>   *Weary and wayworn.*

Such a poem was bound to invite parodies. The nineteenth-century statesman-poet, George Canning, turned to Sapphic verse for his lampoon, "The Friend of Humanity and the Needy Knife-Grinder," with this opening stanza:

> *Needy Knife-grinder! whither are you going?*
> *Rough is the road; your wheel is out of order.*
> *Bleak blows the blast. Your hat has got a hole in't.*
>   *So have your breeches.*

SATIRE. A satirical poem is one that exposes, rebukes, or ridicules an idea or a person, or (to quote Johnson's broader definition) "one in which wickedness or folly is censured." Its method varies from age to age and from poet to poet. Horace's satires are gentle, Juvenal's are scarifying, Dryden's are solemn, Pope's are biting, Byron's are almost blithe.

Here is a segment of Dryden's translation of Juvenal's Sixth Satire, the most vicious attack on women ever made.

> *Now should I sing what poisons they provide,*
> *With all their trumpery of charms beside,*
> *And all their arts of death, it would be known*
> *Lust is the smallest sin the sex can own.*
> *Caesinia still, they say, is guiltless found*
> *Of every vice, by her own lord renown'd;*
> *And well she may, she brought ten thousand pound. . . .*
> *He sighs, adores, and courts her every hour.*

Who would not do as much for such a dower!
She writes love letters to the youth in grace,
Nay, tips the wink before the cuckold's face;
And might do more; her portion makes it good.
Wealth has the privilege of widowhood.

SCANSION. Although scansion purports to be an analysis of metrical patterns, the subtleties of rhythm are so great that no rule of metrical precision is adequate. Scanning a line is a reading which tends to force the syllables into rigidity. In the classroom it can become pernicious, another way of subjecting poetry to mathematics and, worse, to a system of mathematics that can easily lead to a wrong result.

It cannot be said too often that the basis of English poetry is stress, something that cannot be strictly analyzed. There is only one way of reading Latin verse: by "quantity." (See page 255.) However, as John Livingston Lowes pointed out in *Convention and Revolt in Poetry*, there may be three or four ways of reading an English blank verse line. "I venture to say that no two mortals ever read aloud any given long passage of verse with precisely the same rhythms. I seriously question if there is such a thing as a fixed reading." So much for the precise as well as the debatable function of scansion. It must be added that one does not (or should not) read poetry by scansion. One scans according to strict meters, but one reads rhythmically.

SEPTENARY refers to a line of seven metrical feet as distinguished from a Septet, which is a seven-line stanza.

SEPTET. The seven-line stanza is rather uncommon, but it has been employed with subtle variations by various poets. The rhyme combinations are so many that a list of them would look more like a geometrical problem than a poetical examination. Here are two entirely different forms of the septet; the first, which has three rhymes, is the opening stanza of Thomas Traherne's "Eden"; the second, which has only two rhymes, is the first stanza of Robert Browning's "Misconceptions."

A learnéd and a happy ignorance
    Divided me
      From all the vanity,
From all the sloth, care, sorrow, that advance
    The madness and the misery
Of men. No error, no distraction, I
Saw cloud the earth, or overcast the sky.

*   *   *

This is the spray the bird clung to,
    Making it blossom with pleasure,
Ere the high tree-top she sprung to,
    Fit for her nest and her treasure.
    Oh, what a hope beyond measure
Was the poor spray's, which the flying feet hung to—
So to be singled out, built in, and sung to!

One particular version of the septet is called RHYME ROYAL; its rhyme pattern is *a-b-a-b-b-c-c*. The form is associated with King James I of Scotland. He was, however, not the first to use it. Chaucer never tired of it; his *The Parliament of Fowls*, parts of *The Canterbury Tales*, and *Troilus and Criseyde* are built on rhyme royal. For example, this is the beginning of "The Lawyer's Tale":

In Syria once there dwelt a company
Of wealthy merchants, shrewd, but honest, too;
Their foreign trade was large in spicery,
Fine cloth-of-gold and silks of every hue.
Their wares were so desirable and new
That people, always eager for a prize,
Were quick to buy and sell their merchandise.

Shakespeare employed rhyme royal throughout the almost nineteen hundred lines of *The Rape of Lucrece*. This is its rather stately movement:

Now is he come unto the chamber door
That shuts him from the heaven of his thought,

Which with a yielding latch, and with no more,
Hath barred him from the blessèd thing he sought.
So from himself impiety hath wrought
That for his prey to pray he doth begin,
As if the heavens should countenance his sin.

Rhyme royal remained in use for hundreds of years. John Masefield, who became poet laureate in 1930, gave it fresh vitality in *The Widow in the Bye Street* and in *Dauber*, which begins:

Four bells were struck, the watch was called on deck,
All work aboard was over for the hour,
And some men sang and others played at check,
Or mended clothes or watched the sunset glower.
The bursting west was like an opening flower,
And one man watched it till the light was dim,
But no one went across to talk to him.

SESTET.   In its special application, the sestet is the last six lines of the sonnet. (See page 285 for the SONNET.) It is the second part of the sonnet, following the octave (the first eight lines).

In a general sense, a sestet can be any six-line stanza. It can be written in dozens of different ways. It may be formed by three linked couplets (*a-a-b-b-c-c*), by a quatrain with an added couplet (*a-b-a-b-c-c*), by two alternating rhymes (*a-b-a-b-a-b*), or by two couplets separated by rhyming third and sixth lines (*a-a-b-c-c-b*). This last pattern is a stanza form which is capable of great flexibility. In "A Ballad upon a Wedding" Sir John Suckling gives it a pretty sprightliness.

Her feet, beneath her petticoat,
Like little mice stole in and out,
As if they feared the light.
But oh! she dances such a way,
No sun upon an Easter Day
Is half so fine a sight!

In Oliver Wendell Holmes's "The Last Leaf" the form achieves both whimsicality and gravity.

And if I should live to be
The last leaf upon the tree
  In the spring,
Let them smile, as I do now,
At the old forsaken bough
  Where I cling.

In "A Song to David" Christopher Smart, using exactly the same rhyming arrangement, fills the sestet with exaltation and majesty.

Glorious, more glorious is the crown
Of Him that brought salvation down
  By meekness, called thy Son.
Thou at stupendous truth believed,
And now the matchless deed's achieved,
  Determined, dared, and done.

Another arrangement—*a-a-a-b-a-b*—is known as the Burns stanza because Burns used it so often. The following is from his "The Hermit."

In this lone cave, in garments lowly,
Alike a foe to noisy folly,
And brow-bent gloomy melancholy,
  I wear away
My life, and in my office holy,
  Consume the day.

The combination of three couplets is saved from monotony by the seventeenth-century Robert Jones, who varied the length of his lines in song.

Love winged my Hopes and taught me how to fly
Far from base earth, but not to mount too high:
  For true pleasure
  Lives in measure,
  Which if men forsake,
Blinded they into folly run and grief for pleasure take.

In *Cymbeline* Shakespeare, using the arrangement *a-b-a-b-c-c*,
gave his song a somber finality.

> *Fear no more the heat o' the sun,*
> *Nor the furious winter's rages;*
> *Thou thy worldly task hast done,*
> *Home art gone, and ta'en thy wages:*
> *Golden lads and girls all must,*
> *As chimney-sweepers, come to dust.*

In "The Lover Rejoiceth" Sir Thomas Wyatt framed his plea-
sure-pain in sestets consisting of two triplets—*a-a-a-b-b-b*—beginning:

> *Tangled was I in love's snare,*
> *Oppressed with pain, torment with care;*
> *Of grief right sure, of joy full bare,*
> *Clean in despair by cruelty.*
> *But ha! ha! ha! full well is me,*
> *For I am now at liberty.*

Anna Wickham created an unusual arrangement of rhymes—
a-a-b-c-c-b—and varying line-lengths in a poem complete in six
lines, "Envoi":

> *God, thou great symmetry,*
> *Who put a biting lust in me*
> *From whence my sorrows spring,*
> *For all the frittered days*
> *That I have spent in shapeless ways,*
> *Give me one perfect thing.*

SESTINA.   By all odds the most complicated of the French forms,
the sestina is composed of six stanzas of six lines each. The lines of
each stanza, sometimes rhymed but usually unrhymed, end with
the words of the preceding stanza repeated in varying orders. To
make things still more difficult, there is a final stanza of three
lines in which all six words of the preceding stanzas must be used,

three toward the beginning, and three at the ends of the lines. The order of the terminal words varies according to the taste of the poet.

Although the pattern is so extraordinarily intricate as to seem little more than a virtuoso exercise, poets have been fascinated by it. The sixteenth-century Sir Philip Sidney indulged himself with sestinas much praised by the twentieth-century poet and critic William Empson. Swinburne, for whom no form was too complex, wrote a double sestina of twelve verses with twelve lines each, revolving through one hundred and fifty lines—there is a six-line envoy—all on twelve words. Among the more readable modern examples are Ezra Pound's "Sestina: Altaforte," Elizabeth Bishop's "Sestina: September Rain Falls on the House," Richmond Lattimore's "Sestina of a Far-off Summer," W. H. Auden's "Hearing of Harvests Rotting in the Valleys," James Branch Cabell's "The Conqueror Passes," and Rudyard Kipling's "Sestina of the Tramp Royal," which is not only a good example of this usually unrewarding form but also a truly Kiplingesque poem in its own right. It begins:

> Speakin' in general, I 've tried 'em all:
> The 'appy roads that take you o'er the world.
> Speakin' in general, I 've found them good
> For such as cannot use one bed too long,
> But must get 'ence, the same as I 've done,
> An' go observin' matters till they die.

It ends:

> Gawd bless this world! Whatever she 'ath done—
> Except when awful long—I've found it good,
> So write before I die, " 'E liked it all!"

That the sestina can encompass even scientific abstractions was proved in 1968 when Ruby Fogel received a prize from the Poetry Society of America for "E = MC^2: A Sestina Proving the Equation."

WHIRLWINDS, WORLD-WHEELS, *once set in motion*
can have no ending nor beginning:
    must all run clockwise out of Time—
    from some unknown and mystic place;
no counter-clockwise path returning
ever again to primal night.

As day-blind bats awake by night
to stir wing-circled winds to motion,
    stars float through full clouds, overturning
    small drops of light: the day's beginning
streams from a waterfalling place
that turns great sun-wheels around with Time.

But now the curvature of Time
presents a problem to the night—
    confronts it with the timeless place
    whirling before this patterned motion:
what was it like in the beginning,
when wandering worlds began *their turning?*

Perhaps a new concentric turning—
a sudden spiral-point in Time
    (when "Let there be light" *proclaimed beginning*
    and ". . . there was light" *concluded night)—*
Time started on its clockwise motion
from that perpetual starting-place.

It must be circular . . . a place
of whirlwind; always must be turning;
    and spinning from a grand commotion
    the constant, coiling wheel of Time.
A whirlwind's core is calm and night;
a central Calm was The Beginning.

Now far beyond that first beginning,
light-years from that primeval place
    tomorrow circles from tonight—
    from the calm Source of Time and turning,
that wound the clock-wheels of all Time
and set wild worlds in wheeling motion.

>. . . and Time still curves . . . *conformed to turning*
>*like space or night. In curving motion,*
>*each place of ending brings beginning.*

SHAPED VERSE. See the chapter "The Oddities of Poetry" on pages 133–137.

SIMILE. See METAPHOR on page 225.

SONNET. No form has been more exploited and more exalted than the sonnet; none has covered so wide a range of subjects. The sonnet has several distinctive characteristics. It is fourteen lines long. It is rhymed in a definite manner; although there are various rhyme patterns, no sonnet is unrhymed. Its lines are basically iambic and, with few exceptions, are ten syllables long: iambic pentameter. The brevity of the sonnet compels the poet to concentrate his ideas and his imagery; the sonnet is not complicated with digressions like the ode, but is a quintessence that proceeds directly to its final effect. Finally, the relationship between the first eight lines (the octave) and the final six lines (the sestet) is variously effective.

Italian in origin, the word "sonnet" originally meant "a little sound," a short strain, that is, of verbal melody. In the fourteenth century Petrarch established the form with such skill that, although certain variants have become popular, his model has remained to this day the most persistent form.

THE PETRARCHAN SONNET is the strictest of the sonnet forms. It consists of two parts: an octave (the first eight lines) and a sestet (the last six lines). The octave invariably has this rhyme-scheme: *a-b-b-a-a-b-b-a.* The sestet allows a little more latitude; it usually has three rhymes, and the arrangement is either *c-d-e-c-d-e* or *c-d-e-e-d-c*; many of the earlier sestets had only two rhymes: *c-d-c-d-c-d.*

There are two other features which distinguish the Petrarchan sonnet: (1) There is a definite division into two parts; (2) A thought or problem presented in the octave is answered in the sestet, which thus offers a fulfillment or conclusion of the idea.

Many sonnets make this premise-and-conclusion formula explicit by beginning the octave with "As" or "When" and the sestet with "So" or "Then." Here are two sonnets in Petrarchan style. The first is Longfellow's sentimental-philosophic "Nature"; the second, a poet's tribute to a translator and one of the most famous poems in English literature, is Keats's "On First Looking into Chapman's Homer."

> As a fond mother, when the day is o'er,
>   Leads by the hand her little child to bed,
>   Half willing, half reluctant to be led,
> And leave his broken playthings on the floor,
> Still gazing at them through the open door,
>   Nor wholly reassured and comforted
>   By promises of others in their stead,
> Which, though more splendid, may not please him more;
>
> So Nature deals with us, and takes away
>   Our playthings one by one, and by the hand
>   Leads us to rest so gently, that we go
> Scarce knowing if we wish to go or stay,
>   Being too full of sleep to understand
>   How far the unknown transcends the what we know.

*　*　*

> Much have I travell'd in the realms of gold,
>   And many goodly states and kingdoms seen;
>   Round many western islands have I been
> Which bards in fealty to Apollo hold.
> Oft of one wide expanse had I been told
>   That deep-browed Homer ruled as his demesne;
>   Yet did I never breathe its pure serene
> Till I heard Chapman speak out loud and bold.
>
> Then felt I like some watcher of the skies
>   When a new planet swims into his ken;
>   Or like stout Cortez when with eagle eyes
> He star'd at the Pacific—and all his men
>   Look'd at each other with a wild surmise—
>   Silent, upon a peak in Darien.

THE SHAKESPEARIAN SONNET was not invented by Shakespeare—Henry Howard was among his predecessors using the form—but he so enriched it with his powerful line that it bears his name. It differs sharply from the Petrarchan model. Instead of an abrupt division between octave and sestet, there may be a less pronounced break, but the chief difference is that structured by the rhyme-scheme. The Shakespearian sonnet consists of three quatrains and a concluding couplet—*a-b-a-b c-d-c-d e-f-e-f g-g*—a total of seven rhymes contrasted with the Petrarchan four or five. Two examples follow. The first is one of Shakespeare's one hundred and fifty-four sonnets; the second is Drayton's "The Parting."

Shall I compare thee to a summer's day?
Thou art more lovely and more temperate.
Rough winds do shake the darling buds of May,
And summer's lease hath all too short a date:
Sometimes too hot the eye of heaven shines,
And often is his gold complexion dimmed:
And every fair from fair sometimes declines,
By chance, or nature's changing course, untrimmed:
But thy eternal summer shall not fade
Nor lose possession of that fair thou owest;
Nor shall Death brag thou wanderest in his shade
When in eternal lines to time thou growest.
So long as men can breathe or eyes can see
So long lives this, and this gives life to thee.

* * *

Since there's no help, come, let us kiss and part;
Nay, I have done, you get no more of me;
And I am glad, yea, glad with all my heart
That thus so cleanly I myself can free.
Shake hands for ever, cancel all our vows,
And, when we meet at any time again,
Be it not seen in either of our brows
That we one jot of former love retain.
Now at the last gasp of Love's latest breath,
When, his pulse failing, Passion speechless lies,

When Faith is kneeling by his bed of death,
And Innocence is closing up his eyes—
  Now if thou wouldst, when all have given him over,
  From death to life thou might'st him yet recover.

THE SPENSERIAN SONNET is a compromise between the Petrarchan and Shakespearian sonnets. It has the five rhymes of the Petrarchan model, but it also has the Shakespearian concluding couplet. Its innovation is an interlocking rhyme-scheme—*a-b-a-b-b-c-b-c-c-d-c-d-e-e*. Spenser's continuous weaving of paired sounds is like a silver chain of rhyme, neither too loose nor too constricted.

Like as a huntsman after weary chase,
Seeing the game from him escaped away,
Sits down to rest him in some shady place,
With panting hounds, beguiléd of their prey:
So, after long pursuit and vain assay,
When I all weary had the chase forsook,
The gentle deer return'd the self-same way,
Thinking to quench her thirst at the next brook.
There she, beholding me with milder look,
Sought not to fly, but fearless still did bide,
Till I in hand her yet half trembling took,
And with her own good-will her firmly tied.
  Strange thing, me seemed, to see a beast so wild
  So goodly won, with her own will beguiled.

THE MILTONIC SONNET, a form actually invented by Milton, returns to the Petrarchan rhyme-scheme. Also, like the Petrarchan sonnet, it presents a situation and an answering comment. However, it differs from its model in one important detail: there is no break in thought or typography. Milton develops his ideas without interruption; the octave and sestet are molded into a firm unit. The rhyme-scheme—*a-b-b-a-a-b-b-a-c-d-e-c-d-e*—is illustrated by the famous sonnet "On His Blindness":

When I consider how my light is spent
Ere half my days in this dark world and wide,
And that one talent which is death to hide

> Lodged with me useless, though my soul more bent
> To serve therewith my Maker, and present
> My true account, lest He returning chide;
> "Doth God exact day-labor, light denied?"
> I fondly ask. But Patience, to prevent
> That murmur, soon replies, "God doth not need
> Either man's work or his own gifts. Who best
> Bear his mild yoke, they serve him best. His state
> Is kingly: thousands at his bidding speed,
> And post o'er land and ocean without rest;
> They also serve who only stand and wait."

THE COMPOSITE SONNET is, as the name suggests, a combination of different sonnet forms. Many of the most notable English sonnets are in this category, which includes examples as varied as those of Sidney, Shelley, Arnold, Hopkins, Meredith, Frost, and Merrill Moore, one of whose books, accurately entitled *M*, contains one thousand seemingly improvised "American" sonnets. This one is entitled "How She Resolved to Act":

> "I shall be careful to say nothing at all
> About myself or what I know of him
> Or the vaguest thought I have—no matter how dim,
> Tonight if it so happen that he call."
>
> And not ten minutes later the door-bell rang
> And into the hall he stepped as he always did
> With a face and a bearing that quite poorly hid
> His brain that burned and his heart that fairly sang
> And his tongue that wanted to be rid of the truth.
>
> As well as she could, for she was very loath
> To signify how she felt, she kept very still,
> But soon her heart cracked loud as a coffee mill
> And her brain swung like a comet in the dark
> And her tongue raced like a squirrel in the park.

Perhaps the most celebrated composite sonnet, a fusion of Shakespearian and Miltonic, is Wordsworth's "Sonnet on the Sonnet."

Scorn not the Sonnet. Critic, you have frowned,
Mindless of its just honors; with this key
Shakespeare unlocked his heart; the melody
Of this small lute gave ease to Petrarch's wound;
A thousand times this pipe did Tasso sound;
With it Camoëns soothed an exile's grief;
The Sonnet glittered a gay myrtle leaf
Amid the cypress with which Dante crowned
His visionary brow: a glow-worm lamp,
It cheered mild Spenser, called from Faery-land
To struggle through dark ways; and, when a damp
Fell round the path of Milton, in his hand
The thing became a trumpet; whence he blew
Soul-animating strains—alas, too few!

SPENSERIAN STANZA.   Invented by Spenser and used throughout *The Faerie Queene,* this is a majestic nine-line stanza with an
intricately knit rhyme-scheme: *a-b-a-b-b-c-b-c-c.* The last line, an
alexandrine, one foot longer than the preceding eight lines, rounds
out the stanza with final sonority. This is an excerpt from *The
Faerie Queene:*

For take thy balance, if thou be so wise,
And weigh the wind that under heaven doth blow,
Or weigh the light that in the east doth rise,
Or weigh the thought that from man's mind doth flow;
But if the weight of these thou canst not show,
Weigh but one word which from thy lips doth fall:
For how canst thou those greater secrets know
That dost not know the least thing of them all?
Ill can he rule the great that cannot reach the small.

The Spenserian stanza did not die with Spenser. On the contrary, it appears throughout the centuries in such memorable
poems as Burns's "The Cotter's Saturday Night," Byron's "Childe
Harold's Pilgrimage," Keats's "The Eve of St. Agnes," Tennyson's
"The Lotos-Eaters," and Shelley's "Adonaïs," the agonized me-
morial to Keats, which ends:

> *The breath whose might I have invoked in song*
> *Descends on me; my spirit's bark is driven,*
> *Far from the shore, far from the trembling throng*
> *Whose sails were never to the tempest given;*
> *The massy earth and sphered skies are riven!*
> *I am borne darkly, fearfully, afar;*
> *Whilst burning through the inmost veil of Heaven,*
> *The soul of Adonaïs, like a star,*
> *Beacons from the abode where the Eternal are.*

SPONDEE. A two-syllable foot, its two strong accents represented thus—′ ′—the spondee varies the rhythm with its heavy
stress. Certain words (mostly two combined nouns) in themselves are spondees, such as "heartbreak," "childhood," "football,"
"cornfield," "folklore," "wineglass," and "Mayday." Hopkins elevated the spondee into the basis of his "Sprung Rhythm," and
certain nursery rhymes tend to confirm his theory—for example,
"One, two / Buckle my shoe, / Three, four, / Shut the door."
The heavy beat of the repeated spondee achieves an effect of
weighted slowness in Pope's version of Homer, where Sisyphus is
pictured as

> ′   ′   ′ ′   ′   *with many a groan*
> *Up the high hill he heaves a huge round stone.*

SPRUNG RHYTHM. See RHYTHM on page 266.

STANZA. A stanza (also called a verse) is a unit of lines which
decides the shape of a poem. Its pattern is determined by the number of lines, the number of feet in each line, and, if there are
rhymes, the rhyme-scheme. Once the pattern is fixed, it remains as
a rule unaltered throughout the poem, although there are sometimes exceptions; for example, in Coleridge's *The Rime of the
Ancient Mariner*, the stanza form deviates from predominating
quatrains to occasional quintets and even sestets.

STAVE. An archaic synonym for stanza.

STRESS.   Stress is the emphasis or weight put on a particular syllable. Stress determines the meter and the metrical foot. It is also another word for "accent."

STROPHE.   The strophe was the "turning" made by the Greek chorus as the singers circled about the center of the stage. The antistrophe came into being when the singers reversed their steps. Later, the word *strophe* was applied to part of an ode and, later still, it became synonymous with "stanza." Its use in connection with FREE VERSE is explained on page 202.

SYLLABIC VERSE is verse which is measured by the number of syllables instead of by accent or stress. See ACCENTUAL VERSE on pages 141–143.

SYMMETRICS.   A tireless experimenter, David McCord invented Symmetrics. A particularly tight verse form, a symmetric is a quatrain which begins and ends with the same syllabic sound and pivots upon two identical (symmetrical) syllables. Furthermore, as Dudley Fitts pointed out in a note to McCord's sequence of Symmetrics ("Signs of the Zodiac"), "the stanza is composed of two rhyming couplets, and the focal consonance entails, in addition, the mirroring of the last syllable of the first couplet in the first syllable of the second. The poems, then, are little orbits in themselves." Here are "Aquarius: Water-Bearer" and "Pisces: Fishes."

> *Aquarius, the Water-Bearer, bears*
> *The vintage liquid of the world. Who*
> > *shares shares*
> *Life itself, since life however various*
> *Depends on water. Any wine, Aquarius?*

> *Fish. Silvery in themselves. The silver night*
> *Reveals a pair, tails tied, in sorry*
> > *plight: "Plight*
> *Thee my troth," said Eros. "As you wish."*
> *Who said that? Aphrodite? The poor, poor fish!*

SYNECDOCHE, literally "receiving together," is a figure of speech in which a part represents the whole. When Kipling speaks of England holding "dominion over palm and pine" he suggests, by selecting typically southern and northern trees, the extent of the British Empire. When Shakespeare begins the fifty-fifth sonnet "Not marble nor the gilded monuments / Of princes shall outlive this pow'rful rhyme," he is not boasting but employing synecdoche, and the word "rhyme" stands for the poem itself.

> *Not marble nor the gilded monuments*
> *Of princes shall outlive this pow'rful rhyme;*
> *But you shall shine more bright in these contents*
> *Than unswept stone besmear'd with sluttish time.*
> *When wasteful war shall statues overturn,*
> *And broils root out the work of masonry,*
> *Nor Mars his sword nor war's quick fire shall burn*
> *The living record of your memory.*

T

TAIL-RHYME. Sometimes called "caudate rhyme" and *rime couée*, tail-rhyme occurs when two short lines are rhymed among longer lines. Tail-rhyme stanzas are usually six lines long, as in Chaucer's "Tale of Sir Thopas," Drayton's "Agincourt," Smart's "Song to David," Shelley's "To Night," and many of Burns's sestets. It is interesting to compare the use of tail-rhyme stanzas in the first stanza of Fletcher's Elizabethan "Bridal Song" and the last stanza of Auden's thirty-stanza "Under Which Lyre," subtitled "A Reactionary Tract for the Times."

> *Hold back thy hours, dark Night, till we have done;*
> *The Day will come too soon.*
> *Young maids will curse thee, if thou steal'st away*
> *And leav'st their losses open to the day.*
> *Stay, stay, and hide*
> *The blushes of the bride.*

* * *

Thou shalt not live within thy means
Nor on plain water and raw greens.
   If thou must choose
Between the chances, choose the odd;
Read the New Yorker; trust in God;
   And take short views.

For other examples see SESTET on page 280.

TANKA.   Like the HAIKU (see page 205), the tanka is a Japanese
form; but where the haiku is restricted to seventeen syllables,
the tanka has a leeway of thirty-one. This gives it something
of the suggestiveness of the haiku while allowing it more scope. A
five-line poem, its thirty-one syllables are arranged in this order:
5-7-5-7-7, the first three lines being in strict haiku form. A modern
example by the author:

Spring has always known
Whisperers in the woodlands,
   Hands reaching for hands,
Promises made by moonlight,
And forgotten in the sun.

TERCET.   The tercet, or triplet, is any stanza of three lines which
rhyme together. The poem by Herrick quoted under MONOM-
ETER (on page 228) is made of tercets. Here are three, of varying
line-lengths and in different meters. The first is by Richard
Crashaw, the second by Robert Browning, the third by James Russell Lowell.

Who'er she be,
That not impossible she
That shall command my heart and me . . .

* * *

Boot, saddle, to horse, and away!
Rescue my castle before the hot day
Brightens to blue from its silvery gray.

*   *   *

> *But John P.*
> *Robinson, he*
> *Says he wunt vote for Governor B.*

TERZA RIMA, literally "third rhyme," is a form of tercet in which the first and third lines rhyme, while the second line introduces a new rhyme carried on by the first and third lines of the next tercet. The interlocking rhyme arrangement follows this pattern: *a-b-a b-c-b c-d-c d-e-d* and so on until the end. The problem of closing the uncompleted rhyme is solved either by closing the poem with an extra line, making the last verse a four-line stanza, or by ending with a couplet.

Terza rima is Italian in origin; Dante's *The Divine Comedy* is composed entirely in *terza rima*. Although Wyatt introduced it into England as early as the sixteenth century, it did not become popular until Shelley's "Ode to the West Wind" showed how flexibly it could be used. Since then there have been such *terza rima* poems as Robert Browning's "The Statue and the Bust," Elizabeth Barrett Browning's "Casa Guido Windows," Robert Frost's "Acquainted with the Night," a section of W. H. Auden's "The Sea and the Mirror," Archibald MacLeish's alternating half-rhymes in *Conquistador*, James Merrill's "Transfigured Bird," and this fragment from Louis MacNeice's *Collected Poems*:

> *Say Yes instead of No. You need only knock.*
> *There are still doors to open; somewhere hidden*
> *Beneath our clay there lies our basic rock.*
>
> *And many doors. Some may be wormwood-ridden,*
> *Some with a whining hinge and sour with rust,*
> *But still can answer if correctly bidden . . .*

TETRAMETER. Any line of four metrical feet is in tetrameter. It is a common meter, usually broken by a caesura. An example by Byron:

Maid of Athens, ere we part
Give, oh, give me back my heart!
Or, since that has left my breast,
Keep it now, and take the rest!

THRENODY. A threnody, in ancient Greece, was a choral song of lamentation, a dirge mourning a particular person. In English poetry, it is the same as an ELEGY. (See page 193.)

TRIMETER. A line of three feet is in trimeter, as in William Vaughn Moody's "Of Wounds and Sore Defeat":

Of wounds and sore defeat
I made my battle stay;
Winged sandals for my feet
I wove of my delay.

In "A Woman's Last Word," Browning alternates trimeter and dimeter lines:

Let's contend no more, love,
*   Strive nor weep;*
All be as before, love,
*   —Only sleep!*

What so wild as words are?
*   I and thou*
In debate, as birds are,
*   Hawk on bough!*

TRIOLET. Neatest of the French forms, the triolet is a single stanza of eight short lines with two rhymes. The first line is repeated in its entirety as the fourth line, while the first and second lines become the final two lines. With capital letters representing the repeated lines, the formula is A-B-*a*-A-*a*-*b*-A-B. Here is an example by Michael Lewis, in which the form is epitomized:

Modest is the triolet,
*   Short and sweet, that's all.*
Fragile as a violet,

Modest is the triolet.
Winds that wander by, oh let
Fragrance on it fall.
Modest is the triolet,
Short and sweet. That's all.

Most triolets are playful, a bit of badinage turning briefly on its axis. However, a few poets have stretched it beyond mere pertness. Thomas Hardy gave it a background of fallow ground recently sown with wheat and placed against it "three large birds walking about, wistfully eyeing the surface. Wind keen from northeast; sky a dull gray." This is Hardy's "Winter in Durnover Field."

Rook: *Throughout the field I find no grain;*
           The cruel frost encrusts the cornland!
Starling: *Aye: patient pecking now is vain*
           Throughout the field, I find . . .
Rook: *No grain!*
Pigeon: *Nor will be, comrade, till it rain,*
           Or genial thawings loose the lorn land
           Throughout the field.
Rook: *I find no grain:*
           The cruel frost encrusts the cornland!

A more cynical use of the triolet occurs in a book of parodies entitled *Heavens* by Louis Untermeyer.

Goodness and Beauty and Truth—
    Where? Well, but only in song.
Honor, Nobility, Youth,
Goodness and Beauty and Truth
Shrink from man's clutches; in sooth
    No one can hold them for long.
Goodness and Beauty and Truth
    Wear well. But only in song.

The quick turn of grace notes which characterizes the triolet is not readily adapted for anything more than vivacity. Yet Austin Dobson managed to combine seriousness and sentiment in a chain of triolets, Robert Bridges began the eight-line trill with "All women born are so perverse," and Barbara Howes wrote "Early Supper," a triple triolet which is also a charming genre picture.

Laughter of children brings
The kitchen down with laughter.
While the old kettle sings,
Laughter of children brings
To a boil all savory things.
Higher than beam or rafter,
Laughter of children brings
The kitchen down with laughter.

So ends an autumn day,
Light ripples on the ceiling,
Dishes are stacked away;
So ends an autumn day,
The children jog and sway
In comic dances wheeling.
So ends an autumn day,
Light ripples on the ceiling.

They trail upstairs to bed,
And night is a dark tower.
The kettle calls, instead
They trail upstairs to bed,
Leaving warmth, the coppery-red
Mood of their carnival hour.
They trail upstairs to bed,
And night is a dark tower.

TRIPLET.   Another name for TERCET. See page 294.

TROCHEE: Sometimes called a marching foot, the trochee consists of a strong syllable followed by a weak one: / ∪. Complete trochaic feet are found in such words as "heartless," "gather," "going," "softly," "laughter." Isaac Watts' "Cradle Hymn" begins with a pure trochaic line:

Soft and easy is the cradle

while Shakespeare's witches use trochaics for a more sinister enchantment:

> *Double, double, toil and trouble;*
> *Fire burn and cauldron bubble.*

The most relentlessly trochaic poem in the language is Longfellow's "The Song of Hiawatha." It stamps its reverberating feet into the reader's consciousness with the opening tetrameter:

> *Should you ask me, whence these stories,*
> *Whence these legends and traditions,*
> *With the odors of the forest,*
> *With the dew and damp of meadows,*
> *With the curling smoke of wigwams,*
> *With the rushing of great rivers,*
> *With the frequent repetitions . . .*

TROPE. In Greek, the word "trope" meant "a turn." In the eighteenth century the word "trope" was used to denote an elegant and even elaborate style. Today it signifies only a figure of speech. Examinations of certain figures of speech can be found under METAPHOR, SIMILE, METONOMY, SYNECDOCHE, HYPERBOLE, and PERSONIFICATION.

TROUBADOUR. The troubadours flourished in southern France during the twelfth and thirteenth centuries. When they were not attached to a court, they traveled about the country and composed their poems in *langue d'oc*, the dialect of Provence. Their chief topic was love, especially courtly love, a noble passion centering about the courtship of a married and presumably unattainable lady. Closely related to the troubadours were the *trouvères*, the established court poets who wrote not only amatory poems but also *chansons de gestes*. (See page 178.) Arnaut Daniel, Bertran de Born, and Guillaume d'Aquitaine were among the more notable troubadours; they excelled in such lyrics as canzones, aubades and albas. Ezra Pound made a version of an alba (see page 144) which he called "Alba Innominata." It began:

In a garden where the whitethorn spreads her leaves
My lady hath her love lain close beside her,
Till the warder cries the dawn—ah, dawn that grieves!
Ah God! Ah God! That dawn should come so soon!

Fifty years before Pound's forthright rendering, an elaborate
enlargement of the same alba was composed by Swinburne. Ac-
knowledging it as a "Provençal Burden," he entitled it "In the
Orchard" and began his ten stanzas with:

Let go my hands; let me catch breath and see;
Let the dewfall drench either side of me.
   Clear apple leaves are soft upon that moon
Seen sidelong like a blossom on the tree.
   Ah God, ah God, that day should be so soon!

The grass is thick and cool; it lets us lie.
Kissed upon either cheek and either eye,
   I turn to thee as some green afternoon
Turns toward the sunset and is loath to die.
   Ah God, ah God, that day should be so soon!

𝒱

VERS DE SOCIÉTÉ. Literally "Society Verse," V*ers de
Société* once connoted the kind of poeticizing which dealt politely
and sometimes pointedly with social customs. Today the term has
come to mean any variety of LIGHT VERSE. (See page 216.)

VERSE. From *versus*, a turning, the word "verse" indicated the
turn of a single line. It has also come to mean a stanza. In general,
we may say verse is that which is distinct from prose. But the term
is also used sometimes in contradistinction to "poetry." Although
it is difficult to draw a line between verse and poetry, it might be
said that the difference is likely to be one of degree of intensity,
that verse tends to be light in tone and texture, while poetry is
more often elevated in pitch and power.

VERS LIBRE. See FREE VERSE on pages 201–202.

VILLANELLE. A kind of shepherd's song, the villanelle was originally tuned to purely pastoral themes. It soon became stylized and bore the same relation to its origins as Marie Antoinette's beribboned dairy bore to the rough cowsheds of the peasantry. Pastoral or not, it was and remains one of the most musical of the French forms. Although its simplicity is suspect, its art saves it from complete artificiality.

Structurally the villanelle consists of a sequence of tercets which suggest *terza rima*. There are five three-line stanzas followed by a concluding four-line stanza, all of them built on only two rhymes. The stanzas are knit together by a double refrain. The first line of the first stanza does duty as the last line of the second and fourth stanzas; the last line of the first stanza becomes the last line of the third and fifth stanzas; both lines appear in the last (sixth) stanza as a concluding couplet. The formula is:

A_1-b-A_2 a-b-A_1 a-b-A_2 a-b-A_1 a-b-A_2 a-b-A_1-A_2.

Henley described what used to be the character as well as the characteristics of the villanelle.

> A dainty thing's the Villanelle.
> Sly, musical, a jewel in rhyme,
> It serves its purpose passing well.
>
> A double-clappered silver bell
> That must be made to clink in chime,
> A dainty thing's the Villanelle;
>
> And if you wish to flute a spell,
> Or ask a meeting 'neath the lime,
> It serves its purpose passing well.
>
> You must not ask of it the swell
> Of organs grandiose and sublime—
> A dainty thing's the Villanelle;
>
> And, filled with sweetness, as a shell
> Is filled with sound, and launched in time,
> It serves its purpose passing well.

Still fair to see and good to smell
As in the quaintness of its prime,
A dainty thing's the Villanelle,
It serves its purpose passing well.

Gradually the villanelle ceased to be a mere "double-clappered silver bell," a dainty thing that served its purpose "passing well." Poets began using it with serious and even somber intent. Ernest Dowson began his "Villanelle of Marguerites" with "A little, passionately, not at all"; Edwin Arlington Robinson's "The House on the Hill" sounded a note of melancholy with "They are all gone away, there is nothing more to say." William Empson's "Missing Dates" has this solemn opening:

Slowly the poison the whole blood-stream fills.
It is not the effort nor the failure tires.
The waste remains, the waste remains and kills.

W. H. Auden's "Villanelle" begins cryptically:

Time can say nothing but I told you so.
Time only knows the price we have to pay;
If I could tell you, I would let you know.

Theodore Roethke starts his metaphysical villanelle, "The Waking," this way:

I wake to sleep, and take my waking slow.
I feel my fate in what I cannot fear.
I learn by going where I have to go.

Dylan Thomas gave the villanelle a new solemnity and an increased music in this elegiac poem to his father:

Do not go gentle into that good night,
Old age should burn and rave at close of day;
Rage, rage against the dying of the light.

Though wise men at their end know dark is right,
Because their words had forked no lightning, they
Do not go gentle into that good night.

Good men, the last wave by, crying how bright
Their frail deeds might have danced in a green bay,
Rage, rage against the dying of the light.

Wild men who caught and sang the sun in flight,
And learn, too late, they grieved it on its way,
Do not go gentle into that good night.

Grave men, near death, who see with blinding sight
Blind eyes could blaze like meteors and be gay,
Rage, rage against the dying of the light.

And you, my father, there on the sad height,
Curse, bless, me now with your fierce tears, I pray.
Do not go gentle into that good night.
Rage, rage against the dying of the light.

VIRELAY. The Virelay—the name, like the form, is derived from the French—is a poem of indeterminate length, in which the short lines of one stanza dictate the rhymes for the long lines in the succeeding stanza and the short lines of the last stanza rhyme with the long lines of the first. The odd rhyme-structure is this: *a-b-a-b b-c-b-c c-d-c-d d-a-d-a*. English examples of the form are rare. This one is by the author. It is entitled "Finis."

Since now, at last, we understand,
 Why all this feigned surprise?
No time for being blind and bland.
 Open your eyes!

I learned suspicion and surmise,
 Flourished on false alarms,
Fed by deceits and lulled by lies,
 Even in your arms.

Impervious to threatening storms,
 We trifled, hand in glove.
Gone are the lures, the whispered charms.
 I've had enough.

And yet . . . are we past thinking of
 What might be rescued, and
Restored with—shall I say it?—love?
 Give me your hand.

EPILOGUE

ART

All things are doubly fair
If patience fashion them
    And care—
Verse, enamel, marble, gem.

No idle chains endure:
Yet, Muse, to walk aright
    Lace tight
Thy buskin proud and sure.

Fie on facile measure,
A shoe where every lout
    At pleasure
Slips his foot in and out!

Sculptor, lay by the clay
On which thy nerveless finger
    May linger,
Thy thoughts flown far away.

Keep to Carrara rare,
Struggle with Paros cold,
    That hold
The subtle line and fair.

Lest haply nature lose
That proud, that perfect line,
    Make thine
The bronze of Syracuse. . . .

Despise a watery hue
And tints that soon expire.
    With fire
Burn thine enamel true. . . . .

—All things return to dust
Save beauties fashioned well.
    The bust
Outlasts the citadel.

Oft doth the plowman's heel,
Breaking an ancient clod,
    Reveal
A Caesar or a god.

The gods, too, die, alas!
But deathless and more strong
    Than brass
Remains the sovereign song.

Chisel and carve and file,
Till thy vague dream imprint
    Its smile
On the unyielding flint.

THÉOPHILE GAUTIER (1811–1872)
translated by GEORGE SANTAYANA (1863–1952)

A SELECTED BIBLIOGRAPHY

Abercrombie, Lascelles, *The Theory of Poetry*. Harcourt, Brace and Company, 1926.

Adams, Hazard, *The Contexts of Poetry*. Little, Brown and Company, 1963.

Arms, George, and Kuntz, Joseph M., *Poetry Explication*. William Morrow & Company, 1950.

Beaty, Jerome, and Matchett, William H., *Poetry from Statement to Meaning*. Oxford University Press, 1965.

Blackmur, R. P., *Form and Value in Modern Poetry*. Doubleday Anchor Books, 1957.

Bogan, Louise, *Achievement in American Poetry, 1900–1951*. Henry Regnery Company, 1951.

Bowra, C. M., *Inspiration and Poetry*. Macmillan & Co., Ltd., 1955.

Brooks, Cleanth, *Modern Poetry and the Tradition*. University of Chicago Press, 1939.

Brooks, Cleanth, and Warren, Robert Penn, *Understanding Poetry*. Henry Holt and Company, 1938; revised edition 1964.

Burke, Kenneth, *Counter-Statement*. Harcourt, Brace and Company, 1931.

Burnshaw, Stanley (ed.), *The Poem Itself*. Holt, Rinehart and Winston, 1960.

Cunningham, J. V. (ed.), *The Renaissance in England*. Harcourt, Brace & World, 1966.

Daiches, David, *Poetry and the Modern World*. University of Chicago Press, 1940.

Davidson, Carter, and Untermeyer, Louis, *Poetry: Its Appreciation and Enjoyment*, Harcourt, Brace and Company, 1934.

Deutsch, Babette, *Poetry in Our Time*. Henry Holt and Company, 1952.

Dickey, James, *Babel to Byzantium: Poets & Poetry Now*. Farrar, Straus & Giroux, 1968.

Drew, Elizabeth, *Discovering Poetry*. W. W. Norton & Company, 1933.

Eliot, T. S., *The Use of Poetry*. Harvard University Press, 1933.

Empson, William, *Seven Types of Ambiguity*. Chatto & Windus, London, 1930.

Evans, B. Ifor, *Tradition and Romanticism*. Longmans, Green and Company, 1940.

Fitts, Dudley, *The Poetic Nuance*. Harcourt, Brace and Company, 1958.

Fussell, Paul, Jr., *Poetic Meter and Poetic Form*. Random House, 1965.

Geiger, Don, *The Dramatic Impulse in Modern Poetics*. Louisiana State University Press, 1967.

Gregory, Horace, and Zaturenska, Marya, *A History of American Poetry*. Harcourt, Brace and Company, 1946.

Gross, Harvey, *Sound and Form in Modern Poetry*. University of Michigan Press, 1964.

——— (ed.), *The Structure of Verse*. Fawcett Publications, Inc., 1966.

Jarrell, Randall, *Poetry and the Age*. Alfred A. Knopf, 1953.

Lanz, Henry, *The Physical Basis of Rhyme*. Stanford University Press, 1931.

Lewis, C. Day, *Poetry for You*. Oxford University Press, 1947.

Lowes, John Livingston, *Convention and Revolt in Poetry*. Houghton Mifflin Company, 1919.

Murphy, Francis (ed.), *Discussions of Poetry: Form and Structure*. D. C. Heath and Company, 1964.

Nemerov, Howard (ed.), *Poets on Poetry*. Basic Books, Inc., 1966.

Ostroff, Anthony (ed.), *The Contemporary Poet as Artist and Critic*. Little, Brown and Company, 1964.

Preminger, Alex (ed.), *Encyclopedia of Poetry and Poetics*. Princeton University Press, 1965.

Prescott, Frederick Clarke, *The Poetic Mind*. The Macmillan Company, 1922.

Ransom, John Crowe, *The New Criticism*. New Directions, 1941.

Read, Herbert, *Phases of English Poetry*. New Directions, 1951.

Rhys, Ernest (ed.), *The Prelude to Poetry: The English Poets in Defense and Praise of Their Own Art*. Everyman's Library, E. P. Dutton & Company, 1927.

Richards, I. A., *Practical Criticism*. Harcourt, Brace and Company, 1929.

Rosenthal, M. L., *The Modern Poets*. Oxford University Press, 1960.

———, *The New Poets: American and British Poetry Since World War II*. Oxford University Press, 1967.

Rukeyser, Muriel, *The Life of Poetry*. A. A. Wynn, 1949.

Saintsbury, George, *A History of English Prosody*. Russell & Russell, 1923.

Scott, A. F., *The Poet's Craft*. Cambridge University Press, 1957.

Shapiro, Karl, *A Primer for Poets*. University of Nebraska Press, 1953.

Shapiro, Karl, and Beum, Robert, *A Prosody Handbook*. Harper & Row, 1965.

Smith, Chard Powers, *Pattern and Variation in Poetry*. Charles Scribner's Sons, 1932.

Stauffer, Donald A., *The Nature of Poetry*. W. W. Norton & Company, 1946.

Steiner, George (ed.), *The Penguin Book of Modern Verse Translation*. Penguin Books, 1966.

Strong, L. A. G., *Common Sense About Poetry*. Alfred A. Knopf, 1932.

Tate, Allen, *Essays of Four Decades*. The Swallow Press, 1969.

Valéry, Paul, *The Art of Poetry*. Bollingen Foundation, Inc., 1958.

Wheelock, John Hall, *What Is Poetry?* Charles Scribner's Sons, 1963.

Wilson, Edmund, *Axel's Castle*. Charles Scribner's Sons, 1931.

INDEX OF PERSONS

NOTE: Page numbers in *italics* refer to poetry selections.